The Writer's Craft

From the painting by Florine Stettheimer

AVERY HOPWOOD

The Writer's Craft

Hopwood Lectures, 1965–81

Edited and with an Introduction by
Robert A. Martin

Ann Arbor
The University of Michigan Press

The editor would like to thank Dr. Andrea Beauchamp, Hopwood
coordinator, for her invaluable advice and assistance in preparing
this collection, and the following for permission to use copyrighted
material:

Harper and Row, Publishers, Inc., for "Moonshine and Sunny
Beams: Ruminations on *A Midsummer Night's Dream*," from *In
Radical Pursuit* by W. D. Snodgrass. Copyright © 1975 by W. D.
Snodgrass. Reprinted by permission of Harper and Row.

John Simon for "The Word on Film" by John Simon from the
Hudson Review. Copyright © 1977 by John Simon. Reprinted by
permission of the author.

New Directions for "Three Meditations" (excerpt) and "The
Necessity" (complete) from *The Jacob's Ladder* by Denise
Levertov. Copyright © 1961 by Denise Levertov Goodman.
Reprinted by permission of New Directions.

Tom Wolfe for "Literary Technique in the Last Quarter of the
Twentieth Century" by Tom Wolfe. Copyright © 1978 by Tom
Wolfe. Reprinted by permission of the author.

Library of Congress Cataloging in Publication Data

Main entry under title:

The Writer's craft.

    Continuation of 2 previous collections of Hopwood
lectures: The Writer and his craft (1954), and To the
young writer (1965)
    Includes bibliographical references.
      1. Literature—Addresses, essays, lectures.   I.   Martin,
2. Authorship—Addresses, essays, lectures.
Robert A.   II.   Title: Hopwood lectures, 1965–81.
PN45.W7   1982   809   82-4752
ISBN 0-472-06337-5   AACR2

For John W. Aldridge, John S. Martin, and Arthur Miller

Contents

Introduction

Robert A. Martin

The publication of *The Writer's Craft* happily coincides with the fiftieth anniversary of the Hopwood writing awards and the publication of *The Hopwood Anthology: Five Decades of American Poetry.*[1] The lectures collected here are from the last sixteen years (1965–81) of the annual awards ceremony held in Ann Arbor in April. Each year, a prominent writer is invited to deliver a lecture on a subject he or she considers of importance to young writers. Ever since 1932, when Robert M. Lovett gave the first lecture (on "Literature and Animal Faith"), to 1981, when Arthur Miller delivered the fiftieth anniversary keynote lecture. "The American Writer: The American Theater," the Hopwood lectures have served as beacons of inspiration for writers on the craft of writing.

In addition to the distinguished commentary by contributors to the present volume, two previous collections of Hopwood lectures, *The Writer and His Craft* (1954) and *To the Young Writer* (1965),[2] have included lectures by writers such as Carl Van Doren (1939), John Crowe Ransom (1942), Robert Penn Warren (1947), F. O. Matthiessen (1949), Archibald MacLeish (1955), Malcolm Cowley (1957), John Ciardi (1958), Theodore Roethke (1960), Saul Bellow (1961), Arthur Miller (1963), and Alfred Kazin (1964). Together with the prize money of over seven hundred thousand dollars distributed among two thousand award winners over the past fifty years, the Hopwood lectures not only constitute a remarkable contribution to American letters, they also serve as a testimony to the generosity and foresight of Avery Hopwood, a University of Michigan graduate and the founder of the contest.

Although better known today as the benefactor of the Hopwood writing awards than as a playwright, Avery Hopwood

(1884–1928) in his time was one of the most popular dramatists of the American theater. As a writer of light comedies and farce, he was the Neil Simon of his day. Hopwood's present-day obscurity has been attributed by Professor Arno Bader in his article, "Avery Hopwood, Dramatist," to the changing conditions of American drama:

> Hopwood was a man of the commercial theater as distinct from the literary drama. In the opening decades of the present century, when the American theater was groping its way toward maturity, Hopwood wrote plays of a largely ephemeral nature which had two purposes: to please Broadway and to make money.[3]

Hopwood was born in Cleveland, Ohio, and entered the University of Michigan in 1901. He contributed several short stories to the student literary magazine, the *Inlander*, and served as its literary editor during his senior year. A member of Phi Gamma Delta and the Quadrangle Club, Hopwood graduated, Phi Beta Kappa, in 1905. While he was still a student, Hopwood read an article in the January, 1904, issue of the *Michigan Alumnus* by Louis De Foe (class of 1891), who was the drama critic for the *New York Morning World*. Hopwood's account of his reaction to the financial rewards glowingly described by De Foe suggests that he had found his true calling at an early age. Shortly after reading De Foe's article, Hopwood later recalled, he began work on his first play, *Clothes*.

> An intense admiration for the theater, a fondness for writing, and the ambition to make money, contrived to pave the way for my career as a dramatist; but the influence that focused my efforts was an article written by Louis V. De Foe, that appeared in the *Michigan Alumnus*, when I was a student at the University of Michigan. "The Call of the Playwright" was its title, and in it Mr. De Foe told of the fabulous sums that dramatists had made; the more I thought about it, the more determined I became to try my luck in this field.[4]

Hopwood's luck was very good indeed. Following his graduation in 1905, he went to New York as a special correspondent for the Cleveland *Leader*. Shortly after his arrival, *Clothes* was accepted by a producer and opened on Broadway in the fall of 1906. An uneven play by today's standards, it nevertheless had enough appeal to New York audiences to enjoy a run of over one hundred performances and during its lifetime earned a total of $22,000 for its twenty-two-year-old author.

Hopwood immediately resigned his fifteen-dollars-a-week position with the *Leader* and settled down to a career as the "playboy playwright" of Broadway. In her memoir, *What Is Remembered*, Alice B. Toklas describes Hopwood and Carl Van Vechten as together having "created modern New York. They changed everything to their way of seeing and doing. It became as gay, irresponsible and brilliant as they were."[5] In 1920, Hopwood had four plays running on Broadway simultaneously, and in 1922 the *New York Times* described him as "almost unquestionably the richest of all playwrights." Five of his plays did exceptionally well: *Seven Days*, written with Mary Roberts Rinehart, earned $110,000 (1909); *Nobody's Widow*, $110,000 (1910); *Fair and Warmer*, $229,000 (1915); *The Gold Diggers*, $236,000 (1919); and *The Bat*, also written with Mary Roberts Rinehart, $339,000 (1920).[6]

Although Hopwood early and easily achieved financial success as a playwright, his unfulfilled ambition was to write a successful serious novel. His one published attempt, *Sadie Love*, has been characterized as "curiously inept," while the manuscript of a second novel, left unfinished at the time of his death, has been lost. Hopwood once told an interviewer: "There was always the one ambition—to write a novel, and I still have the feeling that fiction is a matter that requires more time than I have been able to give to it." Earlier in his career he had told a Cincinnati newspaper reporter that "I want to write books—fiction if you will, but I want to write something which an intelligent man can sit down and read and think about. I do not care so much about having him say, 'This was written by Hopwood' as to have him say, 'This was worth reading.'"[7] Avery Hopwood's literary legacy is slight, and yet his greatest ambition as a writer was to be taken seriously.

In the summer of 1928, Hopwood was vacationing in France. Following a party he gave in Paris, he sent a postcard to two of his guests, Gertrude Stein and Alice B. Toklas, thanking them for attending. "But there was no stamp on the card," Miss Toklas later recalled; "it was Avery's little way of getting things done for him without any bother. That very day we had news that Avery had been drowned in the Mediterranean."[8] After a dinner with friends on July 2, 1928, at Juan-les-Pins on the Riviera, Hopwood went swimming, was suddenly seized with a cramp, and drowned. Altogether, he was the author or coauthor of thirty-three plays and one novel during a brief but productive period of twenty-two years.

Under the terms of his will, one-fifth of Hopwood's estate ($313,836) was to be left to the Regents of the University of Michigan after the death of his mother, who died a few months later. According to the terms of the bequest, the regents are empowered

> To invest and keep the same invested and to use the income therefrom in perpetuity as prizes to be known as "The Avery Hopwood and Jule Hopwood Prizes" to be awarded annually to students in the Department of Rhetoric of The University of Michigan who perform the best creative work in the fields of dramatic writing, fiction, poetry, and the essay. The number and value of the prizes shall be at the discretion of the Faculty or other governing body of the University, but the income shall be distributed annually or semiannually, and shall not be allowed to accumulate from year to year. In this connection it is especially desired that the students competing for the prizes shall not be confined to academic subjects, but shall be allowed the widest possible latitude, and that the new, the unusual, and the radical shall be especially encouraged.[9]

At a meeting of September 26, 1930, the regents approved regulations authorizing the distribution of prize money as *Major Awards*, open to graduate students and seniors, and *Minor Awards*, open to undergraduates, including seniors and freshmen. A faculty committee was quickly appointed to serve as a policy-making body, and the first Hopwood contest was held in 1930–31. In 1932, Professor Bennett Weaver was appointed as the first director of the contest. He was succeeded in 1934 by Professor Roy W. Cowden, who had also served as assistant director during Professor Weaver's term. Professor Cowden continued to serve as director until 1952, during which time he was largely responsible for establishing the contest's national reputation that has made the words *Hopwood* and *literary excellence* nearly synonymous. Professor Cowden opened the first Hopwood Room in 1934 in Room 3227 Angell Hall, and began immediately to create the unique atmosphere and special collections of books and manuscripts that remain an integral part of the Hopwood presence on the Michigan campus.

In 1952, following Professor Cowden's retirement, the Hopwood Room with its manuscripts, books, tea set, and round oak table was moved to its present location in 1006 Angell Hall under the direction of its new director, Professor Arno L. Bader. Under his energetic leadership from 1952–65, the Hopwood contest continued to refine and build upon the strengths and traditions of the preceding years. From 1965–72, Professor Robert F. Haugh ably served as chairman (the title of director having lapsed in 1965), giving generously of his sage advice and friendly counsel to hundreds of students. In 1973 and 1974, the committee was cochaired by Professors Donald Hall and Sheridan Baker. They were succeeded in 1975 by the present chairman, Professor John W. Aldridge, who has gracefully continued the high standards of Hopwood administration and tradition established by his predecessors.

The Hopwood Room has been extremely fortunate in having a succession of chairmen and secretaries who have given freely of their time, talents, and friendship to Michigan students. In 1941, Miss Mary Cooley became Professor Cowden's assistant, serving as secretary, presiding over the traditional Thursday afternoon teas, and carrying on an extensive correspondence with Hopwood writers until her retirement in 1972. Miss Cooley was followed as secretary by Sister Hilda

Bonham, whose warmth and friendship will be remembered by those who visited the Hopwood Room between 1972–81. The present coordinator, Dr. Andrea Beauchamp, has recently begun her term as the third person to hold the position in forty years.

Since 1939, the Hopwood secretary has compiled and edited the *Hopwood Newsletter*, which is circulated twice a year to all award winners. News of activities, awards, publications, and achievements in the *Newsletter* admirably serves as an extension of 1006 Angell Hall throughout the world to Hopwood alumni from 1931 to the present. In addition to the awards ceremony in April, the Hopwood Committee conducts a summer contest and a winter underclassmen contest, open to freshmen and sophomores only. The underclassmen awards, announced in January, are accompanied by a reading. In recent years writers such as Gwendolyn Brooks, Robert Coles, Maxine Kumin, and Eudora Welty have read from their works at the winter awards ceremonies.

To commemorate the fiftieth anniversary of the Hopwood contest in 1981, the committee sponsored a "Hopwood Festival," held on April 9, 10, and 11, to coincide with the annual awards ceremony.[10] Distinguished winners in each of the four award categories were invited to participate in panel discussions and to give readings from their recent works. Focusing on the theme, "To the Young Writer," the panelists were asked to direct their remarks to the social, artistic, and personal problems confronting the writer in America. All former Hopwood winners who could be located were invited to attend the public conference, and playwright Arthur Miller (class of 1938) accepted the committee's invitation to deliver the keynote address, which is included in this collection. Panel members for the drama were Melvin Gordon, Dennis McIntyre, and Norman Rosten; for poetry, John Ciardi, Dorothy Donnelly, and X. J. Kennedy; for fiction, Max Apple, William Brashler, and Nancy Willard; for the essay, John Malcolm Brinnin, Theodore Solotaroff, and Chad Walsh. The conference was considered a great success by all who attended, not only as a Hopwood celebration and reunion, but also as a public forum in which a greater understanding of the writer's work and position in American society could be analyzed and discussed by writers and readers alike.

During the fifty years of the Hopwood writing awards nearly seventy of the winning manuscripts have been published. In addition, one wall of the Hopwood chairman's office contains over five hundred books representing the later work of only a few of the two thousand winners of the past and present. The exact number of books, articles, essays, poems, plays, and short stories published by all the recipients of a Hopwood award will probably never be known. Numerous winners, however, have publicly praised their teachers and members of the Hopwood Committee for their help and encouragement on the road to publication; an even larger number have expressed their professional gratitude to the Hopwood awards for sustaining their writing ambitions with recognition and money during their student days of apprenticeship. All of them, one would like to think, have at some time reflected on Avery Hopwood's wisdom in encouraging young writers at Michigan to pursue "the new, the unusual, and the radical."

Notes

1. Harry Thomas and Steven Lavine, eds., *The Hopwood Anthology: Five Decades of American Poetry* (Ann Arbor: University of Michigan Press, 1981).

2. Roy W. Cowden, ed., *The Writer and His Craft* (Ann Arbor: University of Michigan Press, 1954), and Arno L. Bader, ed., *To the Young Writer* (Ann Arbor: University of Michigan Press, 1965).

3. Arno L. Bader, "Avery Hopwood, Dramatist," *Michigan Alumnus/Quarterly Review* 66 (Autumn 1959):60.

4. Bader, p. 60.

5. Alice B. Toklas, *What Is Remembered* (New York: Holt, Rinehart, and Winston, 1963), p. 126.

6. Bader, p. 66.

7. Bader, pp. 63 and 68.

8. Toklas, p. 127.

9. At the time Mr. Hopwood made his will (1922) the Depart-

ment of Rhetoric and Journalism was a single department. In 1929 journalism was made a department separate from rhetoric, and in 1930 the Department of Rhetoric merged with the Department of English.

10. See also "Avery Hopwood and the Hopwood Awards, 1931–1981," an exhibition catalog prepared by the Department of Rare Books and Special Collections in the University of Michigan Graduate Library, 1981.

Sincerity and Poetry

Donald Davie

Kenneth Rexroth declares, introducing *Selected Poems of D. H. Lawrence* (Viking, 1959):

> Hardy could say to himself: "Today I am going to be a Wiltshire yeoman, sitting on a fallen rock at Stonehenge, writing a poem to my girl on a piece of wrapping paper with the gnawed stub of a pencil," and he could make it very convincing. But Lawrence really was the educated son of a coal miner, sitting under a tree that had once been part of Sherwood Forest, in a village that was rapidly becoming part of a world-wide disemboweled hell, writing hard, painful poems, to girls who carefully had been taught the art of unlove. It was all real. Love really was a mystery at the navel of the earth, like Stonehenge. The miner really was in contact with a monstrous, seething mystery, the black sun in the earth.

And again:

> Hardy was a major poet. Lawrence was a minor prophet. Like Blake and Yeats, his is the greater tradition. If Hardy ever had a girl in the hay, tipsy on cider, on the night of Boxing Day, he kept quiet about it. He may have thought that it had something to do with "the stream of his life in the darkness deathward set," but he never let on, except indirectly.

This is outrageous, of course. In part, at least, it is meant to be. It is outrageously unfair to Thomas Hardy. But then, fairness is what we never find from anyone who at any time speaks up for what Rexroth is speaking for here. Are prophets fair-minded? Can we expect Jeremiah or Amos or Isaiah to be *judicious?* D. H. Lawrence was monstrously unfair; so were nineteenth-century prophets like Carlyle and Ruskin, so was William Blake unfair to Reynolds and to Wordsworth. And some of them, some of the time—perhaps all of them, most of the time—know that they are being unfair, as I think Kenneth Rexroth knows it. Fair-mindedness, Lawrence seems to say, is not his business; if judiciousness is necessary to society, it is the business of someone in society other than the prophet or the poet.

"The prophet *or* the poet"—for, although I've gone along with Rexroth for the last few minutes in accepting this distinction, I am not really convinced by it. For what *is* the distinction which Rexroth has drawn, between Hardy and Lawrence? As he presents it to us, it has nothing to do with prophecy, though he seems to think it has. The distinction is quite simply that when "I" appears in a poem by Lawrence, the person meant is directly and immediately D. H. Lawrence, the person as historically recorded, born in such and such a place on such and such a date; whereas when "I" appears in a poem by Hardy, the person meant need not be the historically recorded Thomas Hardy, any more than when King Lear in Shakespeare's play says, "I," the person meant is William Shakespeare.

When Rexroth introduces the notion of a tradition of *prophecy*, above all when he puts in that tradition the most histrionic of modern poets (W. B. Yeats), he is shifting his ground abruptly and very confusingly. What he is saying to start with is simply and bluntly that Lawrence is always sincere, whereas Hardy often isn't; and Lawrence is sincere by virtue of the fact that the "I" in his poems is always directly and immediately himself. In other words, the poetry we are asked to see as greater than Hardy's kind of poetry, though it is called "prophetic" poetry, is more accurately described as *confessional poetry*. Confessional poetry, of its nature and necessarily, is superior to dramatic or histrionic poetry; a poem in which the "I" stands immediately and unequivocally for the author is essentially and necessarily superior to a poem in which the "I" stands not for the author but for a persona of the author's—this is what Rexroth asks us to believe.

In asking us for this he is asking us, as he well knows, to fly in the face of what seemed, until a few years ago, the solidly achieved consensus of opinion about poetry and the criticism of poetry. That consensus of opinion seemed to have formed itself on the basis of insights delivered to us by the revolutionary poets of two or three generations ago. It had taken the idea of the persona from Ezra Pound, and the closely related idea of the mask from W. B. Yeats, and it had taken from T. S. Eliot the ideas that the structure of a poem was inherently a dramatic structure, and that the effect of poetry was an impersonal effect. It had elaborated on these hints to formulate a rule, the rule that the "I" in a poem is *never* immediately and directly the poet; that the-poet-in-his-poem is always distinct from, and must never be confounded with, the-poet-outside-his-poem, the poet as historically recorded between birthdate and date of death. To this rule there was a necessary and invaluable corollary: that the question, "Is the poet sincere?"—though it would continue to be asked by naive readers—was always an impertinent and illegitimate question. This was the view of poetry associated with the so-called New Criticism, and (although it has been challenged from other directions than the one we are concerned with) it is still the view of poetry taught in our university classrooms. Must we now abandon it?

I think we must—or rather, that we may and must hold by it for the sake of the poetry which it illuminates, but that we can no longer hold by it as an account which does justice to *all* poetry. It illuminates nearly all the poetry that we want to remember written in England between 1550 and about 1780; but it illuminates little of the poetry in English written since 1780. For my own part, much of the time I bitterly regret having to give it up as regards the poetry of our own time. I see too clearly the grievous consequences of doing so, of having the question of "sincerity," which we thought to be safely scotched, once again rearing its head as a central question. Anyone can see these consequences—*see* them, not *foresee* them, because they are with us already. For the question has been settled already, off campus; and it is only in the university classrooms that anyone any longer supposes that "Is he sincere?" is a question not to be asked of poets.

Confessional poetry has come back with a vengeance; for many years now it is the poetry that has been written by the most serious and talented poets, alike in this country and in Britain. Consider only the case of Robert Lowell, probably the most influential poet of his generation. It is a very telling case indeed: trained in the very heart of New Criticism by Allen Tate, Lowell made his reputation by poems which are characteristically dramatic monologues, in which the "I" of the poet was hardly ever to be identified with the historical Robert Lowell. Then in the mid-fifties came his collection called *Life Studies* in which the "I" of the poems nearly always asks to be taken, quite unequivocally, as Robert Lowell himself. At about the same time, from under the shadow of Rexroth himself, came Allen Ginsberg's prophetic-confessional poem, "Howl!" And ever since, confessional poems have been the order of the day, with the predictable consequences—the poem has lost all its hard-won autonomy, its independence in its own right, and has once again become merely the vehicle by which the writer acts out before his public the agony or the discomfort (American poets go for agony, British ones for discomfort) of being a writer, or of being alive in the twentieth century. Now we have once again poems in which the public life of the author as author, and his private life, are messily compounded, so that one needs the adventitious information of the gossip columnist to take the force or even the literal meaning of what, since it is a work of literary art, is supposedly offered as public utterance. And woe betide that poet whose life, when the gossip columnist–reviewer goes to work on it, does not reveal fornications and adulteries, drug addictions, alcoholism, and spells in mental homes. "What?" the reviewer exclaims, "When it appears that your poems have cost you so little, when the writing of them has apparently disorganized your life hardly at all, can you expect me to give them as much attention as the poems of Miss X here, whose vocation drove her last week to suicide?"

If this is what can happen when the question of sincerity

once again becomes central to the judgment of poetry, how much we must wish that we could hold firm to those precepts of the New Criticism which ruled that question out of order. Why not? If the universities are the bulwarks of that more decorous view of poetry, what more proper than that the universities should resist with disdain the disheveled sensationalism of the literary worlds of London and New York? And after all, aren't most of these new confessional poets very bad poets? Yes, they are; as most poets of any kind, at any given moment, are bad poets. But Robert Lowell isn't. And in fact, it won't wash: the question of sincerity can never again be out of order. For, as we see now, even in the heyday of the persona and of impersonality in poetry there were poets writing who would not fit the doctrine and who came off badly in consequence. Ezra Pound, the very man who introduced the concept of persona, was one of those who came off badly. His *Pisan Cantos*, written late in his career, are confessional poems, and they have been esteemed by many who find all or most of the rest of Pound unreadable. Who shall say those readers are wrong? William Carlos Williams wrote confessional poems which a criticism evolved to do justice to T. S. Eliot could get no purchase on. Thomas Hardy, for all that Kenneth Rexroth herds him in with the poets of the persona, in fact came off badly at the hands of a criticism which based itself on the persona. And there is, indeed there is, D. H. Lawrence. Was Lawrence a poet at all? The New Criticism, true to its lights, decided for the most part that he wasn't. But he wrote, along with too much that is messy and strident, "River Roses" and "Gloire de Dijon" and "Snake," poems which any candid and unperverted taste must applaud, poems which do indeed (and this is the strength of Kenneth Rexroth's case) make us exclaim at finding the business of poetry once again so simple, so straightforward, so direct.

To be sure, Lawrence is not a confessional poet as Lowell and Ginsberg are confessional poets. For the confessional poet comes in two sizes: there are the Wordsworthian poets who confess to virtue (like Pasternak), as well as the Byronic poets who confess to vice (like Baudelaire). Lawrence in this respect is of the Wordsworthian sort, and in fact he was very hard and contemptuous toward writers such as Rozanov who confessed to meannesses and perversities. For myself, I find it easier today to sympathize with the Wordsworthians than the Baudelaireans. For our leaders of literary fashion long ago fell over backward in their determination not to treat the Baudelaires of our day as the pundits of Paris in the 1860s treated Baudelaire. In other words, those who demand most insistently that our poetry be confessional, demand also that its confessions be Baudelairean; they are so determined that the poetic vocation be agonized and disheveled that they are never so affronted as by the Wordsworthian or Pasternakian poetry which confesses, on the contrary, to having found the poetic vocation stabilizing and composing and refreshing. Robert Bly is one contemporary poet who makes this Wordsworthian claim to have gained access through his vocation to sources of refreshment and composure; and however we might differ as to the intrinsic quality of Bly's poems, we can see that it is this pretension which has provoked some of his reviewers to fury.

But there is more than this to be said. *Byronic* is a term we may use lightly; *Wordsworthian* is not, or not in my usage. If it is true, as I am suggesting, that with those of our poets who confess to virtue we have a recovery of the note of Wordsworth, we need to understand just what this means. What is involved is the assumption or the contention (with Wordsworth it was a contention) that the living of a poetic life is more important than the writing of poems; that the poems indeed have their value less in themselves than as pointing back to the life that they have come out of, which they witness to. (It may be indeed that "poetry of witness" would be a better name for what I have called "confessional poetry." "Witness," for instance, fits Williams's poems better than "confession." And "witness," as we hear it used from the pulpit ("a Christian witness"), explains better than "confession" why such poetry is often "prophetic" into the bargain.) This view of poetry is horribly dangerous, especially in our age when publicity is an industry with a fearsome range of techniques for exploiting the personality, distorting it, and destroying its privacy. This view of poetry opens the door to the exhibitionists; to the deceivers and self-deceivers (the conscious and unconscious hypocrites); to the man who will plume himself on his status as a poet, and demand special privileges on the strength of it, without ever submitting to having his qualifications examined. All this is true. These are indeed the lamentable consequences of once again admitting the Romantic pretension that the poetic life is more important than any of the poems which come out of it. Nevertheless these consequences must be accepted, and even gladly accepted. For I want to say now that at those infrequent moments when, as readers or writers, we think really earnestly about what poetry is and means, we cannot regret that the question of sincerity has once again become central. On the contrary we must welcome it; we must welcome the change from poetry seen as the extant body of achieved poems, to poetry seen as a way of behaving, a habit of feeling deeply and truly and responsibly. If poetry is once again making Wordsworthian pretensions, we must be glad of this, whatever the untidy and embarrassing and disconcerting consequences.

In the first place we must be glad to be compelled to recognize that we are all, like it or not, post-Romantic people; that the historical developments which we label "Romanticism" were not a series of aberrations we can and should disown, but rather a sort of landslide that permanently transformed the mental landscape which in the twentieth century we inhabit, however reluctantly. It seems to me now that this was a recognition which I came to absurdly late in life; that my teachers when I was young encouraged me to think that I could expunge Romanticism from my historical past by a mere act of will or stroke of the pen, and that by doing this I could climb back into the lost garden of the seventeenth century. It is not a question of what we want or like; it is what we are stuck with—post-Romantic is what we are.

But there is a more urgent reason why we should welcome *sincerity* back into our vocabulary. And it's for this reason that I have coupled (I think justly) the name of Pasternak with that of Wordsworth. For who of us can doubt, examining the spectacle of Pasternak, that here is a case in which the witness of a poet's life lived through matters more than any of the poems which that poet wrote—poems which most of us can't judge in any case, for lack of adequate translations? It was poets, it was at all events writers, who brought the Hungarians into the streets of Budapest in 1956, as it was a poet, Petöfi, who in 1848 incited the Hungarians into revolt against the Austrian Empire. This is what it means to be a poet, or what it *can* mean, in societies less fortunate than yours or mine. What these extreme situations put to the test is not a poem but a poet; or (more precisely) it is poetry embodied in persons who have dedicated themselves to a life of sincere feeling, not poetry embodied in poems which resist all the guns of the critical seminar. And isn't this indeed what Pasternak spells out for us in his *Doctor Zhivago*, that narrative of a poetic life, a life which, simply by being lived through, challenges and criticizes and condemns the society about it?

To be sure, it is easier to applaud in this way the Wordsworthian poetry which witnesses to virtue, than the Byronic or Baudelairean poetry which confesses to vice. The name of Baudelaire is there to show (and in some measure the name of Ginsberg shows it also) that the latter sort of poetry can challenge and condemn the society it is written from. But over this Byronic sort of poetry there necessarily falls the shadow of a divided purpose: the poet confesses to discreditable sentiments or behavior, but in doing so he demands credit for having the courage or the honesty of his shamelessness. By contrast the Wordsworthian poet is asking for credit quite unequivocally. He may be deceiving himself, he may not have earned the credit which he asks for, and we may withhold it. But at least he knows, and we know, what he is up to; he is not wooing us, coquetting with us, glancing at us sidelong.

If the question "Is he sincere?" is reinstated as a legitimate question to be asked of a poet, what is the consequence of this for those of us who read and write poetry specifically in the universities? The most revolutionary consequence is one that is really counterrevolutionary: the biographer, who a genera-

tion ago was excluded from literary criticism, or at least demoted, must now be reinstalled as a highly respectable figure.
In itself this does not matter much, for in fact we've all continued drawing on the biographies of dead poets, though it's
been important for some of us to pretend that we weren't
doing so. In the case of our living contemporaries, however,
the case is different; for until the biography of a poet is written, his place has to be taken by the retailer of gossip. Or so it
may seem. In fact, however, in the case of a living contemporary poet, we rely not on biography but autobiography; the
confessional poet is his own biographer, and his poems are his
autobiography. Like any other autobiographer, he selects
what he will reveal and suppresses much more. And insofar as
the confessional poet thus presents only a trimmed and slanted
image of himself, he may still be thought to be revealing to us
not a personality but a persona. This is to use the term persona
in an extended but thoroughly legitimate sense. Yet it seems
to me unhelpful, and even a sort of evasion. The poets we are
speaking of are trying to break out of the world of rhetoric; and
although we can spread the nets of rhetoric wide enough to
catch them despite their struggles, in doing so we are being
ungenerous and we are even being dishonest, because we are
refusing to acknowledge what is so patently the impetus behind their writing. Moreover, as critics we need to ask ourselves why we should so much want to do this. Why is it so
important to us as critics to seal off the world of literature from
the adjacent worlds of biography and history and geography?
What are we afraid of?

In any event, however, we are not required to dismantle
the whole body of our current assumptions. In part at least,
the measure of a poet's sincerity is, it must be, *inside his
poem*. This is to say that confessional or prophetic pretensions
in the poet do not absolve him from producing poems that are
well written. This seems too obvious to be worth saying. But
alas! among the hoary fallacies which the new confessional
poetry has brought to life among us is the notion that we know
sincerity by its dishevelment; that to be elegant is to be insin-
cere. To be sure, we must beware of supposing that the marks

of good writing are few and obvious. Confessional poetry, when it is good, is characteristically limpid, thinly textured semantically. And so for instance ambiguity, a high incidence of words with double meanings—this, which we have thought of as a feature of all good writing, we must not recognize as a feature of only *one kind* of good writing. For rather different reasons, irony and paradox are features which we must learn to set less store by. We must learn, I dare say, to give more weight to other features, notably to the *tone* in which the poet addresses us, and to the fall and pause and run of spoken American or spoken English as the poet plays it off against his stanza-breaks and line-division. In short, a poet can control his poem in many more ways, or his control of it manifests itself in more ways, than until lately we were aware of. Nevertheless we were right all along to think that a poem is valuable according as the poet has control of it; now we must learn to call that control "sincerity." For after all, what is the alternative? Are we to collect gossip about his private life? Are we to believe the poet sincere because he tells us so? Or because he shouts at us? Or (worst of all) because he writes a disheveled poetry, because the poem and the experience behind the poem are so manifestly *out* of his control?

To be sure, *control* is a word that may easily be misunderstood. Yet I think we need it in order to acknowledge how much of the poetic activity in the act of composition can be summed up in words like *judgment* and *prudence*. For I should maintain, in the teeth of Kenneth Rexroth, that, as for prophetic poetry (which may be, but need not be, confessional poetry also), it is necessarily an inferior poetry. My reasons I have given already. The prophet is above being fair-minded—judiciousness he leaves to someone else. But the poet will absolve himself from none of the responsibilities of being human, he will leave none of those responsibilities to "someone else." And being human involves the responsibility of being judicious and fair-minded. In this way the poet supports the intellectual venture of humankind, taking his place along with (though *above*, yet also along with) the scholar and the statesman and the learned divine. His poetry supports and nourishes and helps to shape culture; the prophet, however, is outside culture and (really) at war with it. The prophet exists on sufferance, he is on society's expense account, part of what society can sometimes afford. Not so the poet; he is what society cannot dispense with.

1965

That Cloistered Jazz

Peter Taylor

> The Sultan Schahriar, convinced that all women are false and
> faithless, vowed to put to death each of his wives after the first
> nuptial night. But the Sultana Scheherazade saved her life by
> entertaining her lord with fascinating tales, told seriatim, for a
> thousand and one nights. The Sultan, consumed with curiosity,
> postponed from day to day the execution of his wife, and finally
> repudiated his bloody vow entirely.
>
> *—The Thousand and One Nights*

The life of a professional writer has a good deal in common
with that of the Sultana Scheherazade. He must keep on inventing something new and fascinating, or it's off with his
head. But the analogy can be taken only so far, because, alas,
the writer's sultan, the public, never repudiates its bloody
vow. Moreover, the professional writer has not only to produce regularly, lest he be forgotten, he must every year come
up with a better book than the one he wrote the year before,
or else the critics will say his work is falling off. He absolutely
cannot allow that to be said.

If by *professional writer* we mean a writer who earns his
livelihood by writing, then the fellow's situation is truly desperate. Today, it seems almost impossible to prevent professionalism in any field from passing over into commercialism. I
believe the saddest news one has to give any young writer just
setting out is that very few good writers are able to support
themselves by their writing. I do not mean to say that no good
writers can, with great good luck, earn a living by writing. But
they are certainly few. And the important point is that the
quality of their work is not a determining factor. It has, in fact,
nothing at all to do with financial success.

But even if we think of professionalism as meaning something quite different, it still has its dangers for the writer—the artist. One sometimes hears a writer say admiringly of another writer: "I don't like anything he has written very much, but he is a real professional." That means, I suppose, that this professional has very clear ideas about what good writing is. He has standards, and he is faithful to them in his own work and in his judgment of the work of others. It means he is concerned with the literature of his day and, I'm afraid, overly concerned with the literary scene of his day. That is all something quite different from the business of earning a living. But, still, imagine overhearing someone say about you: "I don't like anything he has written very much, but he is a real professional." How much better to hear someone say of you: "He's no professional, God knows, but in such and such a piece of work he *is* inspired!"

My own view is that writers should be freed from any sort of mere professionalism. Individual writers are as different from each other as individual doctors or lawyers are, and their lives can and should be just as different. In fact, a writer—man or woman—may choose to be, or happen to be, a journalist in New York, a doctor in New Jersey, a housewife in Indiana, or a schoolteacher in Ohio. Or he may by temperament prefer the life of a beachcomber. That is his own affair, and happy is the writer who finds early in life an occupation that gives him satisfaction and money and that allows him whatever time he needs for his writing. (Does it even have to be said that some writers require all their time for their writing and that others thrive on an active life into which they somehow manage to squeeze additional hours for their most serious work?) Above all, one should not avoid doing whatever work he finds and likes simply because he has not heard of another writer's doing it or because he fears it might hurt his image as a writer. One's image as a writer is of no importance, of course. Contrary to what one may be led to believe nowadays, the serious writer—the poet, the short story writer, the novelist, the playwright—is not like a movie star. Nothing hurts a good writer but bad writing. I am always amused to hear it said of some novelist or short story writer that he was ruined by teaching, or by the movies, or even by the *New Yorker*. To my ear it sounds even funnier to hear a young writer, one who has as yet published nothing, declare manfully that he intends to avoid those pitfalls. I heard one such young man express his shock at the news that an older novelist of his acquaintance had sold a novel to the movies for two hundred and fifty thousand dollars: "I didn't think *he* would do that!" And I have even, believe it or not, heard published writers say that they don't want to read too much for fear it will hurt them as writers. If one is going to be "ruined" by publishing in the *New Yorker*, or by selling a novel to the movies, or by reading students' themes and talking about literature before a class, then one doesn't have far to go to be ruined. Indeed, one *had* better watch out about reading too much.

I suppose the question one has heard most often during the past thirty years, in this connection, is: "Should a writer teach?" It is a silly question. The good question is: "Should a writer not teach?" Like many another, I began teaching as a way of earning an honest dollar. I say an "honest" dollar because I knew that teaching freshman and sophomore English was something I was capable of doing reasonably well. I must admit, however, that I thought of it then merely as something to tide me over until the day when the vast income from my writing would settle me comfortably on a huge plantation in West Tennessee. A dozen years later, when it seemed finally that I just might eke out an existence on the income from my short stories (and from the foundations), I announced to the world and to the chairman of my department that I was making the great break. I was on leave that year. My wife and I—with our children—were spending the winter in London. When I wrote the chairman about my decision, he replied with a wonderfully warm letter, saying that he understood perfectly how I might have come to such a decision. We had a lovely exchange, telling each other what a pleasure, what a privilege, the association had been. Several months passed. Then one night my wife and I went to the theater with another American writer. The play we saw was written by a young American and

was one of the best, or worst, examples of the Theater of the
Absurd. We were so outraged by the bad writing in it that,
from our seats on the front row of the balcony, we booed and
waved our handkerchiefs. We felt ashamed of ourselves afterward, of course. But in the taxi going home, I suddenly announced that I, for one, was going back to teaching. I knew
that my wife and my friend didn't care to hear me expounding
endlessly upon how bad the play was and why, no more than I
cared to hear them. But I knew that somewhere in the United
States there was a class that would listen, that needed to listen, and that I needed to be heard by. If I could not improve
the taste of students, if I could not encourage good writing
among them, at least I might somehow discourage among
them the sort of bad writing that had gone into that play. I felt
"needed." I got off a letter that night to my former chairman,
and he replied that my place had not yet been filled. I suspect
that he had waited to fill it, knowing before I did that I was
hooked for life by teaching, knowing that such a letter was apt
to be coming along from me any day.

It is interesting to me to think of the chief sources of the
criticism leveled at the writer who teaches. The first person
who comes to mind is Mr. Dowds, the internal revenue man,
in Columbus, Ohio. Mr. Dowds examined my federal tax returns in about the year 1957, and ordered me to report to him
in his office on Gay Street. When I sat down in the straight
chair beside his desk, he asked without looking up at me,
"What is this Fulbright thing? And what made you think you
didn't have to pay the full tax on it?" I explained that it was a
research grant and that my understanding was that it wasn't
taxable—not the full amount. He got up, peered into his filing
cabinet, shrugged his shoulders. Then he looked at me for the
first time and said, "Nothing doing."

That was that. But Mr. Dowds had not finished. Presently
he said, "Now, about this trip down to Nashville to see your
play produced, what about that?" I explained that I was paid
nothing by the producer of the play but that it was very much
to my interest—or might be—as an ambitious playwright to go
down to see it and that I had been urged by the producers to

be there for the opening night as a matter of publicity. "Well, you got to see your play acted, didn't you?" he said. "Nothing doing."

It ended by Mr. Dowds's going over my returns for the two or three previous years and eventually sending me notice to the effect that I owed his department three thousand dollars. Innocent idiot that I was, I paid the amount. But there was more to the inquisition that day in Mr. Dowds's office on Gay Street. In going over my returns, he must have observed that I listed my occupation as "writer-teacher." For presently he put down his pencil and looked me in the eye to say, "Are you a writer *or* a teacher? You had ought to make up your mind." The very idea was too complicated for him, I suppose. He went on to imply that either I was wasting a lot of time by writing or I was wasting a lot of time by teaching. And his final, fatherly advice was this—I quote verbatim: "The truth of the matter is, you ought to give up writing. Now that we've got TV, writing is on its way out. [The conversation took place in Ohio.] Why, I used to subscribe to four or five magazines, but now I've got TV, I only take *Popular Mechanics*, and sometimes I don't even read it." As I have said, that's verbatim. That's the voice of our government speaking to its writers. When Mr. Dowds peered into his filing cabinet looking for instructions on how to deal with my case, he found none. Because none existed. Our Congress had passed the income tax laws without making any provision for artists and writers. So far as they were concerned, we did not exist. Anyway, it was left to the likes of Mr. Dowds, in the isolation of Central Ohio, to decide what to do with us. At the time, I could not help thinking of a sentence I had read in a letter Ezra Pound once wrote to somebody: "A government that does not support its artists is a barbarian dunghill."

But Mr. Dowds's inquisition persisted even a little beyond that. I had the temerity to suggest that perhaps I ought to see a lawyer. It was the wrong thing—or the *very* thing—to say to Mr. Dowds. For then he would not let me go until he had told me what he thought of lawyers and the trouble they make for people in this world. "They're the ones that make it necessary for us to be so tough on you guys." But I can't give you the exact words of the diatribe he then launched against lawyers, farmers, and college professors. (In his wildest dreams he had never thought he would come up against a writer. And he didn't know how lucky he was in the writer he drew. I sat there, perishing in my self-contempt, but keeping my mind on the buck I wanted to save in back taxes. After all, there was the wife and children to think of. For us timid souls, there is always the wife and children for an excuse.) Anyway, those were the people who somehow made life intolerable for Mr. Dowds—lawyers, farmers, teachers, and now, if he didn't nip them in the bud, writers. I do just remember two sentences he had for teachers in a state university: "Why, you college professors are nothing but state employees. Don't forget that. You are no different from my janitor out there, sweeping the corridor."

Mr. Dowds's voice was the voice of our government and also the voice of our philistine society. Such men as Mr. Dowds really feel that writers should have no income, that we should take sustenance from the sweet air we breathe in this best of all possible worlds. Either that, or they believe that if writing doesn't pay, then a man ought to give it up and go into something worth his while. He should *not* seek a congenial means of earning his livelihood and thus manage to continue the work of his imagination. Writing—poetry, that is to say—must reduce its terms. Poetry must come to terms with the world. Perhaps the last word of fatherly advice these men would give us is: "Give up writing, but don't turn to something so shaky, so perilously near the writing of poetry as college teaching."

Strangely enough—and for very different reasons, of course—some of those who are most vocal against the writer-teacher are men who are writers of a sort themselves. How often, on some campus where I happen to be teaching, one of these men turns up, an old acquaintance usually, just passing through town. He works either for *Esquire* or *Playboy* or is connected "temporarily" with a publishing house or even a foundation. At lunch, in the college cafeteria, he whispers his

question in my ear: "How long are you going to continue to
bury yourself teaching in this dull, provincial place?" He, you
see, is where the action is. He is experiencing real life, he—
approaching forty and balding a little and married to a rather
wealthy third wife—is looking still for his subject and knows
only that it won't be found in places with names like Columbus
and Bloomington and Greensboro and Ann Arbor. (He may
say that even his income tax man in New York would not be so
provincial as Mr. Dowds. After all, in New York they are used
to dealing with show people, hoofers, and "other artists,"
or—he might say—"that type thing.") Even more vociferous is
the visiting lecturer—frequently an English poet or novelist.
After his lecture, which followed drinks and a dinner at a
chairman's house, and after more drinks at the president's
mansion following the lecture (since he is an English writer,
the president will probably entertain him), he first insults the
rest of the faculty and then gets you in a corner to ask you how
you can bear "this life" (the one you have freely chosen). Think
what it's doing to your style! Have you thought of getting a
lecture agent and giving up teaching? Six or eight lectures in
one season will bring in about as much as a year's teaching,
that and doing a certain number of omnibus reviews. I am
afraid that to the attacks from those visiting lecturers I remain
as silent as I did with Mr. Dowds. But it seems unnecessary to
defend what you are doing if you like doing it. And besides,
those poor lecturing fellows, what have they in the performance of their duties so satisfying as the rapport one establishes with one's students over the months and years? How
much more real and meaningful our cloistered lives and our
schedules of regular class meetings must seem to us than those
poor fellows' one-night stands seem to them, giving the same
lecture over and over to different seas of faces.

There is yet another critic of the writer-teacher, and he is
perhaps the most severe of all. He is the writer who teaches in
a college or university and is somehow ashamed of the fact. He
had always felt that deep down in his soul he is too "academic"
to be a writer. He likes being around a college but is afraid of
what this liking may mean. Often, instead of making one-night

stands, he makes one-year or one-semester stands as "writer in residence." In the college town, he goes into a shop to establish credit. The merchant asks him politely if he is a professor at "the college." He pales and quickly protests, "Oh, no! I am the writer in residence!" He accepts many invitations out to dinner, hoards his money, and next year he will be off to Paris, or to Connecticut—the real world—where he will tell stories about the "incredible" place where he was cloistered last year.

I remember, one time in New York City, just after World War II, telling a literary friend about my interview for a job at the college where I now teach in North Carolina. It was known then as the Woman's College of the University of North Carolina, and to the ears of my friend it didn't sound like a place where a serious writer could find much satisfaction in life. But what really horrified him was my description of the interview itself. I don't think I need repeat the description. Suffice it to say, there was a long luncheon with six senior members of the English Department—four men and two women—and there were several hours spent in the offices of the chancellor and the dean of students. My friend said it sounded degrading. He would never teach if he had to submit to such an indignity, the indignity of being passed upon by those old fogies. To me, it didn't seem quite so bad as that. Why, I had, so to speak, known those four middle-aged Southern men and those two spinsters all my life. I must admit, even, that for me, the short story writer, they seemed grist for the mill. And, speaking quite literally, I have now known those six for nearly half my life and count them among my good friends. They seem much younger to me today than they did when I was a boy of twenty-eight. Like one's students, they are a part of one's "real" life and also a part of one's literary life. What my outraged friend seems to have been saying, and what a good many fiction writers seem always to be saying nowadays is: "Have nothing to do with old people. Have nothing to do with children or young people. Consort only with those who are of your own age and temperament and profession." And doesn't it show? Unlike Dickens, and Trollope, and Chekhov, and Faulkner, we are not concerned nowadays with observing and rendering a variety of human beings in our novels and stories. We are interested only in observing and rendering one human being, the author.

I suppose that all I am really trying to suggest is that if ever the life of the college teacher in America was a cloistered life, it is no longer so, and that if a writer discovers he is temperamentally suited to teaching he should rejoice in the knowledge rather than suffer any sense of shame. But don't let me give the impression that I think the writer finds no problems in teaching, particularly if he has concluded that what he wishes to teach is creative writing. Don't let me convey the impression that, from the moment I received my first appointment at what is now the University of North Carolina at Greensboro, I was content with my lot. I have left my niche there more than once to teach at other institutions, and each time it was simply because I thought it would be fun to teach somewhere else for a while. (You will notice that I am not going into the problems that writers make for even the most sympathetic college administrators.) The problems for, the pressures on, a writer who is teaching are very great. They are very great for productive scholars also, and for the scholar and the writer they are not so very different either. At the least the two can agree that teaching itself is not the difficulty. And possibly they can agree that committee work is what they find most stifling and time-consuming. I don't propose to offer solutions to any of the troubles with teaching. I am, at the most, only acknowledging that they exist. I used to maintain that when I received in one mail the notices of two committee meetings, I had in effect heard my neighbor's axe and that like Daniel Boone I knew it was time for me to move on.

At one place where I went to teach, I soon discovered that there were ten classes in creative writing and that I was expected to hold regular meetings with the staff involved. Moreover, we were asked to draw up plans for giving graduate degrees in writing and to prepare ourselves at once to direct the theses. I saw that what was needed was a man with talents for administration, which I do not possess. At another place, I discovered after a year that I was going to be asked to edit a literary quarterly, discovered that I had really been hired for that purpose. The purpose seemed always to be something other than teaching and writing. I tried one more place, though, before going home again. And there the problem was entirely different. I was given an office and a light schedule — almost no schedule, in fact (you can't please these writers) — and I felt that I was, in effect, told to make myself scarce. Before long I began to notice that there were only three or four students in one of my two classes and less than a dozen in the other. And I wasn't much longer in getting the word that student advisers were not allowing good students to register for creative writing. The administration had brought in a writer, because it seemed the thing to do nowadays, and it wouldn't matter so long as he refrained from interfering with the serious work of the department. He was a necessary evil that the faculty would simply have to find a way of living with. The students must be protected, however. Above all, the graduate students, those who were going to teach literature, *must not* be permitted to go near the man, must not be subjected to the deadly influence of a live writer.

At this point, I suppose I am bound to say what I think the place of creative writing is in the curriculum of an English department. First, let me say that I think a creative writing course is a course in which one teaches literature. My idea is that students should be expected to read no less for that course than for any other. But even if the student does only a little reading, I regard "creative writing" as a way of teaching literature. It is the complement to the other method that is used in courses in the history and meaning of literature. But I am willing to go further than that. I think it is conceivable that every student seriously interested in literature should be asked to take at least one semester in creative writing, or, if he does not need someone to give him deadlines, then to spend one semester trying to write poetry and fiction which he may possibly never show to another living soul. I am willing almost to say that I believe our departments of literature should become more like our art departments and that our instructors might be expected to have demonstrated a certain proficiency in the different literary forms. I am, in fact, much more inclined to question the wisdom of offering regular period courses in contemporary literature than to question that of offering creative writing courses. In my mind, the novel, the book of stories, the book of poems, which is submitted as a thesis for a Master of Fine Arts degree, is a better indication of the writer's feeling and knowledge of literature than is the usual thesis for the doctoral degree.

But I should like to return to the question of whether a writer should not teach. Whatever his trials, there is the one great consolation, one about which those who have never taught regularly cannot know. I refer to the association with student writers themselves. I refer to the satisfaction of watching their minds and talents develop and the satisfaction of knowing that you are influencing their tastes in literature.

In returning to this question, in attempting to answer it, I want to append a personal memoir, a sort of impressionistic sketch, of a writer who did teach, who thrived on teaching, and who wrote what is undoubtedly the wittiest work yet produced dealing with the writer in the university. He is a much better subject than I would be for a sketch of the writer-teacher, because no one could dare accuse him of being a timid conformist. I am speaking of a beloved friend and colleague of mine, who died last year in North Carolina, at the age of fifty-one—the poet Randall Jarrell.

Randall came to teach at Greensboro the year after I did. He had to face there the same sort of "degrading" interview that I had faced a year earlier. I had known him well for a good many years before this, and I must admit that the day of his interview was a day I had dreaded for weeks. Not that I wasn't looking forward to seeing him again! I was dreading how he might behave at the luncheon, in the dean's office, in the chancellor's office. Among his teachers at Vanderbilt, he had been known for his impudence and his arrogance, as well as for his brilliance as a student. Among older literary people in New York, he already had a reputation as an enfant terrible. At the dinner table of a writer who was then regarded by younger men in New York as the Master, Randall had made an awful

breach. One of the Master's essays was being discussed re-
spectfully when suddenly Randall called out to him from the
far end of the table: "Oh, that's not one of your *good* essays.
Your good ones are . . . ," and he proceeded to list them. He
had not stopped to reflect that at the Master's dinner table all
his essays are good. He was never forgiven, I think. At any
rate, he was never asked back to dinner. At a college where he
taught briefly, just before World War II, he was out skiing one
day with the college president. Neither Randall nor the president had been on skis before. The president found himself
lying in the snow a good deal of the time. Randall, who was
very agile and who was good at almost any sport, went flying
by the president at one of the president's bad moments and
called back to him: "God made me for skis!" And Randall was
not asked back to teach at that college the next year.

The first I ever heard of Randall, when I was a boy in
Nashville, was that he was a boy who knew a lot and that he
had posed for the figure of Ganymede in the frieze of the
Parthenon—*our* Parthenon, that is, in Centennial Park,
Nashville, a full-sized model of the original, with the exact
Athenian dimensions. A sculptor who was making copies of
some of the figures for the frieze—Belle Kinney, I believe it
was—asked Randall to pose as cup bearer to the gods. That
was in 1922. The child Randall is there in Centennial Park
today, perhaps as good a justification as you could ask for the
existence of "our" Parthenon.

Anyway, the first I ever heard of him was that he was a boy
who knew a lot. I heard it from one of my childhood friends in
Nashville. But I didn't really know Randall Jarrell until I was
living in Memphis and came back to Vanderbilt as a freshman,
in 1936. Among the literary students at Vanderbilt, in those
days, there were two parties. Each had taken for its master a
brilliant graduate student. One of these was George Marion
O'Donnell. The other was Randall. The two graduate students
were *not* congenial. They lived very different kinds of lives.
They addressed each other as Mr. O'Donnell and Mr. Jarrell.
O'Donnell and his followers met by night in a beer joint called
Melfi's. Randall held sway, held court, held class—that's the

only word for it—on a grassy plot outside the Student Union Building, either at mid-morning or in the early afternoon. His would-be disciples—for he only tolerated us—met there not to drink beer but to play touch football with the master. By temperament, some present were much better suited to the life at Melfi's, but we gave up all that and tried instead to play touch. It was Randall's talk we wanted, of course, and his talk on the sidelines and even while the game was in progress was electrifying. It was there that I first heard anyone analyze a Chekhov story. I have never since heard anything to equal it. Even then Randall would talk about a story you had read and make you feel, make you realize that you had never really read it before.

The next year, John Crowe Ransom left Vanderbilt to teach at Kenyon, Randall followed Ransom to do his first teaching there, and I more or less followed Randall. Among Randall's friends at Kenyon were the tennis players. There was Don McNeil, and there was Maury Lewis. He played tennis most often with Maury. Maury was a boy from Arkansas, with a high southern voice, who, when they had a tennis engagement, would come to the foot of the stairs in Douglass House and call out, "Randy, are you ready?" I never knew anyone else who presumed to call him "Randy." But by the end of the second year, you would see members of Kenyon's champion tennis team sitting about the soda shop reading Auden and Chekhov and Proust. Apparently, he was able to teach literature on the tennis courts as well as on the touch field.

I enrolled in his eight o'clock class in American literature at Kenyon. It met on the third floor of Ascension Hall. Since it was an eight o'clock, Randall was frequently late. We would look out the third floor windows and see him sprinting down the Middle Path, often eating his breakfast as he ran. At Kenyon, a class had to wait for the professor only until the second bell. The boys would cup their hands and shout to Randall how many minutes or seconds he had; and he kept coming. Sometimes the bell would ring when he was already on the stairs, but regardless of that, when the bell rang, the class, most of it, would stampede down the stairs. I don't know how many times this happened. More than once or twice. Anyhow, I see him standing on the stairs when the stampeding students were gone, smiling and shrugging his shoulders. The good part, though, is that a half dozen students would remain. And those sessions with the devoted half dozen were of course the best sessions. It was more like a literary club than a class. Randall's friends always felt somehow that he was their teacher, and Randall's students always felt that he was their friend. And with good reason in both cases.

After the war, I saw Randall again in Nashville, and then he and I migrated, with our wives, to New York. We lived there only for a short time, but it was then that we became really close friends. I doubt I could ever have got started again after the war without Randall to talk to—or to listen to—then. He was wonderful, of course, about reading what you had written and wonderful about telling you the truth about it—often the terrible truth. His talk was about literature, painting, music, about your own work, seldom about his. I remember once at Kenyon a student had done a painting—a landscape—and had it proudly displayed in his room. When Randall came in and saw it there he exclaimed, "Gosh, that's *good!*" He pointed out all its fine qualities. The painter sat soaking up the praise. They talked of other things for a while, and when Randall got up to leave he said, putting his fist on his hip and frowning, "You know, I've changed my mind about that picture. There's something wrong—*awfully* wrong—about the light in it. You ought to work on it some more. Or maybe you really ought to just throw this one away and try to do another." As usual, of course, he was right about it. He was that way about stories and poems too—never hesitated to tell you what he thought of something you had written, never hesitated to change his mind about what he thought. If you published something he didn't like, he behaved as though you had been disloyal to him in some way, or not that so much more as if you had been disloyal to some other friend of his—your other self, that is. And that he would not tolerate. He might avoid seeing you for days afterwards. But, oh, if you published something he liked! That winter when I was staying in London, I had two ten-page

letters from him about two stories of mine he had seen in
print. And if one were on the same side of the Atlantic with
him, there would be long-distance telephone calls that went
on and on. Or if there were no call or letter when you published something, the silence was awful and seemed bound to
reach out to you wherever you were. Once you were a student
of Randall's, once you were a friend of Randall's, it was for life.

When, in 1947, I reported to a mutual friend that Randall
was coming down to Greensboro to be interviewed for an
appointment, the friend refused to believe me. In effect, he
said that in that "southern female seminary" Randall would be
like a caged beast. But Randall knew what he was doing. He
had already taught for a while in a very advanced, very experimental, institution, where the teaching was done in con-
ferences and where no grades were given. He knew that he
could do with a little more of the seminary atmosphere in the
college where he was to settle down to serious teaching and
writing.

At the luncheon, on the day of Randall's interview, he behaved very well except that he insisted upon talking about
books instead of letting us ramble on about whether we preferred the fish cakes or the roast pork. But I must add that I
think the senior members of the English Department behaved
well too. I know now that their attitude toward Randall was
not too unlike my own attitude toward them the year before.
Why, they had, so to speak, known Randall all their lives.
Other gifted, young, southern, literary men had passed
through their lives. They recognized him. The others had not
been so brilliant in conversation or such gifted writers, but,
still, their having known the others helped. They knew who he
was. Later on, several of those present at that luncheon became friends of Randall's. One of the ladies present boasts
today that she is the original of Miss Batterson in *Pictures from
an Institution*. Not only can she recognize herself, but, after
all, Randall once *told* her that she was the original. It is a very
affectionate portrait that he painted of the sensitive, cultivated
southern gentlewoman, who has given her life to teaching.

Once when I was living in the country in North Carolina

and we were both teaching at Greensboro, Randall came out
to spend the day. When he got out of his car, he was carrying a
briefcase. He didn't often carry a briefcase in those days. My
wife and I eyed it without comment until at last he said,
"Guess what! I've written a novel!"

"You're kidding," I said.

He burst out at me, "Are you crazy? You know I don't kid
about things like that!" And of course he was right. He didn't.
It was *Pictures from an Institution.*

I suppose that nothing is more interesting than to hear what
someone else—especially Randall Jarrell—has said about you.
A friend reported to me once something that Randall had said
of me and my literary efforts: "He is like a great white horse
doing tatting." I loved so hearing him say the witty things he
said about other people that I used to wish I could have been
hiding under the sofa the night he brought forth that about the
white horse. He found gossip tedious and boring, yet it was
worth making him endure it occasionally just to hear the final
word he would come up with, once and for all settling the hash
of the subject. And of course the whole method of *Pictures
from an Institution* is that of letting us hear what the characters in the book have to say about each other. It is mainly a
book of Randall's witty talk, and in it we see to what serious
places his witty talk could take one. And since I have never
done what I always said I intended to do—that is, to write
down the things he said—I should like to conclude with two
passages from *Pictures* that will make us hear his voice as
nothing else can. I have chosen one of the subjects that he was
best on: important people and their fondness for important
people. And I should remind you that this is a novel about a
college with a creative writing program and its resident writers
and its visiting lecturers.

Ordinary people think that very important people get along
badly with one another—and this is true; but they often get
along worse with you and me. They find it difficult not simply
to get along with, but to care about getting along with, ordinary
people, who do not seem to them fully human. They make

exceptions, real or seeming, for school friends, people who flatter them enough, relatives, mistresses, children, and dogs: they try not to bite the hand that lets them stroke it . . . but all power irritates—it is hard for them to contain themselves within themselves, and not to roast the peasants on their slopes. But they eye one another with half-contemptuous, half-respectful dislike: after all, each of them *is* important, and importance, God knows, covers a multitude of sins.

This earth carries aboard it many ordinary passengers; and it carries, also, a few very important ones. It is hard to know which people are, or were, or will be which. Great men may come to the door in carpet-slippers, their faces like those of kindly or fretful old dogs, and not even know that they are better than you; a friend meets you after fifteen years and the Nobel Prize, and he is sadder and fatter and all the flesh in his face has slumped an inch nearer the grave, but otherwise he is as of old. They are not very important people. On the other hand, the president of your bank, the Vice-Chancellor of the—no, not the Reich, but of the School of Agriculture of the University of Wyoming; these, any many Princes and Powers and Dominions, are very important people; the quality of their voices has changed, and they speak more distinctly from the mounds upon which they stand, making sure that their voices come down to you.

The very important are different from us. Yes, they have more everything. They are spirits whom that medium, the world, has summoned up just as she has the rest of us, but there is in them more of the soul-stuff, more ego—the Spirit of Gog and Magog has been summoned. There is *too much* ecto-plasm; it covers the table, moves on toward the laps of the rest of us, already here, sitting around the table on straight chairs, holding one another's hands in uneasy trust. We push back our chairs, our kinship breaks up like a dream: it is as if there were no longer Mankind, but only men.

1966

No More Masterpieces

Robert Brustein

Perhaps one of the most controversial statements of the revolutionary French dramatic theoretician, Antonin Artaud, was his call for "No More Masterpieces." For taken literally, this position implies a complete break with all classical western literature. It was Artaud's conviction that traditional theater had reached a dead end, that the work of Molière and Racine had become less a living heritage than a source of rot and deterioration, and that the theater would never be reborn in modern form until it had burrowed its way back past the written works of civilization to primitive, even preliterary, roots. Like all polemicists, Artaud was overstating his case. Actually, it was not the great French classical writers who disturbed him so much as the stodgy staging of their plays by such companies as the Comédie Française. And it was out of his desire to recapture some of the original vitality of the great ages of theater—including the French neoclassic age of Molière and Racine—that he was compelled to make such a blanket repudiation of all beloved masterworks.

Artaud had become convinced that the greatest enemy of vital theater was the contemporary middle-class notion of "art." In Artaud's mind, art was an excrescence, a limb of man rather than his vital center—it was something cut off from the inmost heart of the people. For the mildewed concept of *art*, Artaud wished to substitute his dynamic notion of *culture*, a word he used in a very special sense. Art was the expression of one man, culture the expression of all; art divided mankind, culture united it. For Artaud, culture was closely related to primitive religion, and would ideally take the form of ritual, ceremony, and sacrificial rites. Connecting with the entire populace and not just the well-fed bourgeois, culture was to produce a theater that would shock and dismay, exteriorizing the dream life through theatrical images dredged from the deepest roots of man's psychic experience.

One does not have to accept Artaud whole, or join him in rejecting the whole corpus of western dramatic literature, to understand his hostility to masterpieces. As a metaphor rather than a literal fact, Artaud's position makes a lot of sense, for it enjoins us to make the maximum demands on the theatrical event, to ask that everything performed on the stage— including classical plays—have the power and immediacy of living experiences, catching the audience up in an emotion of multitude. His is a cry against the institutionalization of dramatic art, against the piety reflected in the very word *masterpiece*. Artaud's battle cry, in short, asks us to free the energies of the great classical plays, asks us to liberate these works from libraries and museums, asks us to explore the hidden links that exist between every successful work of art and the deep sensual life of every spectator.

The questions raised by Artaud are of particular moment to us now that we are caught in a period of theatrical unrest, for until we can answer those questions properly we will never properly formulate an American theater. If theater in this country, which so recently seemed close to extinction, is now shaking itself into wakefulness like a long-sleeping animal, what form will this new awakening take for the production of the classics? If radical departures are now taking place in play writing, acting, and staging, how will these affect the presentation of works from another time and country? Certainly, this seems like the proper time to be raising these questions. The decline of the commercial system has resulted, at least temporarily, in a certain tolerance for experimentation; numerous arts councils are agonizing over the meaning of culture and the nation's responsibility to support it; and, although theatrical boards and paying audiences are still demanding the more conventional forms of entertainment, artistic directors in various resident theaters around the country are searching for a new sense of theatrical identity. We are now in a crisis which will inevitably lead to change, and Artaud's questions must be raised again if we are ever to advance past the safe, the tired, and the predictable in the programming of plays. What is the proper relationship between the past and the present? Is history something to be memorialized or must it be renewed with each succeeding generation? How do we build a bridge to the past without turning into prisoners of culture centers and slaves to masterpieces?

The answers I am going to suggest may at first seem unacceptable to most of you, since the literate community is traditionally opposed to any tampering with the past. But I do not see any way out of our present dilemma unless we are willing to approach classical works with complete freedom, even if this means adapting them into a modern idiom. I should add, by way of a preparatory footnote, that I advance this notion tentatively, and with a little astonishment at myself, since I have often been critical of the extensive liberties directors have taken with masterpieces. As a teacher of dramatic literature, I have always felt that a classical play was relevant to the present by virtue of its concern with universal values and timeless traits of character; and as a critic of production, I have frequently cried out against the mutilation of the classics, either through updating, bowdlerizing, or adapting them to the musical stage.

I still have strong objections to certain of these approaches. But I have also had to concede lately that excessive familiarity with one's favorite plays, either in the study or in the theater, can have the result of neutralizing their power. Certain works that used to have a lot of meaning for me—say, *Lysistrata*, or *Romeo and Juliet*—have by now lost a good deal of their charm. After seeing a dull but respectable enough production of *Measure for Measure*, performed by the Bristol Old Vic, I became curiously reluctant to read that play as well. And I am even growing gradually estranged from *Hamlet*, a work I thought would never lose its magnetism. To put it bluntly, I have sometimes found myself, during an evening at the theater, half inclined to shout, "No More Shakespeare"—and this about an author of the greatest depth and brilliance, whom I have loved since childhood. I think we must conclude that the

"Shakespearean rag," as T. S. Eliot calls it ("It's so elegant, so
intelligent"), is a rhythm that can begin to surfeit like any
rhythm played too often, and that the famous parody of the
history plays, performed by the Beyond the Fringe company
("Oh saucy Worcester") is a form of protest that becomes more
meaningful with each successive conventional production of
Shakespeare's plays.

Actually, we have reached the end of a cycle in the staging
of the classics, and if we don't attempt some renewal in our
thinking about these works, we run the risk of becoming as
paralyzed in the theater as captive husbands now are at
Wagnerian opera. Such renewal should ideally take place
every ten or twenty years, and indeed *has* been taking place
throughout history; in fact, it is only in recent times that literature has assumed the inviolability of scripture—perhaps because it has begun to take the place of scripture. But even
scripture, in previous times, was susceptible to interpretation
and adaptation. Just as the gospels of Matthew, Mark, Luke,
and John were adapted by medieval guilds in the passion
plays, so the Homeric myths—which constituted scripture for
the Greeks—have been in a constant state of development and
change. The Electra story, for example, was dramatized by
Aeschylus, then by Sophocles, and then by Euripides, each
treatment a brand new departure that reflected each writer's
own religious, social, and psychological obsessions. Roman
drama is little more than a free revision of Greek comedies and
tragedies, particularly those of Menander and Euripides, performed in Greek dress, but clearly Latin in tone and temperament. Racine adapted Euripides and Seneca to his own purposes, while Molière Frenchified Terence and Plautus. In
seventeenth- and eighteenth-century France, England, and
Italy, almost every writer with literary pretensions revised or
adapted the Greco-Roman drama; in the nineteenth century,
the Germans joined the parade; and in our own day, the tradition of myth-drama—which is to say, the updating of classical
plays by contemporary hands—reached its peak.

Nobody, for example, dares to produce Greek originals
more radically than Cocteau, Anouilh, Giraudoux, T. S. Eliot,

and Eugene O'Neill dare to rewrite them. To turn Oedipus into a willful neurotic with a mother fixation, as Cocteau did in *La Machine Infernale*, or to make Agamemnon into a returning Civil War officer, as O'Neill did in *Mourning Becomes Electra*, or to bring the Alcestis story into the modern drawing room with Heracles transformed into a spiritual advisor and psychological counselor, as Eliot did in *The Cocktail Party*, is to wreak havoc on the original intentions of the original authors of these plays. But despite the fact that the mania for adaptation possessed the world of literature, art, music, and drama for the first half of our century, no professor of classics has even been anywhere nearly as outraged by the reworking of Aeschylus as professors of literature, including myself, have been by the reworking of Shakespeare.

It could, of course, be argued that the Greeks themselves set a precedent for the elastic interpretation of their plots, and that, anyway, there is a world of difference between the plots of Shakespeare and the myths of the Greeks. But it could also be argued that Shakespeare himself borrowed his plots, and that the great stories of the western tradition—the stories of Lear, Macbeth, Candide, and the Underground Man—are *our* myths, as deeply imbedded in our racial unconscious as the myths of Oedipus, Orestes, and Antigone were in the minds of the Athenians.

As a matter of fact, it is only recently that Shakespeare has become a sacred, inviolable text. In the Restoration period— the first age in which the Elizabethans were revived on anything approaching a significant scale—plays by Shakespeare and his contemporaries were treated with about as much respect as the first story idea for a Hollywood movie. John Dryden, whose admiration for Shakespeare was second to none, had no compunction at all about translating his great predecessor's works into an idiom more acceptable to his formal and decorous age. He made a hash of *Troilus and Cressida;* he totally revised *The Tempest*, with the aid of William Davenant; and he rewrote *Antony and Cleopatra* so as to make it no longer a sprawling colossal epic but rather a well-organized and unglamorous moral lesson, during which Antony's wife, accompanied by her children, arrives on stage to plead tearfully for the preservation of her marriage. Nor was Dryden unique in this; with the exception of *Hamlet* and *Macbeth*, which remained more or less untouched, every play of Shakespeare's suffered a sea change in this period. As Verdi was later to do with *Othello, Henry IV,* and *Macbeth,* Purcell adapted *The Tempest* and *A Midsummer Night's Dream* into operas. Colley Cibber revised *Richard III,* adding new characters and a famous line still mistakenly attributed to Shakespeare ("Off with his head! So much for Buckingham!"). And in a version of *King Lear* that was to hold the style for a century and a half, Nahum Tate gave the play a happy ending which found Lear conquering the forces of Goneril and Regan, Cordelia marrying Edgar, and everyone but the villains living happily ever after.

A similar fate overtook Shakespeare for the next hundred years and yet he managed to survive; in fact, it was not until the Romantic period, when the word *masterpiece* was invented, and when a large middle-class public began seeking cultural improvement through books, plays, newspapers, and magazines, that Shakespeare became an object of jealous devotion. It was at this time—during the late eighteenth and early nineteenth centuries—that Shakespeare developed into "the immortal Bard," and, thus sanctified, was approached in the most conventionalized manner. The famous roles became material for the declamatory acting of actor-managers; scenery became ponderous and extravagant and atmospheric; costumes were made up of velvets and brocades, flowing head pieces, and beautifully carved daggers and swords. It was the beginning of the "historical" Shakespeare, in which audiences were somehow persuaded they were seeing an authentic reenactment of the play in its own period, even though Shakespeare's plays had originally been performed on a bare stage with a minimum of props and with costumes that continually violated historicity (Shakespeare's original Cleopatra, for example, was known to have worn a hoop skirt).

This movement found its apotheosis in twentieth-century England in the institutionalized Shakespeare of the Old Vic

Company and the Stratford Memorial Theatre. Both these institutions produced genuine achievements, particularly the Old Vic during the Olivier years in the late forties and early fifties, when Ralph Richardson, Peggy Ashcroft, Joyce Redman, and Harry Andrews were members of the company, and the great productions of *Oedipus Rex*, *Henry IV*, and *Uncle Vanya* were being organized under the direction of Michel St. Denis and Glenn Byam Shaw. But like the Comédie Française, which was also regenerated from time to time, these companies were more often dedicated to perpetuating the past than illuminating it, and, as a result, ended up looking more like museums than living organisms. The Stratford Memorial Theatre, until its recent transformation by Peter Hall (who took the word *Memorial* out of the title and the atmosphere, renamed the group the Royal Shakespeare Company, leased a London theater, and introduced new plays into the repertory), was invariably overrun by tourists and schoolchildren who had already paid their fealty to the homes of Ann Hathaway and Mary Arden, and to Shakespeare's grave. As for the Old Vic, this company, once it had been abandoned by Olivier and his boisterous companions, degenerated into a collection of effeminate leading men and genteel leading ladies, who offered a Shakespeare calculated to rouse no one from somnolence, and who were ultimately absorbed into the quasi-official National Theatre without the slightest protest even for Bardolators.

The academic approach to the classics suggested by the productions of these two companies was more than a period or a costume problem: it was essentially a problem of attack. In the simplest terms, it amounted to a failure to probe and explore the classics in new and daring ways. This is not to say that institutional Shakespeare was impervious to novelty. Quite the contrary, it was at Stratford, and particularly at the Old Vic, that a practice known as "jollying Shakespeare up"—a particularly noxious form of streamlining—first took hold. The "jollying" techniques were especially adored of directors who were doing a Shakespeare play perhaps for the fourth time in as many years, and who therefore undertook to amuse themselves during a rather arduous chore not by trying to penetrate the play more deeply, but rather by changing its physical environment—not by determining a true modern equivalent for the action, but rather by redesigning its costumes, props, and settings. Tyrone Guthrie—responsible for many genuinely exciting productions of Shakespeare—was also largely responsible for the "jollying" approach, which has always seemed to me one of the emptiest and least concentrated ways to produce a classic.

It was, nevertheless, an approach that soon became immensely popular with many of the classical repertory companies in England and America—not only at the Old Vic and Stratford, but at the Bristol Old Vic, the Minneapolis Theatre, the Phoenix Theatre in New York—in fact, everywhere that Mr. Guthrie visited. "Jollying up" reached epidemic proportions with the American Shakespeare Festival at Stratford, Connecticut, where the plays were almost invariably set during some time and in some geographical location totally foreign both to the spirit and the letter of the text: *Measure for Measure* in nineteenth-century Vienna, *Twelfth Night* in Brighton during the Napoleonic Wars, *Much Ado about Nothing* in Spanish Texas around the time of the Alamo. I myself had no puristic objections to updating Shakespeare: rather I objected to updating Shakespeare for no discernible reason other than the desire for novelty. And when these techniques occasionally worked for comic or thematic emphasis—as did Franco Zefferelli's treatment of *Much Ado about Nothing* at the National Theatre, in which the characters became nineteenth-century Italian noblemen, peanut vendors, and carabinieri, or Guthrie's own production of *Troilus and Cressida*, which analogized the corruption of the Greeks through images from turn-of-the-century Europe—then I felt that this was justification enough. But it was rare indeed when the "jollying" approach illuminated the plot, theme, or characters in the slightest way.

While this was going on in the Anglo-Saxon world, another approach to the classics was being explored elsewhere, particularly by Bertolt Brecht and the Berliner Ensemble, which demonstrated that there was an alternative both to academic conventionality and to irresponsible "jollying up." For what Brecht proved through his own example was the possibility of refreshing the past by fortifying it with a new vision, the possibility of rejuvenating a classical idea by discovering for it a strong modern equivalent. Like T. S. Eliot, Brecht was a writer who used literary fragments to shore against his ruins: his own work is virtually a pastiche of plundered literature. Brecht, in fact, worked very much the way Shakespeare did, striving not so much for originality of plot as for originality of conception, and just as, say, *Hamlet* is a reworking of an earlier play, probably by Kyd, so *The Threepenny Opera* is a modern version of Gay's *Beggar's Opera*, *Edward II* is a new look at Marlowe's play, *Trumpet and Drums* is a modern adaptation of Farquahar's *Recruiting Officer*, and *The Caucasian Chalk Circle* is an elaboration of the old Chinese play, *The Circle of Chalk*. Looting his way through the past, Brecht emerges as one of the great buccaneers of literature, for as he remarked when accused of plagiarizing a contemporary's work without acknowledgement: "In literature as in life, I do not recognize the concept of private property."

Given Brecht's manner of working, it was inevitable that he should turn his attention to Shakespeare himself, just as it was inevitable that the style of the Berliner Ensemble should be based on a distillation of epic Shakespearean production. In the *Little Organum for the Theatre*, Brecht speaks of the need of the theater "to speak up decisively for the interests of its time," and goes on to give a reading of *Hamlet* in which the chief character's internal struggles take second place to the external struggle occurring between Fortinbras and the Polish forces, advising that cuts and interpolations be made to justify this reading. In his adaptation of *Coriolanus*—uncompleted at his death but, finished by another hand, now one of the chief glories of the Berliner Ensemble—Brecht shifts the emphasis of the play from considerations of human fallibility to considerations of economic problems caused by a rise in the price of corn, all played out against a background of battle in which Marcus and Aufidius stalk each other like two Kabuki warriors.

As a Marxist, Brecht's motive for adapting Shakespeare was primarily political—he wanted food and money to replace love and power as the prime dramatic concerns; and, because of his ideology, he was anxious to bring Shakespeare's feudal sense of economics and primitive nationalism into some sort of conformity with the latest "scientific" findings on these subjects. Nevertheless, despite his narrow ideological views, Brecht brought fresh eyes to the staging of Shakespeare's plays, and gave artistic authority to a whole new method of producing the classics.

This authority was soon transferred to England, after a visit of the Berliner Ensemble in the fifties, and is now finding full expression in the work being done by the Royal Shakespeare Company. Under the direction of Peter Hall, and in association with such brilliant directors as Peter Brook, Clifford Williams, Trevor Nunn, and John Barton, this group has been creating a quiet revolution in the production of Shakespeare—a revolution which makes the more glamorous productions of the National Theatre look a little staid and old-fashioned. Like the Berliner Ensemble, the Royal Shakespeare Company is not a company of stars but rather of directors and actors producing out of workshop conditions; projects are initiated less in order to provide roles for lead actors than to establish the identity of the company as a whole. Settings are sparse and abstract, using metal, wire, and aluminum; costumes are constructed out of burlap and leather; the acting is terse, ironic, cold, and contemporary; the style of the new plays (like *The Homecoming*) is almost indistinguishable from the style of the old (like Marlowe's *Edward*).

And indeed the style of the new determines the style of the old. In Royal Shakespeare productions, Shakespeare and his contemporaries are seen through the eyes of Beckett, Pinter, Genet, Brecht, and their contemporaries. A recent production of *Henry V*, for example, directed by John Barton and Trevor Nunn, divested the action of panoply and presented instead a play about the squalor of war and hollowness of military rhetoric. With Ian Holm in the lead (the same actor who played Lenny in *The Homecoming* with such cold grace),

Henry was no longer a glorious warrior, achieving England's manifest destiny on French battlefields (Olivier's approach in the magnificent film version), but rather a frail, diminutive, sensitive youth who grows increasingly brutalized by senseless carnage. Holm's Henry is urged into battle by purely casuistical arguments, becomes an anguished participant in atrocities (personally cutting the throat of a French prisoner before the eyes of the audience), and suffers severely from shell shock and battle fatigue. When the battle of Agincourt is finally won, he is a shivering wreck, scarred inside and out, and crying like a baby. The concept obviously runs flat against Shakespeare's conscious intention, but it adds an interesting dimension which may even have been put there by Shakespeare himself—how else do we explain the shaky morality of Henry's claim to France, his order to kill all French prisoners, his apparent indifference to the hanging of former comrades like Bardolph, and his personal stiffness and lack of scruples?

Peter Brook's celebrated production of *King Lear*—also a project of the Royal Shakespeare Company—was another modernized treatment of Shakespeare based on a serious new reading of the play. Brook, deeply influenced by Jan Kott's unconventional interpretations in *Shakespeare Our Contemporary*, offered *King Lear* in a barren primitive landscape where no birds sang—visually realized by a single geometric sheet of corroded metal suspended near stretched canvas. All action was excised from the play and all empathy forbidden; compassionate speeches, including Edmund's repentance, were simply cut. The battle scenes became offstage cries, and the storm was realized by means of three shaking pieces of metal. Time stood still, activity became meaningless, life inchoate, and the most significant sounds to be heard were the coughing and wheezing of an arthritic old man. It was *King Lear* as if written by Samuel Beckett—a Lear of stasis, ordeals, frustration, in which the repeated negatives of the play (no, never, nothing) became the token syllables of life upon a lonely, abandoned planet.

In America, we are just beginning to probe the possibilities of the modernized classic, though, to be fair, the Living

Theatre was experimenting with new classical styles long before the English. Most of these experiments were dismal failures (I am still trying to forget a production of Sophocles's
Women of Trachis, translated by Ezra Pound into twenty-
three skidoo colloquialisms, which sent me screaming from
the theater), but when the principle was transferred to the
production of a modern classic like Pirandello's *Tonight We
Improvise,* it worked very well indeed (Pirandello's play was
now set in New York, and Doctor Hinkfuss, the Reinhardtian
director, became Julian Beck, a precious avant-garde aesthete). Similarly, the current production of *MacBird* could be
considered a radical reworking of Shakespeare, which uses
Macbeth for its remorseless political purposes as freely as
Brecht's *Arturo Ui* uses *Richard III.*

To speak from closer experience, a recent production of
Volpone at Yale, directed by Clifford Williams of the Royal
Shakespeare Company, made an interesting (though incom-
plete) effort to find analogies for Jonson's play in the modern
experience. Taking note of Jonson's emphasis on distortions
and transformations of nature, Williams set the play in a fantasy Venice out of the imagination of Fellini and Antonioni—a
Venice of aristocratic vice and corrupt daydreams. In this version, Volpone's dwarf, eunuch, and hermaphrodite became a
monstrous pipe-smoking hunchback in a skirt, an outrageously
campy queer, and a shortcropped lesbian in a leather suit who
sang tuneless rock and roll; Mosca became a cunning
Machiavellian pimp, obsessed with a loathed body and its
excretions; Volpone turned into a vulgar middle-class charla-
tan with a bit of the pitchman in him; and the whole parade of
suitors, judges, notaries, lawyers, and whores found their
equivalents among the denizens of *la dolce vita.* Thus, Volpone's famous apostrophe to Celia before the attempted rape
("Come my Celia, let us prove") was sung and danced to the
tune of a bossa nova, and Volpone came before the judges,
impotent, in a hospital gown, being pumped with plasma, and
drawn in a wheelchair by a male nurse.

The dangers of this line of attack are obvious: everything
depends upon the tact, taste, and talent of the director. If

new values are not unearthed by a new approach, then the whole effort is worthless; and if these new values are merely eccentric or irresponsible, then it is careerism rather than art that has been served. Then again, romantic and light comedies do not lend themselves handily to such treatment, and neither do plays with very particularized environments. I do not look forward with any anticipation to the all-male production of *As You Like It* being produced at the National Theatre next season, and I do not look backward with any affection at the APA's translation of Chekhov's *Seagull* into Noel Coward's England.

But when something in the play itself stimulates the director to pursue a radical new line of inquiry, then even the most radical transformations can be justified. I think we might be more tolerant of these modernized interpretations if we stopped regarding each new production as definitive. Changing Shakespeare is not the same thing as painting a mustache on the Mona Lisa, for if an artwork has been desecrated by such behavior, a dramatic work still continues to exist purely, as a text. If we regard each new production of a classical play less as a total recreation of that work than as a directorial essay upon it, then I think we will begin to regard mutilated masterpieces with more permissiveness and relaxation. Peter Brook's production of *King Lear* is no more final than Jan Kott's chapter on the play: it is merely one more perspective on a profoundly complicated tragedy, a perspective that will undoubtedly inspire other productions in reply. And it is this continuing dialogue that keeps masterpieces alive on the stage, just as the dialogue among such Shakespearean critics as Coleridge, Bradley, T. S. Eliot, and F. R. Leavis have helped to keep the plays alive on the page.

What "No More Masterpieces" means for us, then, is no more piety, no more reverence, no more sanctimoniousness in the theater. It means the freedom to approach the most sacred text as if it has just been written. It means trying to recreate not so much the original environment of a work so much as the original excitement with which spectators attended it, and that means establishing a link less with the spectator's educated life—the passages he memorized in school and college—than with his psychic life—the passages burned into his soul by the acid of experience. "No More Masterpieces" means treating the theater as informally as a circus tent, a music hall, a prize ring—a place in which the spectator participates rather than worships, and offers the stage something more than the condescension of applause. "No More Masterpieces" means not a disrespect for the past, but rather an effort to rediscover some of its vitality. For masterpieces are the sedatives of a time half dead at the top, and only when they cease to lull us, will our time begin to come alive.

1967

Origins of a Poem

Denise Levertov

Some time in 1960, I wrote "The Necessity," a poem which has remained, for me, a kind of testament, or a point of both moral and technical reference; but which has seemed obscure to some readers. Since I don't think its diction or its syntax really are obscure, it seems to me their difficulties with it must arise from their unawareness of the ground it stands on, or is rooted in; or to put it another way, the poem—any poem, but especially a poem having for the poet that character of testament—is fruit, flower, or twig of a tree, and is not to be fully comprehended without some knowledge of the tree's nature and structure, even though its claim to *be* a poem must depend on internal evidence alone. What I propose to do here is not to paraphrase or explicate "The Necessity," which I assume to be a poem, but to provide and explore some of the attitudes and realizations to which it is related.

I keep two kinds of notebooks: one is a kind of anthology of brief essential texts, the other a journal that includes meditations or ruminations on such texts. In drawing from these sources, as I propose to do here, I am not implying that all of them are literally antecedents, in my consciousness, of this particular poem. In fact, although most or all of the sources—the quotations I shall be making from other writers—were probably familiar to me by 1960, and in many instances long before, and had been copied out by then into my private anthology, the reflections on them written in my journals are of later date. I am therefore not speaking of simple sequence but of habitual preoccupations, which accrue and which periodically emerge in different forms.

One such preoccupation forms itself as a question. What is the task of the poet? What is the essential nature of his work?

Are these not questions we too often fail to ask ourselves, as we blindly pursue some form of poetic activity? In the confusion of our relativistic age and our eroding, or at least rapidly changing, culture, the very phrase, *the task of the poet*, may seem to have a nineteenth-century ring, both highfalutin and irrelevant. Our fear of the highfalutin is related to the salutory dislike of hypocrisy; but I believe we undercut ourselves, deprive ourselves of certain profound and necessary understandings, if we dismiss the question as irrelevant, and refuse, out of what is really only a kind of embarrassment, to consider as a task, and a lofty one, the engagement with language into which we are led by whatever talent we may have. And precisely this lack of an underlying conception of what the poet is doing accounts for the subject-seeking of some young poets—and maybe some old ones too—and for the emptiness, flippancy, or total subjectivity of a certain amount of writing that goes under the name of poetry.

Years ago, I copied out this statement by Ibsen in a letter.

The task of the poet is to make clear to himself, and thereby to others, the temporal and eternal questions. . . .

In 1959 or 1960, I used these words as the subject of one of "Three Meditations." The three formed one poem, so that in referring to this one alone certain allusions are lost; but it makes a certain amount of sense on its own:

Barbarians
throng the straight roads of
my empire, converging
on black Rome.
There is darkness in me.
Silver sunrays
sternly, in tenuous joy
cut through its folds:
mountains
arise from cloud.
Who was it yelled, cracking

the glass of delight?
Who sent the child
sobbing to bed, and woke it
later to comfort it?
I, I, I, I.
I multitude, I tyrant,
I angel, I you, you
world, battlefield, stirring
with unheard litanies, sounds of piercing
green half-smothered by
strewn bones.

My emphasis was on asking oneself the questions, internalizing them, on coming to realize how much the apparently external problems have their parallels within us. (Parenthetically, I would suggest that man has to recognize not only that he tends to project his personal problems on the external world but also that he is a microcosm within which indeed the same problems, the same tyrannies, injustices, hopes, and mercies act and react and demand resolution.) This internalization still seems to me what is essential in Ibsen's dictum: what the poet is called on to clarify is not answers but the existence and nature of questions; and his likelihood of so clarifying them for others is made possible only through dialogue with himself. Inner colloquy as a means of communication with others was something I assumed in the poem but had not been at that time overtly concerned with, though in fact I had already translated a Toltec poem that includes the line, "The true artist / maintains dialogue with his heart."

What duality does *dialogue with himself, dialogue with his heart,* imply? "Every art needs two—one who makes it, and one who needs it," wrote Ernst Barlach, the German sculptor and playwright. If this is taken to mean *someone out there* who needs it—an audience—the working artist is in immediate danger of externalizing his activity, of distorting his vision to accommodate it to what he knows, or supposes he knows, his audience requires, or to what he thinks it ought to hear. Writing to a student in 1965, I put it this way:

... you will find yourself not saying all you have to say—you will limit yourself according to your sense of his, or her, or their, capacity. In order to do *all that one can* in any given instance (and nothing less than all is good enough, though the artist, not being of a complacent nature, will never feel sure he *has* done all) one must develop objectivity: at some stage in the writing of a poem you must dismiss from your mind all special knowledge (of what you were *intending* to say, of private allusions, etc.) and read it with the innocence you bring to a poem by someone unknown to you. If you satisfy yourself as *reader* (not just as "self-expressive" writer) you have a reasonable expectation of reaching others too.

This "reader within one" is identical with Barlach's "one who needs" the work of art. To become aware of him safeguards the artist both from the superficialities resulting from overadaptation to the external, and from miasmic subjectivities. My reference to "self-expression" is closely related to what I believe Ibsen must have meant by "to make clear to himself." A self-expressive act is one which makes the doer feel liberated, "clear" in the act itself. A scream, a shout, a leaping into the air, a clapping of hands—or an effusion of words associated for their writer at that moment with an emotion—all these are self-expressive. They satisfy their performer momentarily. But they are not art. And the poet's "making clear," which Ibsen was talking about, *is* art: it goes beyond (though it includes) the self-expressive verbal effusion, as it goes beyond the ephemeral gesture: it is a construct of words that *remains* clear even after the writer has ceased to be aware of the associations that initially impelled it. This kind of "making clear" engages both the subjective and objective in him. The difference is between the satisfaction of exercising the power of utterance as such, of *saying*, of the clarity of action; and of the autonomous clarity of *the thing said*, the enduring clarity of the right words. Cid Corman once said in a broadcast that poetry gives us "not experience thrown as a personal problem on others but experience as an order that will sing to others."

The poet—when he is writing—is a priest; the poem is a temple; epiphanies and communion take place within it. The communion is triple: between the maker and the needer within the poet; between the maker and the needers outside him—those who need but can't make their own poems (or who do make their own but need this one too); and between the human and the divine in both poet and reader. By divine I mean something beyond both the making and the needing elements, vast, irreducible, a spirit summoned by the exercise of needing and making. When the poet converses with this god he has summoned into manifestation, he reveals to others the possibility of their own dialogue with the god in themselves. Writing the poem is the poet's means of summoning the divine; the reader's may be through reading the poem, or through what the experience of the poem leads him to.

Rilke wrote in a letter:

> art does not ultimately tend to produce more artists. It does not mean to call anyone over to it, indeed, it has always been my guess that it is not concerned at all with any effect. But while its creations having issued irresistibly from an inexhaustible source, stand there strangely quiet and surpassable among things, it may be that involuntarily they become somehow exemplary for *every* human activity by reason of their innate disinterestedness, freedom, and intensity.

It is when making and needing have a single point of origin that this "disinterestedness" occurs. And only when it does occur are the "freedom and intensity" generated which "involuntarily become exemplary"—which do, that is, communicate to others outside the artist's self. That is the logic of Ibsen's word *thereby* ("to make clear to himself and *thereby* to others").

I'd like to take a closer look at this word *need*. The need I am talking about is specific (and it is the same, I think, that Rilke meant when in the famous first letter to the Young Poet he told him he should ask himself, "*Must* I write?"). This need is the need for a *poem;* when this fact is not recognized, other needs—such as an undifferentiated need for self-expression, which could just as well find satisfaction in a gesture or an action, or the need to reassure the ego by writing something that will impress others—are apt to be mistaken for specific poem-need. Talent will not save a poem written under these misapprehensions from being weak and ephemeral.

For years, I understood the related testimony of Jean Hélion, the contemporary French painter, only as it concerned "integrity" and as an affirmation of the *existence* of an "other" within oneself, when he wrote:

> Art degenerates if not kept essentially the language of the mysterious being hidden in each man, behind his eyes. I act as if this hidden being got life only through the manipulation of plastic quantities, as if they were his only body, as if their growth were his only future. I identify him with his language. Instead of a description, an expression, or a comment, art becomes a realization with which the urge to live collaborates as a mason.

But when I reconsidered this passage in relation to how the transition from the inner world, inner dialogue, of the artist, to communication with any external other, is effected, I came to realize that Hélion is also implying that it is through the sensuous substance of the art, and only through that, that the transition is made.

The act of realizing inner experience in material substance is in itself an action *toward others,* even when the conscious intention has not gone beyond the desire for self-expression. Just as the activity of the artist gives body and future to "the mysterious being hidden behind his eyes," so the very fact of concrete manifestation, of paint, of words, reaches over beyond the world of inner dialogue. When Hélion says that then art becomes a realization, he clearly means not "awareness" but quite literally "real-ization," making real, substantiation. Instead of description, expression, comment—all of which only refer to an absent subject—art becomes substance, entity.

Heidegger, interpreting Hölderlin, says that to be human is to *be a conversation*—a strange and striking way of saying that communion is the very basis of human living, of *living humanly*. The poet develops the basic human need for dialogue in concretions that are audible to others; in listening, others are stimulated into awareness of their own needs and capacities, stirred into taking up their own dialogues, which are so often neglected (as are the poet's own, too often, when he is not actively *being* a poet). Yet this effect, or result, of his work, though he cannot but be aware of it, cannot be the *intention* of the poet, for such outward, effect-directed intention is self-defeating.

Man's vital need for communion, his humanity's being rooted in "conversation," is due to the fact that since living things, and parts of living things, atrophy if not exercized in their proper functions, and since man does contain, among his living parts, the complementary dualities of needer and maker, he must engage them if they are not to deteriorate. That is why Hélion speaks of "the urge to live collaborating as a mason" in the realization of art. The two beings are one being, mutually dependent. The life of both depends not merely on mutual recognition but on the manifestation of that recognition in substantial terms—whether as "plastic quantities" or as words (or in the means of whatever art is in question). The substance, the means, of an art, is an incarnation—not reference but phenomenon. A poem is an indivisibility of "spirit and matter" much more absolute than what most people seem to understand by "synthesis of form and content." That phrase is often taken to imply a process of will, craft, taste, and understanding by which the form of a work may painstakingly be molded to a perfect expression of, or vehicle for, its content. But artists know this is *not* the case—or only as a recourse, a substitute in thin times for the real thing. It is without doubt the proper process for certain forms of writing—for exposition of ideas, for critical studies. But in the primary work of art it exists, at best, as a stepping-stone to activity less laborious, less linked to effort and will. Just as the "other being" of Hélion's metaphor is *identified*, in process, with his language, which is his "only body, his only future," so *content*, which is the dialogue between him and the "maker," *becomes* form. Emerson says, "insight which expresses itself by what is called Imagination *does not come by study*, but by the intellect being *where and what it sees*, by sharing the path or circuit of things through forms, and so making them translucid to others" (emphasis added). Goethe says, "moralists think of the ulterior effect, about which the true artist troubles himself as little as Nature does when she makes a lion or a hummingbird." And Heidegger, in "Hölderlin and the Essence of Poetry" writes:

> Poetry looks like a game and is not. A game does indeed bring men together, but in such a way that each forgets himself in the process. In poetry, on the other hand, man is reunited on the foundation of his existence. There he comes to rest; not indeed to the seeming rest of inactivity and emptiness of thought, but to that infinite state of rest in which all powers and relations are active.

"Disinterested intensity," of which Rilke wrote, then, is truly exemplary and affective intensity. What Charles Olson has called a man's "filling of his given space," what John Donne said of the presence of God in a straw—"God is a straw in a straw"—point toward that disinterest. The strawness of straw, the humanness of the human, is their divinity; in that intensity of the "divine spark" Hasidic lore tells us dwells in all created things. "Who then is man?" Heidegger asks. "He who must affirm what he is. To affirm means to declare; but at the same time it means: to give in the declaration a guarantee of what is declared. Man is *he* who he *is*, precisely in the affirmation of his own existence."

Olson's words about filling our given space occur in a passage that further parallels Heidegger:

> . . . a man, carved
> out of himself, so wrought he
> fills his given space, makes
> traceries sufficient to

others' needs . . .
here is
social action, for the poet
anyway, his
politics, his
needs . . .

Olson is saying, as Heidegger is saying, that it is *by* being what he is capable of being, *by* living his life so that his identity is "carved," is "wrought," *by* filling his given space, that a man, and in particular a poet as a representative of an activity peculiarly human, *does* make "traceries sufficient to others' needs" (which is, in the most profound sense, a "social" or "political" action). Poems bear witness to the manness of man, which, like the strawness of straw, is an exiled spark. Only by the light and heat of these divine sparks can we see, can we feel, the extent of the human range. They bear witness to the *possibility* of "disinterest, freedom, and intensity."

"Therefore dive deep," wrote Edward Young, author of the once so popular, later despised, "Night Thoughts,"

dive deep into thy bosom; learn the depths, extent, bias, and full fort of thy mind; contract full intimacy with the stranger within thee; excite and cherish every spark of intellectual light and heat, however smothered under former negligence, or scattered through the dull, dark mass of common thoughts; and collecting them into a body, let they genius rise (if genius thou hast) as the sun from chaos; and if I then should say, like an Indian, Worship it (though too bold) yet should I say little more than my second rule enjoins, *viz.*, Reverence thyself.

What I have up to now been suggesting as the task of the poet may seem of an Emersonian idealism (though perhaps Emerson has been misread on this point) that refuses to look man's capacity for evil square in the eyes. Now as perhaps never before, when we are so acutely conscious of being ruled by evil men, and that in our time man's inhumanity to man has swollen to proportions of perhaps unexampled monstrosity, such a refusal would be no less than idiotic. Or I may seem to have been advocating a Nietzschean acceptance of man's power for evil, simply on the grounds that it is among his possibilities. But Young's final injunction, in the passage just quoted, is what, for me, holds the clue to what must make the poet's humanity *humane*. *Reverence thyself* is necessarily an aspect of Schweitzer's doctrine of Reverence for Life, the recognition of oneself as *life that wants to live* among other *forms of life that want to live*. This recognition is indissoluble, reciprocal, and dual. There can be no self-respect without respect for others, no love and reverence for others without love and reverence for oneself; and no recognition of others is possible without the imagination. The imagination of what it is to *be* those other forms of life that want to live is the only way to recognition; and it is that imaginative recognition that brings compassion to birth. Man's capacity for evil, then, is less a positive capacity, for all its horrendous activity, than a failure to develop man's most human function, the imagination, to its fullness, and consequently a failure to develop compassion.

But how is this relevant to the practice of the arts, and of poetry in particular? Reverence for life, if it is a necessary relationship to the world, must be so for all people, not only for poets. Yes; but it is the poet who has language in his care; the poet who more than others recognizes language also as a *form of life* and a common resource to be cherished and served as we should serve and cherish earth and its waters, animal and vegetable life, and each other. The would-be poet who looks on language merely as something to be used, as the bad farmer or the rapacious industrialist look on the soil or on rivers merely as things to be used, will not discover a deep poetry; he will only, according to the degree of his skill, construct a counterfeit more or less acceptable—a subpoetry, at best efficiently representative of his thought or feeling—a reference, not an incarnation. And he will be contributing, even if not in any immediately apparent way, to the erosion of language, just as the irresponsible, irreverent farmer and industralist erode the land and pollute the rivers. All of our common resources, tangible or intangible, need to be given to, not exclusively taken from. They require the care that arises from intellectual love—from an understanding of their perfections.

Moreover, the poet's love of language must, if language is to reward him with unlooked-for miracles, that is, with poetry, amount to a passion. The passion for the things of the world and the passion for naming them must be in him indistinguishable. I think that Wordsworth's intensity of feeling lay as much in his naming of the waterfall as in his physical apprehension of it, when he wrote:

> ... The sounding cataract
> Haunted me like a passion. ...

The poet's task is to hold in trust the knowledge that language, as Robert Duncan has declared, is not a set of counters to be manipulated, but a Power. And only in this knowledge does he arrive at music, at that quality of song within speech which is not the result of manipulations of euphonious parts but of an attention, at once to the organic relationships of experienced phenomena, and to the latent harmony and counterpoint of language itself as it is identified with those phenomena. Writing poetry is a process of discovery, revealing *inherent* music, the music of correspondences, the music of inscape. It parallels what, in a person's life, is called individuation: the evolution of consciousness toward wholeness, not an isolation of intellectual awareness but an awareness involving the whole self, a *knowing* (as man and woman "know" one another), a touching, a "being in touch."

All the thinking I do about poetry leads me back, always, to Reverence for Life as the ground for poetic activity; because it seems the ground for Attention. This is not to put the cart before the horse: some sense of identity, at which we wonder; an innocent self-regard, which we see in infants and in the humblest forms of life; these come first, a center out of which Attention reaches. Without Attention—to the world outside us, to the voices within us—what poems could possibly come into existence? Attention is the *exercise* of Reverence for the "other forms of life that want to live." The progression seems clear to me: from Reverence for Life to Attention to Life, from Attention to Life to a highly developed Seeing and Hearing, from Seeing and Hearing (faculties almost indistinguishable for the poet) to the Discovery and Revelation of Form, from Form to Song.

There are links in this chain of which I have not spoken, except to name them—the heightened Seeing and Hearing that result from Attention to anything, their relation to the discovery and revelation of Form. To speak intelligibly of them would take more time and space than I have. But I hope that I have conveyed some idea of the true background of a poem, that have helped to define for others much that they have already intuited in and for their own labors, perhaps without knowing that they knew it:

The Necessity

From love one takes
petal to *rock* and *blesséd*
away towards
descend,

one took thought
for frail tint and spectral
glisten, trusted
from way back that stillness,

one knew
that heart of fire, rose
at the core of gold glow,
could go down undiminished,

for love and
or if in fear knowing
the risk, knowing
what one is touching, one does it,

each part
of speech a spark
awaiting redemption, each
a virtue, a power

in abeyance unless we
give it care
our need designs in us. Then
all we have led away returns to us.

1968

Exploring Inner Space

Peter De Vries

There is more than a faint element of imposture in my standing before you in the role of lecturer, since to discharge that function creditably is to play the critic, which is not at all my speed—or bag, as one should perhaps say today. I suppose it's hard to know what to say about my books. Some think of them as caricatures of the white race. Others assign them to their classes as suggested or required reading, and even approve them as subjects for dissertations. All of which I think vindicates me by bearing out what I've been saying in those books all along—that everything is going to hell in a hand-bucket.

At least some of you out there are scholars, full-blown or in embryo, and I'm sure you're thinking to yourselves, possibly even murmuring to one another, "This character will talk for half an hour about the creative process, or some such, without telling us a damned thing." I shall not disappoint you. You may return to your classrooms and studies confirmed in the knowledge that what goes on in an artist's head is something about which he hasn't the slightest personal comprehension, but is the proper concern of scholars, and after I have returned home you can write crisp notes to the Hopwood Committee saying, "Why do you invite cows to analyze milk?"

Nevertheless, I can ask intelligent questions, furnishing answers of whatever caliber. Simply as readers we periodically wonder, by way of taking inventory, what the literature of the hour is up to. We know what our scientists are up to: one mechanistic triumph after another. By contrast, our artists grow more determinedly humanistic, private, and, as the cries of lay protest occasionally have it, obscure. That the twain will never meet, that the gulf grows ever wider, is a concern of course formally expressed by C. P. Snow, articulating for all of us with his idea of the two cultures, the scientific and the intellectual running full speed away from each other, or at best in irreconcilable parallels. Still, it's important to remember that over the long haul men do work together whether they work together or apart, as Robert Frost reminds us in the poem "The Tuft of Flowers." In the distant future, or even now in some larger perspective, there may be somewhere an ultimate fusion of the two seemingly hopelessly divergent elements. For the time being, I have at least mentioned Frost and Snow in the same breath, which will have to suffice us as a token unity.

The rickety spirits and demoted egos whose inner space our best novelists navigate in the name of characterization are very good counterparts of our own, and whether we shall be vicariously enlarged by our astronauts' exploration of outer space, or merely shrunk into punier earthlings by contrast, depends on our individual makeup. There will certainly, in any case, be further feats to leave us magnified or dwindled, for make no mistake about it: our arrival on the moon and our departure for points more distant will without a doubt be counted among the scientific miracles of this century of the common cold. The humanistic scruple remains, "Should we spend all that money on trips to other astral bodies when there's such a heap still to be done on this one?" Should man go to the moon? The romantic instinctively replies, "Yes. He must have been put on this earth for a purpose."

In any event—to get this so-called lecture in orbit—it's fair to say that literature has found the exploration of private consciousness and even unconsciousness, which I am calling inner spece, enough of a challenge. It is perhaps just as well that our poets and novelists—and you can name them for yourselves—concern themselves principally with the microscopic half of the full human reality, leaving the telescopic to science. It would take a combined Homer, Milton, and Shakespeare to dream our cosmological dream in an epic commensurate with the commonplaces of the front page. But to think of the "two cultures" as absolutely polarized is too neat, too slipshod, as I tried to say a moment ago. That men do work together whether they work together or apart, that there are points of similarity between such seemingly irreconcilable endeavors as the artistic and the scientific, is suggested by our very attempts to understand the one in terms of the other. Some of you may remember how, in the first blush of Virginia Woolf's vogue, terms like "rain of atoms" and "atomic dance" were applied to the minute and seemingly random thoughts, associations, and particles of memory out of which she constructed, particular by particular, the evocations of individual consciousness that in turn collectively made up, for her, a novel. Rereading her now, as I recently did, one would be lured a step farther into the metaphor and say that she was bent on a kind of psychic fission, which releases the energy of the association.

Edmund Wilson first elucidated Proust to us as the literary counterpart of Einsteinian relativity, with time so clearly a fourth dimension as to make *Swann's Way* end: "remembrance of a particular form is but regret for a particular moment; and houses, roads, avenues are fugitive, alas, as the year." If Joyce's stream of consciousness is no stream at all but precisely the sequence of disconnected droplets it appears on paper, it may suggest to us that psychic energy flows as quantum physics tells us physical energy does, not continuously but in individual packets. A Joycean association—a Planckian ergsecond? Why not? And as though this were not enough, even as a humble humorist scurrying back to his proper depth, I might define the self-disparagement in which modern humor almost exclusively consists as the human counterpart of what is known in atomic physics as the loss of unstable carbon isotopes—and if *that* doesn't hold the boys on the academic quarterlies, I don't know what will. If from here on in I talk about myself a lot, you will understand that I do so out of insecurity. There goes an unstable carbon isotope already!

I thought that in the remaining minutes I might perform a kind of public exercise aimed at showing how the writer can only explore the inner space of his characters by perceptively navigating his own, and that this, and this alone, results in anything worth calling characterization. To say that literature illuminates life is platitudinous enough, and I haven't come nine hundred miles to sock that apocalypse to you; but it may be instructive to suggest how the sheer *practice* of fiction as such can sometimes help the practitioner understand what he is writing about, that is to say living with, and to conduct the experiment by recalling an incident that recently befell me—or rather, to focus the point down to where I want it, a character I ran foul of, and he me, and whom I misjudged completely at first and did not comprehend until I had spent some time trying to put him down on paper, though he may have had my number from the beginning on a somewhat more primitive level.

The purpose of fiction is still, as it was to Joseph Conrad, to make the reader see. That is our quarrel with television, is it not? That it is not visual enough? It cannot make us *see* Jeeves, the butler, entering the room, "a procession of one." It cannot make us see the woman in *Dorian Gray* whose dresses always looked as though they had been designed in a rage and put on in a tempest. It cannot make us see the character in Ring Lardner who served what he thought was good Scotch though he may have been deceived by some flavor lurking in his beard. Least of all can it ever hope to begin to make us see anything like the young girl in Elizabeth Bowen's *The Death of the Heart*, who "walked about with the rather fated expression you see in photographs of girls who have subsequently been murdered, but nothing so far had happened to her." Such wild rich subtleties require transmission from one mind to another via the written word upon the printed page, and remain beyond the power of the boob tube to convey.

The task I recently set myself was to make the reader see—and now for the next few minutes to make you see—a character who was nothing if not flamboyantly vivid on the merely visual plane in real life. I was prepared for him by my wife, whom I saw, as I came home one evening, waiting for me at the front door, not with a smile of greeting but somewhat grimly, her arms folded on her chest, holding in one hand a magazine that she had rolled into a truncheon.

"Wait till you see this one," was her first remark after my bestowal of the greeting kiss, and something in her tone made me know exactly what she meant, and made me hurry on past her into the house and head straight upstairs for my predinner bath. Scars left by hospitalities recently extended to my fourteen-year-old son's friends were an aid to the instinctive understanding that this elliptical opening referred to the latest specimen he had brought home, in the way of an overnight guest. "Remember the last one?" my wife pressed on, close at my heels.

I did indeed. This was a thirteen-year-old character who excoriated the false values my generation had given his, and who expressed his disapproval of bourgeois criteria by keeping his chewing gum in his navel. He believed in the abolition of money. Not that he conclusively infected my son with any of those iconoclastic notions. I still keep missing dollar bills and an occasional fin from my wallet just the same. "So cheer up," I said to my wife, summarizing the episode briefly in those terms as I hurried down the passage to the bedroom. "Things aren't always as bad as they seem."

"And the one before that?"

Him I remembered too, him indeed. Lad who brought a gerbil. Lad who also believed in the primacy of instincts, and who pursuant thereto got up some time during the night and ate all the breakfast Danish, and who in his freedom from the tyranny of material possessions inadvertently walked off with one of my derby hats.

"Well, when you get a load of *this* one," said my wife, "you'll wish you had either of *them* back, *if not both.*"

"I love the way you talk in italics," I said, throwing a fond smile over my shoulder as we sped down the passage toward the bedroom.

There I had a moment to catch my breath and get my bearings, the dinner my wife was preparing requiring, presently, her attention in the kitchen. But it was only a moment. I was pulling off my clothes and flinging them in every direction in my haste to get into the tub before hearing anything else that might qualify the peace in which I planned to luxuriate there, for a bit, when the door I had shut behind me opened and she reappeared, again nursing the cudgel. She tapped it mysteriously in a palm as she sat down on the bed to resume the interrupted dossier. (What such a cylindrical elongation might mean to a housewife I have no idea, having lost my taste for symbolism with the two steel balls the crazy captain in *The Caine Mutiny* kept rolling in his palm.)

"We're used to kids who live with one or the other of their parents, right? Well, *this* one doesn't live with *either* of *his*. Oh, he's with the mother technically, because she has custody of him, but he only goes there to sleep because he can't *stand* her, while his *father* can't stand *him*. So he likes to farm himself out to *other* people."

"Abrogation-of-the-family-pattern bit, eh? And must you speak in italics all the time, dear? It gives a man such a sense of stress."

"The father," she continued, crossing her legs, "says the mother lost the toss, so let her see to him. That's how he puts the custody decision. Apparently this one likes to sleep with the phonograph going—he's brought along an album of some group called The Burning Bananas that'll make you hanker after the gerbil days—and is said to make passes at his school teachers." I cleared my throat, kicked my shoes about, and in general made as much noise as possible in order to hear as little of this information as I could before gaining the safe haven of the bathroom. "Now, as to the father, *he's* currently shacked up with some cookie half his age in a cottage by the beach. She's about twenty, and models for—"

I sprang into the bathroom, clapped the door shut and turned the tub faucets up full blast, instantly cutting off all further data. I lolled as best I could in the promised warmth, for five minutes, perhaps ten. She was waiting for me when I emerged.

"—and models for these."

She opened the magazine and exhibited a picture of the baggage he was knit up with. I pored over it as she held it out for my inspection, nodding as I dried my shoulders with the towel. It showed a girl of the age specified, posing at the water's edge in a polka-dot diaper and nothing more—half a bikini. I set up in a small waffle shop in the east Fifties, read aloud to her evenings from my favorite authors, and in general exposed her to something better than was intimated by the evidence in hand.

"A face that could launch a thousand ships, all right," I murmured, dropping the towel on a chair. "To say nothing of the topless towers of Ilium."

"You don't ask how I got this magazine. Aren't you curious? Well, Mike—that's your guest's name, Mike Hackett—carried it around with him to show people. *As though it's something about his father to be proud of.*"

"*Stop talking in italics.*"

A knack for dramatic construction will have been discerned in my narrator. Nothing more displayed this gift than the manner in which she now inserted the keystone in her expository arch. Setting the magazine down on a table, she waited until I had finished extracting a clean pair of shorts from my bureau drawer, then yet a moment while I drew them on. Then she said:

"So that is what the father is lollygagging around with, leaving it to other people to raise—*that.*" She pulled aside a corner of the curtain and pointed down into the yard. I stepped to the window to look out.

I saw an Old Testament prophet dressed in loose-fitting vestments of muslin, or perhaps hopsacking, haranguing my attentive son. A lighted cigarette hung in one corner of his mouth, flapping briskly as he spoke. He talked with apparent authority, judging from the rapt, nodding concentration he received. He seemed to be denouncing something, possibly the garage against which he slouched, because once or twice he poked a thumb at it over his shoulder, as though he opposed it on some ground or other, possibly as symbolic of something he must deny his personal approval—such as the two cars it normally houses. Presently, and rather abruptly, the diatribe ceased, and the two gazed about them at the waning day. The prophet drummed the side of the garage with the palms of his hands. Then he took a last drag on the cigarette and snapped it into the shrubbery.

"Well," I said, turning from the window, "we can't judge all our young people by the behavior of most of them. But what's with the long hair? I thought that was on the way out."

"Huh!"

I swam into a pullover shirt of bleeding Madras, paused at the glass to brush my displaced hair, and then from the closet selected a pair of mulberry slacks. Leaning against a wall with folded arms, much in the manner of the prophet against the side of the garage, my wife coldly watched these sartorial preparations. My feet I slipped into a pair of white calfskin Belgian casuals.

"So you say his father won't have him around. It's probably his way of atoning for his adultery. Denying himself the pleasure of his children."

"Oh, will you stop being perfect!" my wife snapped with unaccustomed zest. "Nothing is more irritating than that. And all that I-would-never-sit-in-judgment cool is really a form of holier-than-thou, you know." Then she began slowly to pace the room. "But how to handle the boy is the problem now. The thing is, he doesn't let on his old man won't have any part of him. His story is that he's there with him all the time, that they're real pals, go for rides together in the father's Porsche roadster and what not. Skippy told me the real dope on the side—that the old man hauls off on him whenever he shows up. So we play dumb about that."

"All in all then, what the boy seems to need is some good normal family life. Let's give him a little of that, shall we?" I said, signaling that I was ready to go down.

"All right, but one thing. Don't go being incomparable at table. Nothing confuses children more than that. It upsets them. They don't understand it, and so they resent it. So lay off the savoir faire for tonight, shall we?—the style?"

Hardly. Standards must be upheld, a tone set at all costs, that setting, in turn, an example. That was especially important for those hailing from environments so lamentably lacking in it as that of which I had just been vouchsafed a glimpse. One must put one's best foot forward at all times.

Proof of how the grossest origins may be transcended lay allegorically in wait for us in the very soup to which we sat down—four cups of that vichyssoise whose genesis in the lowly potato of peasant France may be forgotten in the elegant restaurants (and fine homes) in which we sip it. I opened the table talk on just that point, in a properly oblique and subtle fashion of course. We were disposed round a circle of gleaming marble set with showy napery and hereditary plate, the prophet on my right, Skippy on my left, and my wife visible across from me above a floral centerpiece. Her lips delicately puckered to a spoonful of her soup, she watched the boys drink theirs, not to say listened to them, for they made hydraulic noises as they fed. "You may pick up your cups if you wish," she said, addressing to both boys an assurance aimed principally at the prophet, whose hair was hanging in his soup.

"You like this?" Skippy asked him.

"Yar's like groovy. But whassat like bee-bees?"

"We like to float a few grains of caviar in it," I said. "Gives it a certain zing, don't you think? Tell me," I continued in a pleasantly rambling fashion, "has anybody here been to that new diner on the Post Road yet? Teddy's. I dropped in there for a hamburger the other day and noticed something on the menu that struck me as funny. Among the desserts was listed a Jello du Jour. I thought that rather amusing."

"Kina flavor's that, man?"

I opened my mouth to explain, but a terse headshake from my wife persuaded me to shove along to other matters. The subject of mothers somehow came up, and I noticed a play of pained grimaces cross the prophet's face. A reference to his father, however, brought a broad smile to it. "He's got this cool place on the water," he related. "Man, you get up mornings and jump right in. Then he takes me for rides in his Porsche. He's got a Porsche that's like really where it's at."

No one taking as sacred the obligation to evolve—the progressive refinement of sensibility of which Henry James was so exquisitely a stage, now restated as Pierre Teilhard de Chardin's principle of "complexification"—will ever unrealistically blind himself to the impediments everywhere awaiting this long and uphill climb. The struggle to elevate our guest's temper was beset at every turn by a commensurate threat: I mean the decline of our host's. For the next quarter-hour we heard little but paeans of praise to the prophet's father, deluded as we know. He told of waterside sport (with or without Miss Twin Peaks was never said), of camaraderie in the open Porsche and convivial hands of rummy. Throughout the encomium, the prophet sat hunched over his plate with his hands around it, as though it were itself the steering wheel of a motor car in which he and, indeed, we all were traveling at high speed, his hair streaming behind him like a witch's instead of depending like a beagle's ears into his food.

The conversation at some point turned to hippies, and their ironical migration to Boston.

"You think they're really like the early Christians, Pop?" Skippy asked. "You buy that?"

"I do indeed," I said. "And I would like to see the parallel completed by having them thrown to the lions. If not the Kiwanians. Fix both sides."

"The idea is to live as though every day is Christmas, right?"

"Right. And dress as though every day is Halloween. Where did you get that chiropracter's tunic and those bare feet?" He had been given dispensation to come to the evening board unshod, in deference to his guest status.

"Timothy Leary's got charisma," said the prophet contentiously.

"Aw, I'm sorry to hear that," says I. "He certainly doesn't look well. I hope he's taking something for it."

The prophet shot a look into the kitchen over his shoulder. "Like I have some beer? My father lets me have it."

"Mine doesn't let me. But there are plenty of soft drinks out there," I said, seeing he hadn't touched his milk. "Coke, Seven Up, Like. Ever had Like? You might like like Like."

My wife was noting that he had also, in all this time, scarcely touched his food, since the soup. "Don't you like lamb chops?"

"Well, no. I don't seem to care much for chops of any kind."

"Maybe he'd like a karate chop," I said, looking into my wine glass.

There was no doubt I was being worn thin. The odds seemed too great at least so far. We had by midnight not discernibly evolved. Indeed, the backslidden state apprehended above increasingly marked the scene. The hour found me hammering my pillow and hissing the name of the Nazarene into it at the sound, issuing faintly but remorselessly from the boys' bedroom, of the Burning Bananas. The struggle for men's minds was not going at all well. Perhaps a battle must be granted as lost while bearing the war in mind. I tossed onto my back with a fresh oath as the vocalist, apparently pursuing a technique of singing the "words" of a song other than that being performed by the instrumentalists, belted out: "Atsa mah wah dig muh baby, lemme rock ya frunks!" or some such.

I sprang out of bed and thudded down the passage to the other bedroom. I snapped off the light, switched off the machine, and barked, "OK, that's it. That wraps it up, know what I mean? No more playing, talking, nothing. Good night!"

This night's sleep was a sequence of snoozes from the next of which I awoke to the murmur of voices below my chamber window. Leaning out of which I saw them sitting on the doorstep leading to the flagstone terrace. They were both smoking cigarettes, and the prophet was sucking on a bottle of Löwenbräu.

I suppose my manner, as I thundered down the stairs again in the Belgian casuals, resembled that of the movie actor Franklin Pangborn, whose thirty years of apoplectic fits still checker the Late Late Show. No later than this one, this was the Late Late Show too. They parted to let me storm down the stoop between them. I marched out to the terrace and wheeled to face them.

"Now then. You will go back in there—right in that house,"

I said pointing to it so there would be no mistake about which house was meant, "you will go back in there and get to bed. And if I hear one more peep out of either of you it'll be the razor strap. Now git!"

My kid skedaddled. The prophet, however, hung back a moment, gesturing with his free hand. "But like we couldn't sleep, so we just—"

I snatched the bottle from his grasp and flung it into the bushes, dealing a generous spray of foam about, and flecking us both with it. "Goddamn you, get in there!" With that, I drew my right foot back and let fly with all my might.

We use the term *good swift kick* with an everyday familiarity, as though delivering one were a regular occurrence, whereas in fact most of us go to our graves without experiencing the solid satisfaction of doing so. This one was well planted. But in planting it, I lost my balance and sat down on the terrace with an impact at least equal to that felt in the prophet's case. Also, in finding its target my foot lost its slipper, one of the white Belgian casuals, which sailed an inch past his head, through the open doorway, and straight at my wife, who had by now been awakened by the ruckus and come down herself to see what was going on. She ducked just in time, the slipper spinning end over end into the room giving onto the terrace, which is the library, where it struck a far row of bookshelves with a flat *splat* and dropped to the floor behind an easy chair. "Son of a *bitch!*" I said, closing the generation gap.

That did it. That turned the trick. The prophet from then on was nice as pie. I set to work the very next day on a story about the incident, about how young people really do want a firm hand (if that's the mot juste); discipline; a sense of authority. But when I reached the turning point of the narrative, the crisis I've just described, something about it didn't ring right. Some sneaking doubt about my grasp of the prophet's motivation nagged me. It was his grin as he bade me goodbye, thanking me for my hospitality, that hung me up. Each time I reread my interpretation of the prophet's sudden shift of attitude, as exhibiting the masculine adolescent's need for the authority principle, it rang hollow. The grin became a laugh, remote but unnerving. The principle was true enough, but not in this case. Something told me it was not relevant to this story. The author himself did not quite dig what he was illuminating.

I put it aside, and, as one often does, let the unconscious get in its licks. The badgering question on which the conscious agenda remained stuck was: why had my central character become nice as pie if not for the reason so far stated? Why had he come to like like me? The firm-hand theory didn't seem right in the exposition, any more than the best-foot-forward hypothesis.

The key to his sudden change lay, of course, in his relationship with his own father, so obviously that it is still a matter of embarrassment to me that light didn't break over me sooner. It broke, at any rate, in the form of an incident involving my own son and me, of no significance in itself; a minor traffic altercation between me and another motorist, in which he got decidedly the best of me. He had made what I thought a dumb move, for which I undertook to rebuke him with what I regarded as a rather neat thrust while we were both waiting for a green light. His riposte still makes me think of the cartoon of the prizefight manager saying to his battered boxer between rounds, "The next time you think you see an opening, duck." Having sent his repartee home, he shot away through the intersection and disappeared—leaving my son, who was sitting in the front seat beside me, blushing a brick red. I was startled to find how my humiliation stung him, until I remembered from my own boyhood how keenly a father's shame can become the son's. In the twinkling of a split second I had orbited all those memory-miles of inner space, and in that splinter of time my literary problem was illuminated. I understood what had made the prophet so happy.

His boasts of companionship with his father were only a cover-up, a shell carefully concealing an inner hurt, a wound that throbbed anew with every fresh evidence of parental decency and familial integrity elsewhere, stilled only by any proof, again at last, that his own old man wasn't so bad after all, relatively speaking. The last thing he needed was the civilized domestic environment I had egotistically striven to supply. Confronted with such another hazard to his self-esteem, he had spent that whole damned evening, and then half the night as well, reducing it to the shambles his own private life had become; in particular, reducing me to a clod at least as bad as his old man, if not worse. He had proved—or I had proved—the truth of Mark Twain's remark, that there are few things in life harder to bear than the irritation of a good example. That example liquidated, he could get on with the business of behaving toward me with comparative decency.

He still does, though it is now I who find the example hard to bear. I catch glimpses of him about town, always nodding politely to me and with a grin behind which lurks the gleam of cunning, the secret knowledge that I know what he knows.

That is the story of how I restored one boy's faith in his father. Little wonder it remains unwritten! I had sat down to write it without the faintest idea that was what it was about. I had surmised it to be about something else altogether. Thus it was the practice of my craft that, ultimately, enabled me to understand the reality the craft was intended to illuminate. Light did not break as I sat at the typewriter. That's not what I mean. I simply mean that my struggle with the literary problem kept my mind and spirit open to the revelation when it came, in the shape of real persons, places, and things.

To say that the story remains unwritten is to ignore its unexpected culmination in lecture form. It is in that form that I may now analytically equate my loss of heart for the narrative with the loss of my role in it as the hero. For the flash of illumination entailed, of course, my sudden switch to that of villain. In real life, the story with its transferred function remains unresolved, since I keep seeing the putative villain, now its martyr. Indeed, I saw him only last week when he was once more an overnight guest, and this time I had to steel myself for the confrontation in quite another manner than in the original instance when my wife's exposition had set up the drama to follow. Perhaps it is thus not a story after all, much less a novel, or a play, but the subject of a poem, and that, indeed, already written, put down not by a latter-day exponent of the surburban mores, or an interpreter of corroded metropolitan egos, but by the white-clad recluse of Amherst, Emily Dickinson, who a hundred years ago said:

> What fortitude the soul contains
> That it can so endure
> The accent of a coming foot,
> The opening of a door.

1969

Modern African Writing

Nadine Gordimer

There are two kinds of writers in Africa: the testifiers and those who are actually creating a modern African literature. But perhaps I ought first to explain a little more fully on what criteria I base the distinction between the testifiers and the creative writers. The testifiers supply some fascinating folklore and a lot of useful information about the organization of traditional African life, and the facts of social change in Africa. Like their counterparts, lesser writers all over the world, they take stock-in-trade abstractions of human behavior and look about for a dummy to dress in them, a dummy put together out of prototypes in other people's books rather than from observation of living people. They set these dummies in action, and you watch till they run down; there is no attempt to uncover human motivation, whether of temperament, from within, or social situation, from without. Such writers do not understand the forces which lie behind the human phenomena they observe and are moved to write about.

In passing, there is one difference between these writers in Africa and their European counterparts which is interesting because it relates so closely to Africa in its present state of transition. Elsewhere, people who are ill equipped creatively write out of vanity or because there is a profitable reading public for the third-rate. In Africa, a literature is still seen largely as a function of the benefits of education, automatically conferred upon a society which has a quota of western-educated people. The West African Pidgin English concept "to know book" goes further than it may appear; many school teachers, clerks, and other white-collar workers seem to write a novel almost as a matter of duty. The principle is strongly reinforced, of course, by the fact that the shortage of western-educated people means that Africa's real writers all, I think, without exception, have to perform some other function in addition to their vocation—from Africa's greatest poet, Leopold Sedar Senghor, who is also the president of Senegal, to T. M. Aluko, a fine Nigerian novelist, who is director of public works.

But this is by the way. Let me give some examples of the work of writers whose factual material is interesting but whose ability falls short of that material. The would-be writer says to himself, "All over Africa village boys have become prime ministers and presidents: Kenyatta, Obote, Toure, Banda, Launda. I will write a book about a village boy who, like them, leaves home, struggles for an education, forms a political party, resists the colonial authorities, wins over the people, and moves into Government House." Another would-be writer, aware of the move to reestablish the validity of the African way of life, says to herself, "It is one of the customs of my country for the husband of a childless woman to take another wife; I will write about a childless woman whose husband takes another wife." The result is, at best, something like the Sierra Leonian William Conton's *The African*, and the Nigerian Flora Nwapa's *Efuru*. While Conton's hero, Kisimi Kamara, progresses from village bright boy through the care of gin-tipping missionary ladies to Cambridge certificate, England, lodgings, urban poverty, and midnight oil, enlivened by boyish plans for African liberation, he has a certain autobiographical veracity behind him. When he returns to his country and becomes a public, less subjective figure, his author, lacking the creative insight into the complex motivation—psychological, political, and historical—needed to give his hero substance in this situation, resorts to sudden bald statements to be taken on trust by the reader—"Six months later I was Prime Minister"—and finally turns in desperation (and wild defiance of the political facts of life) to having Kamara resign office, buy an airline ticket, and land in South Africa to organize a boycott to bring down apartheid.

Flora Nwapa's *Efuru* is a childless woman whose bewilderment and frustration are stated and left unexplored. Again, not knowing enough about her own creation, the author has to resort to something to fill the vacuum. She uses rambling details of daily life, mildly interesting but largely irrelevant. Among them the key to the objective reality of *Efuru* lies half buried and less than half understood. Efuru is presented as beautiful, clever, a successful trader, and she performs all the rites and neighborly duties without which these attributes would not be valid in a tribal society, but she has had two unsuccessful marriages and seen her only child die. In a somewhat offstage incident, a sage diagnosis that a river goddess has chosen Efuru as her honored worshiper, it seems that other women chosen by the river goddess have been childless, too. Are we then being shown, through the life of an individual, how sublimation of frustrated natural instincts takes place in a woman of a particular type, and how an African society invents or employs religious or mystical conventions to reconcile her to her lot and give her a place within the society despite the fact that she cannot fulfill the conventional one? Is this novel really about an interesting form of compensation, not merely personal, but also social? The answer is yes, but Flora Nwapa, the author, only dimly senses the theme of her novel; all she has seen is the somewhat disparate series of events in the life of Efuru. Perhaps you remember E. M. Forster's famous definition of the difference between story and plot. "The king died and then the queen died"—that is a story, a series of events arranged in their time sequence. "The king dies and then the queen died of grief"—that is a plot; the time sequence is preserved but the emphasis is on causality. If I carry the definition one step further and suppose the author sets out to explore the questions, "What sort of woman is it who dies of grief and what sort of social and historical context shaped her?" we reach a definition of theme, the third dimension of the novel, and the one where it fulfills art's function of eternally pushing back the barriers of understanding in order to apprehend and make sense of life.

Flora Nwapa is one among the many African writers who are not able to do this for African life because she is not capable of dealing with theme. But she is a countrywoman of one of the few African writers whose name already belongs to world literature—Chinua Achebe. He handles the dominant themes of African writing, commanding all the resources of a brilliant creative imagination, from a classical sense of tragedy to ironic wit. In his first novel, *Things Fall Apart*, he shows at once a comprehensive insight into his characters. Their psychological makeup is never seen in isolation, as a neurotic phenomenon; his historical sense sets them at the axis of their time and place. He knows who they are, and why they are as they are; he shows them as stemming from the past, engaged with the forces of the present, and relevant to a future. He chooses as his hero what Hegel calls a world-historical figure, a man who, though not obscure, is not a king, not a history maker in the obvious sense, but someone through whose individual life the forces of his time can be seen to interact.

Okonkwo is a person of authority and achievement in his eastern Nigerian village. He was born the son of a failure and is self-made; by his own efforts he has a reputation as a fine wrestler, has distinguished himself in tribal wars, has an excellent yam crop, two tribal titles, and can afford three wives. A hostage of a tribal skirmish, a young boy, Ikemefuna, is given into his care until the council of tribal elders decides the boy's fate. Ikemefuna becomes so much a member of Okonkwo's family that he often has the honor of carrying Okonkwo's stool; yet when the elders decide Ikemefuna must die, Okonkwo is expected to be present when the deed is done, and, indeed, to dispatch him in his final agony. Okonkwo tries to put the dead boy out of his mind. Then later, at the funeral rites for an old man, the gun with which Okonkwo is to fire a salute explodes and fatally wounds another young boy. It is a crime to kill a clansman, and so Okonkwo is exiled from the village for seven years.

These are the disparate facts of the narrative; in Achebe's hands they grow out of one another with the surging inevitability of a Greek tragedy. Okonkwo's own son, Nwoye, was a disappointment; Ikemefuna had come to stand in his place. Yet when Ikemefuna received his deathblow and turned to Okonkwo, calling out "My father, they have killed me!"

Okonkwo, afraid of being thought weak, drew his machete and cut him down. The curse of Okonkwo's guilt over Ikemefuna hangs over subsequent events; the man at whose funeral Okonkwo inadvertently killed a young clansman was Ezuedu, the same old man who had said to Okonkwo at the time of Ikemefuna's killing, "That boy calls you father. Bear no hand in his death." So ends the first part of the novel. In it we have seen the personal psychological makeup of Okonkwo stemming from his private situation and background: the forces of the past which have combined to make him the man he is.

The second half brings the man into engagement with the specific politico-historical situation of his time. The seven years of Okonkwo's exile coincide with the infiltration of white missionaries and the colonial administration that follows, the flag close behind the cross. When Okonkwo returns to his village, his crime against the clan expiated, he finds that the white man's religion has come and "led many of the people astray"; the white man's government has built a court where he judges cases "in ignorance" of African law, and a store has been opened where for the first time palm oil and kernel have become "things of great price." Okonkwo's son, Nwoye, has become a Christian convert, and disowns his father. Okonkwo, whose exile has cost him his position of authority in the clan— "The clan was like a lizard; if it lost its tail it soon grew another"—regains authority when, on his advice, the church is burned down because an *egwugwu* (an ancestral spirit impersonated by a clansman) has been unmasked and desecrated by a Christian convert. As a result, Okonkwo and five other leaders are summoned by the district commissioner for a discussion and are then arrested and held hostage for a fine to be paid by the villagers. Lashed and humiliated by underlings of his own race while he was in prison, Okonkwo decides that if the clan will not fight to drive the white man away, he will avenge himself alone. At a meeting of the clan, he kills a government messenger who comes to declare the meeting illegal. Before the district commissioner arrives with soldiers to arrest him, he hangs himself.

Again, the train of events falls into a more profoundly mean-ingful arrangement than that of causality when Achebe's deep understanding of the nature of the white man's impact on Africa is brought to bear on them. Okonkwo kills himself be-cause the authority he takes up again is already a broken thing; there can be no real return to the clan, for him, because the African ethos that held it together has faltered before the attraction-repulsion of the white man's ethos. When Okonkwo kills the government messenger,

> The waiting backcloth jumped into tumultous life and the meeting was stopped. Okonkwo stood looking at the dead man. He knew that Umofia would not go to war. He knew because they had let the other messengers escape. They had broken into tumult instead of action.

The white man's gods more than the white man's guns— Achebe shows how, above all, these were what no one was armed against, at this stage in Africa's history.

Tumult instead of action: *No Longer at Ease*, the title of Achebe's second novel, at once takes up the theme of the era for which the scene was set at the close of *Things Fall Apart*. *No Longer at Ease* begins in a courtroom in Lagos where Obi Okonkwo (I don't know whether the suggestion is that he is a later generation of the dead Okonkwo's family) is on trial for taking bribes. The time is still pre–Nigerian independence. Obi is a been-to, a civil servant educated in England, person-able, with a taste for poetry and Scotch, and a car. Friends, white administrators—all discuss his downfall: "Everyone wondered why." The book explores the irony of the statement, working back to it through the conflict of social pressures that have made this courtroom almost a predestination for young Obi. When he returned from England, full of enthusiasm for the new Africa his generation is going to build, and deter-mined to set an example of dedication, honesty, and disin-terest in the Africanized civil service, he was at once burdened with two incompatible sets of obligations: on the one hand, to pay back to his village the money advanced for his overseas education and the necessity to assist his family; on the other, to live in a European style befitting his position as a civil servant. With a terse ironic touch, Achebe places him not between some sweeping abstraction of "natural" forces of past and future, but between social stresses, as he extends himself docilely on the rack of the bourgeois values his society has taken over from the white man, values totally unreal in the economic and social conditions of that society. It is not that Obi cannot do his work efficiently, but that he accepts the necessity for the trappings of a European bourgeois life that, during a European administration, went along with it. Even the obligation to support his family is not measured in accordance with their actual needs, but with what is thought to befit the family of a man who lives according to European white-collar values.

In his third novel, *Arrow of God*, Achebe turns back to the early colonial era, predating that of *Things Fall Apart*. There are similarities between the first and the third; but, in the first, the conflict between the white man and Africa is overt, whereas in the third, African confidence is still unshaken and the African ethos intact, a positive value not yet brought into question by others. It is significant that whereas Okonkwo loses his son as a convert to Christianity, Ezeulu in *Arrow of God* sends *his* son to the mission school in cold calculation that it is useful and necessary to acquire the white man's magic— his skills. Although the threat of the white man's presence hangs over these people, they have not yet realized that they could ever be anything but masters of their own destiny. In *Things Fall Apart*, Achebe's purpose was to show traditional life disintegrating; in *Arrow of God* his purpose is above all to reinstate the validity of life *without the white man*. He examines, through the ordinary devices of the psychological novel, the stresses and emotional problems of that life and the social order created to contain them. They are presented in themselves, in the tension of their own order, rather than in conflict with another. Although the actions of colonial administrators precipitate events in the novel, it is the events themselves and

the Africans who deal with them who take up the foreground—
the white men, prominent in Achebe's other books, this time
remain curiously unimportant and remote.

The scene is a complex of villages in eastern Nigeria and the
people are Ibo. Ezeulu, chief priest of Ulu, local deity of the
Umuaro people, is the protagonist. The central narrative is his
double struggle: against rivalry among his own tribesmen, and
the incomprehensible demands (scarcely recognized as authority, yet) of the district officers and missionaries. This story line
is so richly overlaid with the intrigues, counterintrigues,
ceremonies, customs, feasts, and legends of the Umuaro, not
to mention character studies of Ezeulu's wives, children, in-
laws, and friends, and the brilliantly observed relations among
them all, that it comes as something of a shock, in the last
chapter or two, to realize that while this abundance of life has
been occupying one's mind, Ezeulu has been moving toward
one of those Lear-like destinies of defeat before social change
that Achebe understands so well. This novel attempts the
complete evocation of African life—not an exoticist exploita-
tion of local color and strange customs, but the total logic of a
particular way of life. Only *The Dark Child*, an autobiographical novel by the French African writer, Camara Laye, can
compare with it, and then only as an exquisite detail can be
compared with the superbly realized complete canvas. For
Achebe has succeeded superbly, even though he has perhaps
not solved all the technical problems of fitting this particular
theme into the form of the conventional modern novel.

In his latest novel, *A Man of the People*, he turns to comic
irony as the best approach to the theme of political corruption
in an independent African state—and he is almost the only
English-writing African able to use it. Again, so far, one has to
look to French African writers for comparison—the rather
clumsy satire of Mongo Beti's attack on the Catholic Church in
King Lazarus, and the immensely stylish, sophisticated bite of
Ferdinand Oyono's *Houseboy*, written in the form of a diary
which records the servant's-eye view of the private life and
loves of the white master race.

James Ngugi of Kenya is another novelist who attempts

important African themes on a scale of complexity and depth, although he does not always manage to bring them off with the skill of an Achebe. He attempts to relate the African past—not just historical but also mythological—to the present-day life of the Gikuyu people. The period of his novel, *The River Between,* is immediately pre-Mau-Mau—or pre-Kiama, to give the movement its proper name. The approach is that of an exploration of the background of social and historical forces that led to the formation of a liberation movement. The novel begins with a scene setting in which the mythological origin of the Gikuyu—their Adam and Eve story—is invoked, and the prophecy of an ancient Tikuyu seer is recalled: "There shall come a people with clothes like butterflies." Now they have come; the familiar struggle is on between the clanspeople who remain within tribal disciplines and the white missionaries and their black converts. The young boy Waiyuki, like Ezeulu's son in *Arrow of God,* goes to the mission school to learn the secrets of the white man; but for Waiyuki this is seen as part of the fulfillment of a political destiny. His father is a descendant of the seer and believes that his son is the chosen one whom it was also predicted would come from the hills to save the Gikuyu. The feud between the mission and the clan finds its martyr in Muthoni, daughter of the convert pastor, Joshua. The issue is, not surprisingly, her circumcision—white condemnation of female circumcision coming second only to the settler appropriation of the White Highlands in the canon of Gikuyu resentment of colonial rule. Muthoni is a devout Christian, but she cannot accept the Christian edict against a rite without which she will not belong, in the true sense, to her people. She says "I want to be a woman made beautiful in the manner of the tribe." Waiyuki realises that Muthoni "had the courage to attempt a reconciliation of the many forces that wanted to control her" from the tribal past and the westernized future. She dies of the operation: to the tribe, a saint; to the mission, a pagan punished for her sins. Waiyuki, while he follows his father's admonition to remain true to his people and the ancient rites, becomes a teacher and believes that the salvation of the people before the threat of annihilation by the white man's ethos lies in western education, the organization of the Tikuyu independent schools movement. He joins the Kiama at its inception, when it is chiefly a society to keep Gikuyu cultural traditions alive, but resigns when it takes on a more militant character, putting off the political mission that he sees is necessary: to unite the people, both Christian and tribal, in a common purpose of liberation from white rule. Later he rejoins the Kiama but fails to commit himself fully to leadership. Finally, he is expelled when he goes to warn the mission of an impending attack by the Kiama. The conflict is now between Waiyuki and the tribe; like other saviors before him he is threatened with crucifixion at the hands of those he has come to save. He understands at last that no evasion is possible—"the new awareness of the people wanted expression at a political level," and no other would do.

This overlong and clumsy novel does analyze with considerable insight the spiritual conflict between the values of tribal life and those imposed by white conquest. Ngugi creates a world-historical figure. The man who seeks to go beyond the either-or and believes that a new synthesis is necessary if Africa is to take her place in the modern world becomes a victim of the force of nationalism. Waiyuki is seen as a failure because he cannot fulfill the demands of his time; Ngugi understands the forces of that time and places him squarely in it.

A Grain of Wheat, James Ngugi's latest novel, is an extremely interesting piece of work because it brings a new theme to African literature—the effects on a people of the changes brought about in themselves by the demands of a bloody and bitter struggle for independence. How fit is one for peace, when one has made revolution one's life? Set in the immediate post-Mau-Mau period, the novel looks back to the personal tragedies of a number of people who were active in Mau-Mau, and examines how the experience now shapes their lives. In the uneasy peace, they have to come to terms with one another, but their relationships are determined by the experience that has put all human relationships through the test of fire—the guerilla revolution itself. Here are the wild-looking bearded men who lived in the Aberdares for years, emerging after the revolution with almost all their instincts for normal life lost; brave men half-broken by the experience; and men accepted as brave men who must live the rest of their lives with the secret knowledge that they were traitors. Mugo, a local small farmer, is such a man. He has betrayed a fellow Gikuyu to the British; as a result of various events which enmesh him in the sense of his own guilt, he brings his own world crashing down around his head by confession, and the words of one of the Mau-Mau veterans who are his judges at a private trial sum up the light in which Ngugi presents him: "Your deeds alone will condemn you. No one will ever escape from his own actions." It is the measure of James Ngugi's development as a writer that none of the protagonists in this novel is marred by the pseudo nobility of some of the characters in his earlier work, and yet he succeeds in placing the so-called Mau-Mau movement in the historical, political, and sociological context of the African continental revolution. What the white world perhaps still thinks of as a reversion to primitive savagery (as opposed, no doubt, to civilized savagery in Nazi Germany) is shown to be a guerilla war in which freedom was won, and which brought with its accomplishment a high price for the people who waged it.

Wole Soyinka, another Nigerian, made his name as a poet and Africa's finest playwright. He deals with a postindependence Africa in an extraordinary first novel, *The Interpreters*. Sagoe the journalist, Sekoni the engineer, Lasunwon the lawyer, Egbo the aristocrat working in the Foreign Office, Bandele the academic—these are the friends that the painter Kola is using as models for the pantheon of Nigerian gods in an ambitious canvas. These contemporary Africans are interpreting, through their lives, modern Africa, and the painter is interpreting the old godhead anew, through them. These men are western-educated, but they are certainly not been-tos—far from being precariously extended between two worlds (African life and the cities of Europe), they have reached the synthesis of both which many Africans writing before Soyinka have seen as the ideal solution to the problem of modern African identity. But it is a critical synthesis: it turns out that the spiritual inadequacies of both worlds become clear to those who, at long last, have come into the heritage of the two as one. The journalist Sagoe's scatalogical philosophy of Voidancy ("the most individual function of man")—a lavatory philosophy with the smallest room in the house as its temple of meditation—is a send-up of negritude along with the hairsplitting of orthodoxy and revisionism in the fad philosophies of East and West. Sekoni, the engineer, has a nervous breakdown (the first one I've come across in African writing) when a power station he has built is never used because of some piece of political finaglery. Dr. Faseyi has problems with his English wife, not because she is not acceptable to his family, but because she forgets her white gloves and asks for palm wine instead of a cocktail at an embassy reception, behaving, he says, "like a bush-Cockney." Egbo, taking his friends on a visit to his ancestral home, where his family is still a great one, casts a cold eye on both his grandfather's feudal dignity and his own sycophantic life at the Foreign Office: "What is my grandfather but a glorified bandit? Only that doesn't help either. Sooner a glorified bandit than a loudmouthed slave." And Sagoe, watching a Lagos crowd in pursuit of a wretched young pickpocket, says to himself, "Run, you little thief, or the bigger thieves will pass a law against your existence as a menace to society. . . . run from the same crowd which will reform tomorrow and cheer the larger thief returning from his twentieth Economic Mission, and pluck his train from the mud, dogwise, in its teeth."

Nothing is what it seemed—what it seemed it would be before African emancipation; even the prophet of a new Christian sect in Lagos, a Lazarus claiming to have risen from the dead, turns out to have as his disciples a gang of thieves. Does Soyinka see him as the symbol of the new African society? Perhaps. But this magnificent novel, with its poet's command of the torrents of language, its wit both fiery and laconic, is not defeatist. One cannot do justice to its complexity in a brief summary and discussion; but it is significant that episodes most meaningful—whether as fulfillment or disillusion—to the protagonists are often those rooted in Africanness, in the subsoil of the new society.

It is interesting to compare for a moment the total involvement—in both Europe and Africa—of Wole Soyinka's people with the almost total disengagement of Doumbe in a novel called *A Few Nights and Days*, by the Cameroonian Mbella Sonne Dipoko. Doumbe is just another one of the deracinated young everywhere, moving through the cafés, dance halls, and beds of Paris. To him, the moment, privately tangible, is all that matters; so that one might take him as an example of the African depersonalized by the West. In traditional African societies, the welfare of the tribe is the concept of ultimate concern, and the constant presence of the spirits of the ancestors, influencing daily life, makes the western division of life into secular and spiritual a meaningless concept. Soyinka's sophisticated protagonists are fully engaged in attempting to interpret this concept in modern terms.

Ezekiel Mphahlele, the South African writer, maintains that the cultured elite of black Africa is becoming middle-class because the diplomas of its members give them access to positions of responsibility, whereas in South Africa the Negro intellectual is still a member of the proletariat because racial segregation prevents his obtaining white-collar jobs and privileges reserved for whites. This applies to African literature and writers, too, of course; he implies that there is no proletarian literature in black Africa, only in South Africa. If he has in mind an urban proletariat, what he says is true; apart from Cyprian Ekwensi's *Jagua Nana,* the story of a Nigerian prostitute, and perhaps one or two others, the literature of black Africa, where it deals with urban life, deals with the African middle class. But consider novels dealing with rural life, such as John Munonye's *The Only Son*, Ekwensi's *Burning Grass*, Ghanaian S. A. Konadu's *A Woman in Her Prime*, and James Ngugi's novels as well as Achebe's *Things Fall Apart* and *Arrow of God*—if subject and theme, and not the manner of life of the author, are the criteria, then surely this is the literature of an agrarian proletariat?

Apart from a very few notable exceptions (Mofolo's *Chaka,* Abrahams's historical novel, *Wild Conquest*) imaginative African writing in South Africa is overwhelmingly a proletarian literature in a society where color and class are identified. It ranges from Peter Abrahams's countryman-comes-to-town story, *Mine Boy* with its view of the violent baptism of a mineworker into city life seen through the saving grace of individuals and individual racial attitudes, to Alex La Guma's *A Walk in the Night* in which the debasement of life on the wrong side of the color bar hangs a pall of degradation over every human activity, so that every relationship is demeaned in the generalization of an overwhelming inhumanity: the color bar itself. Alex La Guma's protagonists in District Six do not talk about inequality; they bear its weals. In this novel, Michael Adonis is a colored boy who has just lost his job in a society where his ambitions are limited by job reservations and his security as a worker is not ensured by a trade union. He wanders the streets around his Cape Town tenement room, and in an atsmophere of cheap wine, sex, and the meaningless aggression of frustrated human beings, unintentionally kills a decrepit old white man who has sunk too low for acceptance among whites. Adonis's moral dissolution culminates when he lets his friend, Willieboy, be blamed for the crime, while Adonis himself joins a gang of thugs. In his short stories, Alex La Guma shows the same ability to convey the sight, sound, and smell of poverty and misery, so that the flesh-and-blood meaning of the color bar becomes a shocking, sensuous impact. His stories are set in prisons, cheap cafés, backyards, yet eschew the cliché situations of apartheid—the confrontations of black and white in the context of the immorality act or liquor raids, which are done to death by lesser writers. He is able to make a subtle piece of social comment, in his slight story "Nocturne," out of a colored delinquent attracted upstairs into a white house by the sound of music he has never heard before. James Matthews, in the same story collection, *Quartet,* shows the other face of deprivation in a brilliantly observed story "The Portable Radio," in which the black man's desire for material possessions, cynically fostered across the color bar by the white man, becomes yet another fake foisted upon the black man in place of the self-respect discrimination denies him. Both these stories convey more about the particular social situation in which they occur than the too obvious allegory of a story like Richard Rive's version of the nativity in color bar dress, with a white village hotel owner, and Mary and Joseph as black laborers. When James Matthews deals with political action, as in his bus boycott story "Azikwela" ("We Will Not Ride"), he shows not generalized heroic or saintly figures, but ordinary, frightened men, driven to find themselves through experiences they half shrink from, tempted to prefer deprived life to the danger of risking what little they have in the hope of attaining something better; coming slowly to the discovery that it is the intangibles, a sense of one's innate dignity and an indentification with the hopes of one's fellows, which become both means and end, and give one the courage to act. Throughout South African black literature—in the autobiographical writings of Mphahlele and Lewis Nkosi, Bloke Modisane, and others, as well as in fiction—it is these protagonists and these qualities that are taken to represent the only true values for a dispossessed proletariat.

What are the most striking features of the way Africa sees itself and its relation to the rest of the world, emerging from African literature in English? Well, to begin with, some attitudes that are likely to be surprising to the white world. The way Africa sees the role of Christianity in Africa's history, for example. The general view of Christianity is as intrinsically alien and destructive. Whether Christian values did or did not offer any spiritual advance on those of African religions is not seen as the issue; the church is evil because it lures the people away from their own gods. When the missionaries brought the gospel to Africa, so far as traditional African society was concerned they were the devil's disciples: to be a convert was to be damned, not saved—an attitude that sets on its head the traditional white view of Christianity, leading the dark continent into the light. Well, one's own god is always the true one; the other man's is the pagan idol. Of course, one also sees how the African view of Christianity was conditioned first by the slave trade, when certain bishops were zealous in baptizing slaves before they were shipped off, and then later—when missionaries like Livingstone had influenced the white world to outlaw slavery, and had brought white administrators in their train instead—by resentment against the interlopers for whom the white man's religion had opened the way. On the other hand, where Islam enters African literature it is not presented as a foreign religion at all, so easily, it seems, it was assimilated. And the fact that Arabs bought and sold Africans both before the whites began and after the whites had ceased to do so brings no trace of resentment into acceptance of the Arab's Mohammedanism. What is striking is the religious fatalism that pervades the protagonists in novels about arabized Africans—Ekwensi's *Burning Grass*, for example— and the submissiveness of the woman portrayed, in contrast with the vigor and initiative of those remarkable women who often dominate fiction about societies which still worship their ancestors.

The African view of white colonial administrators—apart from the missionaries, Africa's entire experience of the white world for several decades—is seen to change, from the monstrous bad-man figures of some African writers, through the figures of fun drawn by others, to the picture being presented in postindependence literature of the white administrator as a man who, although he may have had a genuine wish to be useful in Africa, an integrity of purpose fully granted, is completely unable to make real contact with African life. It is as if the man who for so long claimed to "know the African" can now never hope to get to know him in any meaningful way. As for the white liberal, in the main he or she appears in African fiction in the role summed up by the South African political thinker, Majeke, as "conciliator between the oppressor and the oppressed." (Nosipho Majeke, "The Role of the Missionaries in Conquest"). A notable exception is Lois, the Englishwoman in Peter Abrahams's *Wreath for Udomo;* he makes a heroine of her.

But then writing from black South Africa is different from

that of any other part of the continent. As Wole Soyinka said recently, "the experience of the South African writer is approached by that of other Africans only remotely by the experience of colonial repression." The difference in experience is reflected in the picture of the African that emerges from South African black literature, compared with that of the rest of the English-writing continent. It is as a dispossessed proletariat that the Africans emerge in black South African literature, a people struggling under the triple burden of industrialization, color, and class discrimination, in a capitalist economy which orders their lives as if they were still living in a feudal age. It is as a people dealing with the problems of power that the rest are shown, exercising the right even to misgovern themselves and struggling not to live an anachronism, but to reestablish the African past as something contiguous with the drastic, profound, and necessary change of the present.

What main trend does African English literature show in its development? George Lukacs, the Hungarian philosopher and one of the two or three important literary critics of our time, discerns three main trends in modern world literature in his *The Meaning of Contemporary Realism:* first, the literature of the avant-garde—experimental modernism from Kafka and Joyce to Beckett and Faulkner, which he condemns for its subjectivism, its static view of the human condition, its dissolution of character, its obsession with pathological states and its lack of a sense of history; and second, socialist realism, which he criticizes for its oversimplification, its failure to see the contradictions in the everyday life of society, and its view of history—"Utopia is already with us" under communism—a view he finds no less static than that of the western avant-garde. He contrasts with these two systems of artistic dogmatism the trend of critical realism—work in which the social changes that characterize our era are most truly reflected, character is not sacrificed to artistic pattern, the human condition is understood dynamically, in a historical context, and the pathological aspects of modern life are placed in a critical perspective. George Lukacs sees the critical realists as the true heirs, through writers such as Thomas Mann and Conrad,

of the great realists of the nineteenth century—Balzac, Sten-
dhal, and Tolstoy—and critical realism as not only the link with
the great literature of the past, but also the literature that
points to the future. There seems to me no doubt that African
English literature's best writers are critical realists, and that
this is the direction in which African literature is developing.

                                                            1970

The Practical Critic: A Personal View

Theodore Solotaroff

The invitation to give this lecture is the most gratifying one
I've ever received, for at this very moment one of my longer-
standing fantasies is being fulfilled. The fantasy began during
one of the four afternoons I sat in Rackham—my short stories
once again having gone down to defeat—and consoled myself
with the thought that someday I would show them. Someday,
the Hopwood Committee would be saying among themselves,
"My God, how could Solotaroff have written those tremendous novels and not have won even a minor award in fiction
when he was here?" And so, to make amends, I would be
invited to give the Hopwood lecture, and back I would come
to Ann Arbor in modest triumph, my suitcase full of crow.
Well, it didn't quite work out like that. But here I am anyway.
Though I'm about ten years behind the timetable I'd set and
have made the journey not along the high road of fiction but
the low one of literary journalism, my vanity is well content
and advises me not to quibble.

In the Hopwood lecture that I would compose during those
years after leaving Ann Arbor and living in Greenwich Village
and other lonely places, I would always find time to say a few
words in consolation to my fellow losers who would be sitting
in the audience. In fact, as those years dragged on and the
Hopwood judges were joined by a lengthening line of
magazine editors, my fellow losers became exceedingly real to
me: more real than I was to myself, since in my fantasy lecture
I was transformed into a winner, a state that was very pleasant
but not very real. By the same token, my tremendous novels
still being unwritten, my only basis for being there in my
fantasy as a writer was my growing pile of rejection slips. So

my thoughts turned easily to the sweet uses of adversity and to those who most needed to be reminded of them.

All of which, of course, was a bit crazy: a kind of vain (in both senses of the word) and glum effort to rise above the mire of rejection. "Fame is the spur," as Milton said, but still one needs a horse: otherwise there's not much to kick but yourself. There was lots of future glory for me in writing fiction but not much present substance or energy, for reasons which I've already written about ("Silence, Exile, and Cunning," *New American Review* 8 [January, 1969]:201–19) and will spare you this evening. Instead, I'd like to talk a bit about why I went into literary journalism, or practical criticism, why it provided me with a horse of sorts, or, to put it less metaphorically, a positive motive for writing. Perhaps you plan to stay away from criticism like the plague, in which case you may want to set your mind for forty-five minutes from now, when I finally get out of the way of the awards, and drift off into composing your own future Hopwood lecture. But perhaps I may say something, sooner or later, that applies to your situation too, for all forms of writing share a certain identity as physical and metaphysical labor: like this lecture, each is a bridge of words being led across an abyss of doubt.

One of the courses I took at Michigan was called "Practical Criticism." I think I was a junior at the time, and know that I was full of newfangled complexities, a kind of New Critic in training, an ingenious reader between the lines, where all of the ironies and paradoxes and symbols were hidden from common view. Reading between the lines also meant between one's actual gut responses, but armed with the magical lamp of ambiguity one forged on into the darkness. I'm not putting down the New Criticism, which has become kind of a mug's game—the standard form of parricide among critics of my generation—I'm merely saying that it was the way I found to be pretentious, of which each generation has its own modes. Ten years before, I would no doubt have come on like a Marxist, twenty years later, perhaps, as a wild and woolly trasher of literature, or a stoned farmer, or a media freak, or all rolled into one. Anyway, I took this course in Practical Critcism because I was getting out of my depth and not a little screwed up. A few months before, I'd been asked to write a review for the *Michigan Daily*, of a collection of stories by William Carlos Williams. I had given it the big treatment, as though Williams was sort of like Borges (he was really like an American Chekhov—all eyes and heart), and the review was rejected. Very put out, I took it to my friend Herbert Barrows, who read it and said he felt like he had been hanging by his suspenders for two minutes. So since he was teaching Practical Criticism I decided to take it.

It was a swell course, or rather, class, or better, group: that is to say, a course that became a kind of little community that assembled three hours a week so that we could all learn from each other. At first, Herbert would read us a story or poem, and we would jot down what struck us as significant. The first few times I was left at the post in a kind of panic. I could barely make out the lines on one reading: how was I supposed to read between them? This, of course, was the point of the exercise, which had to do not with ingenuity but with a kind of primary responsiveness, known as paying attention, and with letting a central impression grow inside you, and with articulating it.

Clearly, I had a lot to learn, beginning with the distinction between having an impression and making one. The pretender critic (same root as pretentious) in myself didn't have impressions: that was to be impressionistic, which was the last thing a New Critic could afford to be in his pursuit of order and complexity. But someone with my name had better begin to have some impressions, I realized, if he was to stop handing in this desperate gibberish.

As I said, I had a lot of help from our group. I remember one student in particular who almost regularly came up with an amazingly sharp and interesting response. He seemed older than most of us, and was very quiet, and wore a hearing aid, which I thought might be really a secret miniature tape recorder by which he would play back to himself what the rest of us had heard only once and were stumbling to remember. But, as I began to see, his secret advantage lay elsewhere. Instead of groping about to describe and judge the poem or story—"This poem is about X; what I liked about it was Y," and so forth—he would find an image which, as he deftly developed it, characterized the work and stated its appeal in such a way that it came back from his mind as freshly and distinctively as it had entered. I remember his speaking of a poem by Frost or Lawrence as being like a patch of ocean where two mighty warships had fought and gone down, leaving a single empty lifeboat floating on the surface. So I began to see that practical criticism was not only trusting your own impressions but also using your imagination to take the measure of a work and to locate it in the world of experience.

All of which, as time went on, was like being let off a leash, one's mind running free among its natural interests and with its natural energy. Or, to put it another way, by making criticism practical, Herbert brought it level with one's taste and experience rather than setting it on a higher, more abstract plane. Or, to put it a third way, he brought literature back to the reasons I'd had for being interested in it in the first place. The course didn't make me into a practical critic or even make me desire to become one, but it did help to straighten me out a bit and planted certain seeds that were to crop up later.

My second encounter with practical criticism came about six years later and also took place in a classroom. By then I had pretty well given up writing fiction, was now a graduate student at the University of Chicago, and had just begun to teach composition and a literature course at a two-year college called Indiana University Calumet Center. It was located in East Chicago, Indiana, which was known as "The Workbench of America," and most of my students worked in local oil refineries and steel mills. The center was one grim brick building just off Route 12, a major trucking route, and as the diesels roared by outside, we talked about comma faults and dangling modifiers and other "gross illiteracies," and about such immediately relevant writers as Homer, Plato, Dante, and Chaucer.

For a time, we were miles apart—I with my sense of being in an academic slum, my Flaubertian notion of style and my Aristotelean approach to structure, which I was learning at

Chicago and, faute de mieux, teaching at East Chicago; my students, half-awake after eight hours of tending an open hearth furnace or a catalyst cracker and otherwise puzzled, intimidated, or hunched defensively in their leather jackets, staring at their copy of *The Agamemnon* as though it were still in the original Greek. I struggled and groped, cajoled and bitched; none of it did much good.

In one of my composition courses was a boy named John Dovitch. Dovitch was from Calumet City, another garden spot, whose main industry was vice, and he looked like he had grown up on the street corners there: the DA haircut, the motorcycle boots, the swagger. He was small and tough and smart as a whip. He liked to sit in the front and give me the fish-eye, and every so often he would contribute to the discussion:

> "What's the matter with repeating a word?"
> "It makes your writing monotonous."
> "But that other word was two sentences back."
> "Well, it's still not good style."
> "Who says so? I mean besides you?"
> "It's not a question of who says so. It's a question of varying your word choice, of finding the precise word."
> "I read a story by this guy Hemingway and he repeats himself all the time."
> "That's different... He does it for an effect."
> "Yeah... so?"

And so on and so forth. Dovitch's next theme was sure to be full of repetitions, just as it was sure to be full of comma faults and dangling modifiers and misspellings—taunting me. The only problem was that he could write. He wrote a composition on the gang he'd belonged to that could have been written by Nelson Algren. I didn't know what to do, so I gave him an A for content and a D—for mechanics. He came up to see me after class.

> "You want to know about your grade," I said, steeling myself.

"It's pretty screwy, but what I want to know is where you're from."

"Chicago."

"Yeah, I know that. You're one of those graduate students. I mean where did you grow up?"

"Elizabeth, New Jersey."

"That's sort of like around here."

"That's right," I said, "lots of refineries."

"Then why do you talk like you grew up at Harvard?"

I took that one home with me. After a good deal of brooding, I decided that he was telling me to wise up. To realize where I was. Why the airs and graces? Mainly because I was so wrapped up in teaching composition and literature as though I were selling Omega watches at Woolworth's that I hadn't realized that I was teaching persons. And meanwhile there was a whole side of me that knew these persons, had gone to high school with them, buddied with them in the Navy, worked with them in restaurants. And clearly the burden of relating to them was on me, and so was the burden of interest. They were rightly interested in their accounting or lab courses, for through them they might someday have jobs that wouldn't break their backs. But what did using precise transition words or understanding the tragic form have to do for them? What had they to do for me when I had started college, only a little less in the dark than they were, and also bent on moving up in the world?

I make this sound like a moment of truth, but the realities of teaching in East Chicago dawned on me in stages, as I settled into the work and began to see my way, which was to make use of the common ground between us and to make it pertain. Instead of teaching grammar, say, as rules and regulations, I tried to teach it as thought, a kind of rock-bottom logic. We tried to imagine what the dawn of language was like and how a grammar came into being as a way of sorting out chaos of phenomena. Instead of teaching the dicta of correct usage, we played around with etymologies, giving words their weight and color as artifacts, placing them in the affairs of men. In the literature course, we compared Odysseus with

Davy Crockett, a big pop-cult hero at the time, to figure out what an epic hero was. We put together a modern scenario of *Agamemnon* with Douglas MacArthur as the tragic hero. We tried to imagine why Socrates wasn't just a sucker to stay in prison and get executed and why even the laws in East Chicago had something to be said for them. But this puts the experience too pedagogically. Much of the time, I simply plunged in, letting a line of inquiry develop of its own course. I free associated and improvised, stimulated mainly by those faces in front of me that I wanted to amuse and involve, to wipe the film of dullness away from their eyes. And of course I was stimulated myself by all that I was learning by going back to the fundamentals and letting them fill with useful content.

What did all of this have to do with practical criticism? A good deal, as I was subsequently to find out. For one thing, I had begun to learn what an audience was: a group of people who were waiting to be interested, which was within their right. I had also begun to learn what the terms of the appeal were: that one addressed them as a man among men rather than as a highly literary type who had just parachuted in from graduate school. I was also learning that the main problem and opportunity was to be clear: to approach the unfamiliar by means of the familiar, the abstract by the concrete, the concept by means of the example. I was also learning something about tone: the right one coming from the natural play of individuality, the wrong one from role playing. Finally, I was beginning to learn that to make matters interesting you had to first make them interesting to yourself. That was where imagination came in: seeing something in another way. As a corollary of this, I was beginning to understand that the truly interesting was likely to have an element of risk in it.

Obviously, I didn't reach all of these students, and I learned from that too. I remember one exam in which I asked which was the more tragic play: *Agamemnon* or *Oedipus*. Back came my definitions, distinctions, and examples in more or less garbled form. One student told me that the play about the general was more tragic because he was like MacArthur getting bumped off during the San Francisco Parade in 1954,

which was very unusual, but the other play by Socrates wasn't
very tragic because for someone to kill his father and marry his
mother, that happens all the time. So there was no common
denominator: you tried to keep a vision of the best possibilities
in the class—or audience—and address them. This would also
come in handy later.

Meanwhile, there was Dovitch, who turned up the next fall
in the second half of the literature course, a little less daunting
but still up in the front seat, his skepticism still intact. To what
did I owe this privilege of teaching him again, I asked. He told
me that I fitted into his schedule. So we went round and round
again until one day he stayed behind after class.

> "You've gotten a little smarter," he said.
> "Thank you," I said, "maybe I have."
> "Yeah, you said some interesting things now and then."
> "Maybe you're getting smarter too."
> He shrugged, summoning his truculence.
> "It takes two to communicate," I said.

Or something like that. Anyway, from then on the tension
between us diminished; we continued to play each other tough
but there was a rapport that kept each of us from his form of
crapping around. By the time we got to the last two novels,
Crime and Punishment and *Huckleberry Finn*, I was much
more interested in discovering how their two renegades established themselves in his mind than in imposing my own
analogies and structure. Once I knew what was reaching him,
what was charged for him, we could try to figure out the
circuits. I had been trained to work the other way around: find
the form and you'll find the power. It was a much tidier way of
teaching; there is nothing like the word *structure* to cool out a
class. But it was more interesting to teach an alert class, beginning with myself.

The next semester I passed Dovitch on to a friend who was
teaching the sophomore literature course. By the end of the
year, Dovitch had won a scholarship to Illinois and another to

Southern Illinois. He decided to go to Carbondale. "I'd be lost with all those fraternity guys at Champaign," he told me. "I mean, I don't have the right clothes, or table manners." I said that Illinois probably wasn't all fraternities. "Nah, I'm better off with the other hunkies."

Meanwhile, I was still a Ph.D. candidate at Chicago, which was a very different thing from teaching at East Chicago. The main task seemed to be to depersonalize your mind, to sound like a scholar, to write prose that was mostly dull factuality and timidity, as reserved as a corpse or, to quote myself: "I have chosen to continue my discussion of Thoreau's theory of poetry to its more practicable aspects: that is, to the ideas and opinions that appear to bear directly upon what Thoreau presumably wanted to achieve when he sat down to write a poem."

One of the last courses I took was in Contemporary Criticism. It was taught by Norman Maclean, the stylist of the Chicago Critics, a man with a passion for Hemingway as well as Aristotle. There was a five-minute quiz each week; the first was on Croce's *Esthetics:* "What does Croce mean by an 'intuition'?"

So, following my practice of giving them what I thought they wanted to hear, and aping Croce as much as possible, I scribbled down something like, "An intuition, in the Crocean view, partakes of the relational aspect of consciousness..." and continued on in that vein.

The next class meeting, Maclean read a few of the answers.

"'An intuition is a perception,'" he began and stopped. "That's good," he said. "Right to the point. She puts up a clothesline she can hang the washing on. Listen. . . ." and he read it to the end.

"Now, I want to read another. 'An intuition, in the Crocean view, . . .'" He read a few more of my sentences and stopped. "I'm sorry," he said. "I love the English language too much to read this kind of hokum." After a despairing pause, he went on. "Why does a young person want to write like a broken-down philosophy professor in a third-rate teacher's college?"

I didn't know whether to be angry or crestfallen. After all,

Croce didn't sound so different. I'd even gotten that "partake" expression from him or his translator. As I was leaving class, Maclean caught my eye and I walked over to him.

"You seem pretty bright," he said, "when you talk in class. But if you don't learn to write clearly by the end of this course, I'm going to flunk you."

It hurt but it was what I needed to be told. Under Maclean's goading and encouragement, and especially under the influence of his teaching that went to the center of a subject like an arrow ("Eliot's criticism is that of a lyric poet, the two main issues being a writer's sensibility and style"), I labored to write as accurately and cleanly as possible. I thought of it as "coming clean," and "going straight," expressions that suggested the true nature of my project. How difficult it was to cut out the crap. And what a relief. For the first time in my life, I found myself writing for someone—a good voice in my head that drew out my better nature and gave it backing. So Chicago and East Chicago began to come together, two tasks connected by a common aspiration.

Two years passed. One summer morning I was sitting in the office I used at the University of Chicago where I had been teaching and was now finishing up my thesis and getting ready to move on. A young man strolled into the room. He was wearing a nice suit and a rep tie and smiling broadly, and it took me a few seconds to recognize him. It was Dovitch. We chatted for a while about what we had been doing and then he told me why he had looked me up. "I'm going to graduate school," he said.

"You don't say."

"Yeah. I'm going to be an English teacher."

As it turned out, my own teaching career ended a few weeks later when I was offered a job at *Commentary*. So I went to New York and became an editor and a literary journalist. I still had a lot to learn but thanks to Dovitch and Maclean, I pretty well knew what my purpose was.

They way I still see it, eleven years later, is that a great many Americans are in a peculiar bind. They've grown up in

homes, and communities, and schools which provide little intellectual nourishment and go off to college, mainly because
that's where one goes if he can. And there with practically no
preparation or basis—except possibly in math and science—
they study the liberal arts. And if they are bright and fortunate, sooner or later, they are turned on to one another of
these arts, and like Plato's slaves, are led from the cave into
the light. And like them are led back again. For once they
graduate and go off to Middle America, the mass society and
the mass culture take over again, and the deprivations resume,
all the more sharply for being made conscious. Or to put it
another way, education in America tends to be a brief, discon-
tinuous or else solitary activity.

All of which is perhaps a fifties view. There's now the coun-
terculture. But I wonder where most of its members will be
five years from now and how much "greening" they will be
achieving. And it may be that my view of college education is
also from the fifties. But I wonder if the tremendous demands
that students make today on the institution aren't generated
partly, at least, by the recognition that these four or five years
must be made vital to their lives, for there's not much else in
the society that has been or will be.

Be that as it may, it's how I see my work as a practical critic:
the opportunity to teach literature in the public forum. This is
not the way I would have viewed it if I had taken up criticism
twenty years ago. I would have dismissed the reading public as
hopelessly shallow and vulgar and tried to write for the Happy
Few who subscribed to *Partisan Review.* But having followed
the road I have, the notion of fostering an avant-garde has
come to seem rather precious and beside the point. (If there is
an avant-garde. What I tend to see is a lot of writers, in
Richard Howard's phrase, "alone in America.")

I have spoken a lot about the transaction that the practical
critic makes with an audience and said almost nothing about
his transaction with the books and authors he writes about.
Obviously, the claims of the audience are general and those of
the writer are specific and pressing, and most of the time one

is too embattled with the problems of trying to characterize him justly to worry about how all of these uncertainties and approximations of judgment will be taken. A good review, it seems to me, does three things—it describes a book, judges it, and identifies a context, the place it may occupy in contemporary consciousness. I used to think that the last was more crucial than I do now: i.e., gauging the book's relevance to the general reader. Mostly that can be left to him to figure out, once the writer and the book are placed against the ground of one's own interest in them. The rest is often just sniffing the zeitgeist, which grows wearisome to everyone and deflects attention from the task, which hasn't changed since Matthew Arnold defined it, as seeing the object as it truly is.

But if your primary obligation as a practical critic is to the writer and his work, he is not the audience you write for. You aren't there to cheer him up or put him down or set him straight. You're there to listen and respond and to develop your image of the book, the actual impressions it has made on you, into a description and an inquiry; that is to say, a learning process of your own. Unless you're learning something yourself as you write, the chances are that you are merely going through the motions of literary journalism and plodding along one of the ruts in your mind. That is why it is best to risk a line of inquiry that starts in uncertainties rather than assurances, to go off the deep end rather than the shallow. The main thing is to be clear, but an easily won clarity is likely to be superficial.

So you yourself make up the beginning of your audience. But unless you get a great deal of satisfaction out of talking to yourself, you need others—not many, a few good faces and voices will do. By now, the face I see is of no one I know. He belongs to my generation and has come to ideas the hard way and on his own; he is in this society but not quite of it, his face being sensitive as well as practical; he likes books but is not, strictly speaking, literary. He is keenly conscious of the "scrimmage of appetites" in America, and he is stimulated by alternative possibilities. He is fundamentally straight and positive, is put off by posturing, malice, and bad faith. Several people I've mentioned have contributed to this composite, and I've also encountered him as an apple grower, a psychoanalyst, a novelist, and as the head of a steel construction company. He keeps me company as a practical critic and keeps me going.

1971

The Shape of the River

Caroline Gordon

Some years ago the Vanderbilt University Press published an anthology under the title *Reality and Myth*. A young critic, Ashley Brown, contributed an essay to the anthology called "The Novel as Christian Comedy." Very little notice has been taken of this essay but I think it is based on an insight which is of great importance to all fiction writers and serious readers of fiction.

In his essay Mr. Brown maintained—what is no news to scholars of Dante—that in *The Divine Comedy* Dante was the first writer to synthesize certain fictional techniques which were, so to speak, in the air. Dante was, indeed, the first writer of his time to combine these techniques in order to achieve effects he desired. But he was not the first writer to use them. For us of the western world they were first used (in a way that approaches perfection) by the Greek tragedians, Aeschylus, Sophocles, and Euripides. Their plays survive because their characters are archetypal. There may be at this moment in Detroit or San Francisco or Norfolk, Virginia, a young woman who hates her husband enough to conspire with her lover to murder him. But she cannot claim to be original. In our western world Clytemnestra, the wife of the Greek hero, Agamemnon, was the first woman to commit a crime that so fired the imagination of a whole race that to this day she remains the archetype—that is to say, "the first model for such a character."

I cite the great tragedians to make *my* point. But Mr. Brown illustrated *his* point by reference to characters in a novel I had just published, *The Malefactors*. A psychiatrist in that novel, he reasoned, played the same archetypal role that Virgil plays in *The Divine Comedy*. A woman in the book was, he felt, a Matilda who, in *The Divine Comedy*, goes singing and plucking "the flowers by which her path was painted everywhere." I was delighted to hear this—the vanity of authors (as you may have observed) is insatiable—but in this case delight soon yielded to astonishment. Honesty compelled me to inform this critic that I had never really read *The Divine Comedy*. Like most half-educated persons, I had read all of *The Inferno* and half of *The Purgatorio*. But I had never read a word of *The Paradiso*. My young friend—he was younger then than he is now—did not seem surprised. He said only. "Well, you'd better read all three of them!"

I followed his advice and have been reading all three of them ever since. And on this occasion I am going to try to talk about one fictional technique which is used in *The Divine Comedy:* the cosmic metaphor. The metaphor antedates literature; it is a part of the furnishings of the memory of every one of us. The metaphor is also my title: "The Shape of the River." Man had a voyage down a great uncharted river in mind as a figure for the journey every human soul makes from birth to death long before he learned to make letters. Dante uses this metaphor in a twofold way and in a way that is primarily fictional. He uses it not only as a figure of the progress of any human soul but also as a figure for the creation of the poem in which he portrays that progress. Francis Fergusson, in his study of *The Divine Comedy*, has pointed out that in this respect Dante anticipated our own great novelist, Henry James, in what James called "a Central Intelligence."

The metaphor of the river as a figure for the conduct of a human life underlies the "plot" of *The Divine Comedy*—if I may use this term in connection with the poem. But Dante, being a very great poet, subsumes other cosmic metaphors to his action. I will ask your indulgence long enough to abstract from the plot incidents that will serve my purpose. I hasten to add that I will cite only a few incidents. There is nothing more boring than to have some one *tell* you the plot—of anything. When I was trying to teach that unteachable subject, creative writing, at Columbia I would not permit my students to tell me the plots of their novels or short stories. I could not stand

the boredom. At the time I justified this high-handed proce-
dure (to myself, at least) by reasoning that the prohibition was
for their own good. Looking back, I believe I was right. But we
must get back to Dante.

Dante, soon after he comes to himself "in the dark wood,"
which is his metaphor for our mortal life, looks up and sees
before him the Mount of Perfection. He imagines himself as
starting to climb it, but his progress is slowed by a fear that he
holds in "the lake of his heart."

> And as he, who with panting breath has escaped from the
> deep sea to the shore, turns to the dangerous waters and gazes:
>   so my mind, which still was fleeing, turned back to see the
> pass that no one ever left alive.

He has no sooner started up the desert slope than he encounters three beasts: a leopard, a lion, and a she-wolf. He is
rescued from them by the poet, Virgil, whom he acknowl-
edged as his master in the world. Dante asks him, "Art thou
then that Virgil, and that fountain which pours abroad so rich a
stream of speech?"

Here we get our second water image—of a spring that instead of threatening death, promises life, since it flows over a
whole countryside. And it is a stream of *speech*. The image is
prophetic of Dante's future fame. The poem he has set about
writing—*his* stream of speech—will flow, has, indeed, flowed,
as widely as Virgil's stream of speech.

Virgil tells Dante that he has been sent to guide him up the
Mount of Perfection by Beatrice, the lady Dante loved in life.
But Beatrice was impelled to send Virgil to Dante's rescue by
St. Lucy, who, in turn, came to Beatrice at the bidding of the
Blessed Virgin. To persuade Beatrice to leave the Mount of
Perfection and descend into Hell and then to Limbo, where
Virgil reposed with other great pagans, St. Lucy says:

> Beatrice, true praise of God; why helpest thou not him who
> loved thee so, that for thee he left the vulgar crowd?

Hearest thou not the misery of his plaint? Seest thou not the
death which combats him upon the river over which the sea has
no boast?

Beatrice is so moved by the thought of Dante's plight that
she makes the dreadful journey to the underworld, and Virgil,
at her request, leaves Limbo and comes to Dante on the slope
of the Mount of Perfection. Dante and Virgil then make their
way to the shores of Acheron, the river which runs through the
underworld. Charon, "the demon with the eyes of coal," who
ferries condemned souls across this river, recognizes that
Dante is not yet dead and so cannot be his passenger. He says:

"thou who are there, alive, depart thee from these who are
dead." But when he saw that I departed not,
    He said, "By other ways, by other ferries, not here, shalt
thou pass over: a lighter boat must carry thee."

The "lighter boat," figuratively speaking is, of course, the
poem in which Dante will portray what he sees in Hell, Purgatory, and Heaven, "the little bark of my wit" he calls it, in
which he will "hoist sail to course o'er better waters."

Dante and Virgil stand and watch until Charon has loaded
his boat with his sad passengers. Virgil explains to Dante that
Charon's passengers are all of Adam's seed who perished in
the wrath of God. But Dante has been called upon to sing of
that second realm where the human spirit is purged and becomes worthy to ascend to Heaven, so he and Virgil leave the
shores of the "dusky river." As they turn away the whole plain
quivers as if from an earthquake. Dante, like our Father
Abraham in a similar situation, loses consciousness. When he
comes to himself he is on the brink of the "dolorous Valley of
the Abyss, which gathers thunder of endless wailings."

But he still has Virgil for his guide. Virgil, his face pale with
apprehension, then conducts Dante down into Hell and up
through Purgatory to a certain point on the Mount of Perfection. Here I will interrupt our tour of these shadowy realms

and call your attention to another work of fiction. Not a
poem, though it is deeply poetical in conception, not a novel,
though it is intimately concerned with the conduct of life. It is
hard to classify Mark Twain's *Life on the Mississippi*. However, it is certainly one of the most exciting and original works
of the imagination that have been produced in this country. As
I have said, it is deeply poetical in conception and in execution, too—at least as far as the first half of the book goes. The
last half of the book seems almost as if it had been written by
another man. I want to talk about that later. But let us first
consider the plan or plot of the whole work.

In conceiving the book Mark Twain seems to have had in
mind or imagination the same cosmic metaphor which Dante
bases his poem on: a voyage down a vast river as a figure for
man's life. Both authors are at once narrators and actors in
their respective dramas. And Mark Twain, like Dante, plays
the part of a Central Intelligence. Like Dante, he is at once
narrator and protagonist.

I hope that I am not wholly motivated by patriotic ardor
when I say that the Missouri boy seems to have "come to
himself," as Dante puts it, earlier than the Florentine. Mark
Twain's longing to become a steamboatman crystallized into
one burning ambition long before he was twenty-one years
old. He wanted to become a steamboat pilot—to become
"master of the marvelous science of piloting." "I believe," he
said, "that there has been nothing like it elsewhere in the
world." In his book he says that he is trying

> to carry the reader step by step to a comprehension of what the
> science consists of; and at the same time I have tried to show
> that it is a curious and wonderful science, too, and very worthy
> of his attention. If I have seemed to love my subject, it is no
> surprising thing, for I loved the profession far better than any I
> have followed since.

For him there was only one river, the river the Indians
called "the Father of Waters." He calls it "the majestic, magnificent Mississippi, rolling its mile-wide tide along, shining in
the sun, the dense forest away on the other side; the point

above the town and the point below, bounding the river-glimpse and turning into a sort of sea, and withal a very brilliant and lonely one."

But since the boy, Samuel Clemens, was to turn into the novelist, Mark Twain, the river is seen in a fictional context, in the conduct of a life. Or in the conduct of lives.

Dante covers a good deal of history, as well as Hell and Purgatory and parts of Heaven, in his great work. Mark Twain gets over a good deal of ground, too. The action of *Life on the Mississippi* begins (long before either Samuel Clemens or Mark Twain was born) in 1542, according to Mark Twain's reckoning, when the river was first viewed by a white man, the Spanish explorer, De Soto. At that time, Mark Twain reminds us, "the order of the Jesuits was not yet a year old; Michelangelo's paint was not yet dry on his 'Last Judgment' in the Sistine chapel. . . . Elizabeth of England was not yet in her teens. . . . Shakespeare was not yet born; a hundred years must elapse before Englishmen would hear the name of Oliver Cromwell."

Francis Parkman tells us that the merchant, Joliet, and the Jesuit, Father Marquette, reached the banks of the Mississippi in 1673 and

> turning southward, paddled down the stream, through a solitude unrelieved by the faintest trace of man. . . . They did this day after day and night after night; and at the end of two weeks they had not seen a human being. The river was an awful solitude then, and it is now.

Nevertheless, Mark Twain says that when he was a boy "there was but one permanent ambition among comrades in our village. That was to be a steamboatman. We had transient ambitions of other sorts. . . . These ambitions faded out, each in its turn; but the ambition to be a steamboatman remained." All steamboatmen seemed godlike to these boys but the most godlike of all was the pilot. Mark Twain says that

> a pilot in those days, was the only unfettered and entirely independent human being that lived in the earth. Kings are

but hampered servants of parliaments and the people; parliaments sit in chains forged by their constituency; the editor of a newspaper cannot be independent but must work with one hand tied behind him, and be content to utter only half or two-thirds of his mind; no clergyman is a free man and may speak the whole truth, regardless of his parish's opinions; writers of all kinds are manacled servants of the public. . . . In truth, every man, woman and child has a master and worries and frets in servitude; but in the day I write of the Mississippi pilot had *none*. . . . His movements were entirely free; he consulted no one, he received commands from nobody.

The most dazzling of these embodiments of free will—if I may use the term in this connection—is Horace Bixby, who, when young Clemens first encounters him, is the pilot on the *Aleck Scott*. Mr. Bixby is finally persuaded to take young Clemens on as a pupil or apprentice. He does not undertake to make him a pilot. He says only that he will "learn him the river."

I would like to make a brief digression here. After all, I am speaking metaphorically, for the most part. I am speaking metaphorically still, I suppose, when I say that when a young man or woman comes to me and says that he or she wants to *become* a novelist or short story writer, I find myself thinking of Mr. Bixby. He did not undertake to make his pupil a pilot but only to *learn him the river*. I could not undertake to do even that much for any young person who asked my advice. All I can ever undertake is to *try* to learn him as much of the river as I, myself, have learned. And since the river is the shape it is and, moreover, is always assuming different shapes, that undertaking is almost too much for me!

Mr. Bixby, however, is made of sterner stuff. His poor young cub pilot soon finds out that "the marvelous science of piloting" is quite different from what he had thought it was. For Mr. Bixby, learning the river means learning the *shape of the river* by day, by night, in fog, in mist, in flood tide or low tide, in every conceivable circumstance which the dedicated imagination and memory of Mr. Bixby can conceive of. He tells the cub:

My boy, you've got to know the *shape* of the river perfectly. It is all there is left to steer by on a very dark night. Everything else is blotted out and gone. But mind you, it hasn't the same shape in the night that it has in the daytime.

"How on earth am I going to learn it then?" the cub asks. "How do you follow a hall at home in the dark?" Mr. Bixby says. "Because you know the shape of it. You can't see it."

The cub says, "I can follow the front hall in the dark if I know it *is* the front hall but suppose you set me down in the middle of it in the dark and not tell me which hall it is; how am I to know?"

Mr. Bixby says, "Well, you've got to, on the river." And so, Mark Twain tells us

> I went to work . . . to learn the shape of the river; and of all the eluding and ungraspable objects that ever I tried to get mind or hand on, that was the chief. I would fasten my eye upon a sharp wooded point that projected far into the river some miles ahead of me, and go to laboriously photographing its shape upon my brain; and just as I was beginning to succeed to my satisfaction, we would draw up toward it and the exasperating thing would fold back into the bank. . . . Nothing ever had the same shape when I was coming down-stream that it had borne when I went up.

When he mentions these difficulties to Mr. Bixby, that dedicated soul says:

> That's the very virtue of the thing. If the shapes didn't change every three seconds they wouldn't be of any use. Take this place where we are now, for instance. As long as that hill over yonder is only one hill, I can boom right along the way I'm going; but the moment it splits at the top and forms a V, I know I've got to scratch to starboard in a hurry, or I'll bang this boat's brains out against a rock.

There comes a time when the cub feels that the undertaking is too much for him. He tells Mr. Bixby that if he could learn all the things he says he has got to learn he would be able to raise the dead. "And then," he says, "I won't have to pilot a steamboat to make a living. I want to retire from this business. I haven't got brains enough to be a pilot; and if I had I wouldn't have strength enough to carry them around."

Mr. Bixby says: "Now drop that. When I say I'll learn a man the river, I mean it. And you can depend on that. I'll learn you the river."

He is as good as his word. Mark Twain learns to "read the face of the water," as he puts it. He says:

> The face of the water, in time became a wonderful book—a book . . . which told its mind to me without reserve, delivering its most cherished secrets as if it uttered them with a voice. And it was not a book to be read once and thrown aside, for it had a new story to tell every day. . . . there was never a page that was void of interest, never one that you could leave unread without loss, never one that you would want to skip. . . . There never was so wonderful a book written by man.

Literary critics agree, I believe, that the second half of *Life on the Mississippi* is inferior to the first half. We sometimes speak of that part of the book as being "journalistic." But that seems to me unfair to that profession. A competent reporter would be ashamed or afraid to turn in as poorly observed and as haphazardly organized a story as the second half of *Life on the Mississippi*. Some pages would not be out of place in a report from a Chamber of Commerce; for instance:

> The scenery from St. Louis to Cairo—two hundred miles—is varied and beautiful. . . . Cairo is a brisk town now; and is substantially built and has a city look about it. . . . Cairo has a heavy railroad and river trade, and her situation at the junction of two great rivers is so advantageous that she cannot help prospering.

He no longer cares to read the face of the water, and the shape of the river itself is unfamiliar to him. He tells us that when he revisited it:

there was nothing anywhere that I could remember having
seen before. I was surprised, disappointed and annoyed.

I do not believe that this change of attitude is wholly the
result of the twenty years which intervened between his writing of the two halves of the book. It seems to me that this
about-face of vision was foreshadowed in one of the early
chapters—in chapter 9, the same chapter in which Mark
Twain tells us that Mr. Bixby finally succeeded in "learning"
him the shape of the river. Almost immediately after learning
to read this wonderful book—"the face of the water" as he calls
it—Mark Twain begins to wish that he had not acquired this
knowledge.

> Now when I had mastered the language of this water, had come
> to know every trifling feature that bordered the great river as
> familiarly as I knew the letters of the alphabet, I had made a
> valuable acquisition. But I had lost something too. I had lost
> something which could never be restored to me while I lived.
> All the grace, the beauty, the poetry had gone out of the majes-
> tic river! . . . A day came when I began to cease from noting the
> glories and charms which the moon and the sun and the
> twilight wrought upon the river's face; another day came when
> I ceased altogether to note them. . . . the romance and beauty
> were all gone from the river. All the value any feature of it has
> had, for me now was the amount of usefulness it could furnish
> toward compassing the safe piloting of a steamboat.

Indeed, all he has to show for his apprenticeship "to the
marvelous science" is a memory of the river,

> a certain wonderful sunset which I witnessed when steamboat-
> ing was new to me. A broad expanse of the river was turned to
> blood; in the middle distance the red hue brightened into
> gold. . . . The surface was broken by boiling, tumbling rings
> that were as many tinted as an opal. . . . The shore on our left
> was densely wooded, and the somber shadow that fell from the
> forest was broken in one place by a long ruffled train that shone
> like silver. . . . I stood like one bewitched. I drank it in, in a

speechless rapture. The world was new to me, and I had never seen anything like this at home. But, as I have said, a day came when I began to cease from noting the glories and the charms which the moon and the sun and the twilight wrought upon the water's face; another day when I ceased altogether to note them. Then, if that sunset scene had been repeated, I should have looked upon it inwardly, after this fashion: 'This sun means that we are going to have wind tomorrow, that floating log means that the river is rising, small thanks to it'.

He finishes by comparing himself to a doctor who cannot enjoy contemplating the beauty of a young woman who sits next to him at a dinner party because he could, if necessary, articulate her skeleton.

Mark Twain, like Dante, is both narrator and protagonist in the first half of *Life on the Mississippi*. Both authors employ the same figure: a book. Mark Twain sees the Mississippi river as a great book in which he no longer cares to read. Dante has a vision of God. He sees God as a great book in which all creatures and all the diverse modes of being are bound, like leaves in a volume. Then his vision fails him: he says

To the high fantasy here power failed; but already my desire and will were rolled—even as a wheel that moveth equally—by the Love that moves the sun and the other stars.

Dante, one of the most competent craftsmen who ever lived, has taken the measure of his own genius and even as he marks its limitations, he recognizes that he has achieved something that he could not have achieved if he had not "braved the watery deep" in his frail craft—if he had not tried to write the poem, which, it seemed, no man *could* write. As a result, he has had a vision which will stay with him all his life. He calls it "the general sum of perfection" and tells us that he has preserved the memory of his vision in the hope of helping his fellow man.

The young man or woman who aspires to write fiction professionally has a difficult and dangerous voyage before him. I believe, however, that if he has had a glimpse of what Dante calls "the general sum of perfection," he has a tremendous advantage over navigators who have to discover "the shape of the river" for themselves. It may take him all his life to gain any understanding of what has been revealed to him, but at least he has discerned its outline and, like Dante, can keep it in memory if he tries hard enough. This knowledge—the knowledge of the *shape* of the river—will stand him in better stead on his voyage than any other knowledge he can acquire. Or shall I say that all the techniques of navigation are included in this "marvelous science"? Mr. Bixby found that knowledge enough to steer by on the darkest night!

1972

The Transformation of the Avant-Garde

Robert W. Corrigan

One of the more commonplace and romantic definitions of the artist is that one which characterizes him as an adventurous explorer. He is described as one who crosses the frontiers of our common life and through his work he gives definition to those boundary situations of man's mind and spirit. In this role he is a maker of maps for the rest of the community, and these maps, in turn, celebrate the best and the worst, the most beautiful and most painful experiences that men have thought and felt. I have always liked this metaphor of the artist as map-maker, but I am not so sure I can use it any more. You see, in recent years more and more artists have decided that cartography is a much too menial trade. They really want to be a combination of Christopher Columbus, Daniel Boone, and astronaut. What's more, they are rejecting their metaphoric role altogether. Many of them have decided that they are explorers. They think of their art not as something about life, but rather as an immediate social transaction which not only changes the world but also enhances their own humanity. And this new image that the artist has of himself has created many problems—problems for confused audiences, for befuddled critics and scholars, and even for artists themselves.

Indeed, the thorniest problem in the art world today is the growing tendency in all of the arts to break down or dissolve those distinctions that have heretofore existed between art and life. This condition has occurred before in the history of western culture, but only for brief periods of time and always as a local and aberrant phenomenon. Today it is already widespread and it continues to grow—some would say like a giant cancer, while others would describe it as a glorious liberation movement. The fact is, this tendency toward dissolution has been in process for a long time now and its coming was probably inevitable. But our awareness of this does not make it any less of a dilemma for most of us. In this essay I should like to discuss some of the more significant aspects of the problem not only so as to understand it better, but also because I wish to point to certain critical strategies which, it is hoped, will resolve it.

Art and Paradigmatic Experience

All art is based on some form of what Karl Mannheim referred to as "paradigmatic experience." He defined such experiences as those "basic experiences which carry more weight than others, and which are unforgettable in comparison with others that are merely passing sensations." A paradigm, then, is a compelling vision of reality which creates—as it does in language—a hierarchy of being and value which permits us to shape and judge experience in its terms. Insofar as we believe in paradigmatic experiences it is possible for us to say about an object, idea, or event, "this is true or false, good or bad, better or worse." Thomas Kuhn, in his influential book, *The Structure of Scientific Revolutions*, describes what happens in science in the same way. Scientific theories are, in fact, paradigms that are the most economic and complete models for synthesizing the known evidence about the physical world. In characterizing scientific advance, Kuhn describes those periods in which evidence begins to be assembled which the reigning paradigm cannot explain; that is, under the terms of the existing paradigm the new evidence appears anomalous and freakish. But it is the pressure of this anomalous evidence that characterizes scientific advance; calling not only for its acknowledgment, but demanding as well the invention of an entire new paradigm, or as Kuhn puts it, an explanation of what has by then become a "new world." When we deny the validity of paradigmatic experiences, or when the governing paradigms of a culture seem to have broken down, then nothing is revealed as having decisive importance. We are ruled by a kind of kaleidoscopic concept of life which, in giving equal significance to everything, attributes no radical significance to anything.

The most important shift in paradigms in the past several centuries, the shift which created what we now refer to as modernism, occurred in the second half of the eighteenth century and the first part of the nineteenth century when the industrial revolution combined with the political revolutions both in this country and on the continent to destroy the validity of those dominant paradigms that had governed western art and thought since the middle ages, if not from the times of classical Greece. Today we can look back and see that this process had actually been going on at a gradual rate since the fifteenth century. But by the nineteenth century our world was committed to the compelling vision of a democratic egalitarianism and we could no longer accept—at least in principle—a paradigm of social order based on a hierarchy of rank or class. Similarly, the industrial revolution had created the possibility of an economy of sufficiency which made it impossible for a paradigm based on an economy of scarcity to be maintained. This condition led to the emergence of new paradigms, the most important of those being the idea of unlimited economic growth through some form of industrial capitalism and the idea of progress as an alternative to judgment day. In the arts these major changes are reflected in the emergence of a marked pluralism of styles, a tendency to subordinate aesthetic style to more significant ethical and social concerns, the disappearance of genres, and the eventual devaluation of the art object. But most importantly, it created the idea of the avant-garde.

The Nature and Development of the Avant-Garde

We tend to forget what a recent idea this is. To the best of my knowledge, this Napoleonic military term was first used in reference to the arts by Saint Simon in 1825. It is an ambiguous concept. On the one hand, all of the literature of the avant-garde—whether you choose Wordsworth or Shelley, Pater or Fry, Ionesco or Grotowski, Cage or Robbe Grillet—reveals that it is at heart conservative and in a sense even reactionary. Avant-garde artists are "radical" only in the original sense of that word—they want to go back to the old roots. In using new techniques to return to these old truths they hope to be more real and direct, to be more truly communal and involving. Thus, more often than not, what appears in their work to be a shattering of tradition is actually a reaffirmation of it.

But the avant-garde has also had a compelling need to repudiate the past, and particularly its own immediate past. Conceptually it is inextricably linked to the idea of progress and its origins can be traced to the emergence of the Romantic movement. It is interesting to note that before Romanticism insofar as styles in art were categorized they were invariably described as "schools." The notion of a school presupposes a master and a method, the criterion of tradition, and the principle of authority. Furthermore, the nature of a school is defined solely in aesthetic terms. Movements, on the other hand, are activist and future-oriented. They are "moving" toward the realization of something. Whatever goal a school might have, it is transcendent; its central commitment is to the mastery of what has already been achieved, believing that such mastery combined with inspiration will create a future that need not, nor cannot, be precisely defined. The followers of a movement always work in terms of an end which resides in the movement itself. Moreover, this end exists beyond the limits of art and is essentially ethical and social rather than aesthetic in nature. It is for this reason that *movement* conceives of culture not as increment but as creation.

As I said, the idea of movement is linked to the idea of progress. Progress, which had heretofore been millenary and allegorical, had become by the beginning of the nineteenth century a realizable expectation. After the French Revolution there was a decision to start a new calendar for human affairs. This was, in effect, saying that the metaphor of renewal was now seen as a reality so that, as George Steiner puts it, "the eternal tomorrow of utopian political vision became, as it were, Monday morning." And if it can be Monday morning, then the sooner we get started the better. The members of the avant-garde were the early starters, the cutting edge, the first wave—you name it. If culture is something created constantly anew, and if art is conceived as revolution and movement, then there has to be an avant-garde. We are just now coming to comprehend the full significance of this basic change in thinking about the arts and to assess its effects not only on what happened in the arts, but also on the artist's view of himself and the nature of his work.

There have been many studies of the avant-garde published in recent years, but unquestionably the most challenging and imaginative of them is the late Renato Poggioli's *The Theory of the Avant-Garde*. While I don't agree with some of Professor Poggioli's basic premises—and, therefore, some of his conclusions—no one has better described the nature of the avant-garde than he. To catalog these characteristics, even in the most summary way, is to outline the mainstream of the arts in the nineteenth and twentieth centuries. Poggioli's major thesis is that the particular tensions of our bourgeois, capitalistic, and technological society provide the *raison d'être* for all avant-garde movements. Because in a democratic society the artist no longer has the Maecenas of an aristocratic culture to direct his work, he is forced to create not only the work but the audience for that work as well. Of necessity he becomes as much a "producer" for a market as he is a creator, and this puts the artist in a strange and antagonistic relationship to his audience, a relationship which creates both his sense of alienation and isolation and his tendency to become self-serving, partisan, proselytizing, narcissistic, and even subversive. In such a situation, he cannot help but think of himself as superior—the true aristocrat of middle-class culture—and yet he is also a kind of huckster who must be accepted by those "beneath" him if he is to be successful on his own terms. Furthermore, since he is committed to originality rather than renewal, the new and the novel are the hallmarks of his creativity. For the avant-garde artist genuineness of vision means a new vision which avoids anything that has been done before; and genuineness of craftsmanship is the refusal to repeat old techniques. But this inevitably makes him almost completely dependent upon what is fashionable, even as he thinks of himself as the governor of fashion. Fashion's task is to maintain a continual process of standardization, and it does so by creating constantly shifting new norms. Thus, the avant-garde is condemned to conquer through the influence of fashion the very popularity it disdains. But its victories are hollow, for fashion moves with inexorable force. The very success of an avant-garde movement creates the opposition that will eventually put it out of fashion. This is why so many traditional critics argue that the whole history of avant-garde art is finally reducible to an uninterrupted series of fads.

This is only a half-truth, but it does point to another of the avant-garde's most significant characteristics: that it, like progress, is futuristic. Poggioli, with tongue in cheek, wryly observes that "the art of the twentieth century seems to have one desire only, to get to the twenty-first century as soon as possible." Have you ever noticed that whenever teachers, scholars, and critics are talking or writing about any given period or work of art of the past 200 years they invariably refer to it as being in some way transitional? This is not just some tic of the academic imagination. One of the key ideas of modernism is that the present is valid only by virtue of its potentialities for the future. Carl Jung expressed it well when he wrote: "Today is a process of transition which separates itself from yesterday in order to go toward tomorrow." Because the avant-garde sensibility believes that all potentiality is capable of being actualized in the more or less immediate future, it must reject the past (although it unquestionably yearns for what it believes is the lost centrality of more primitive times) and embrace the vision of apocalypse. It is important to understand that the avant-garde artist is not really opposing traditional forms of art; rather he is seeking a radically new experience, one in which the ideal can be made immediate and tangible; one that permits him to believe that the gap between the possible and the real—which heretofore had been bridged by works of art—can be closed. Thus, in rejecting art as a derivative experience in favor of the myth of art as an immediate experience, the avant-garde is constantly mixing up aesthetic and ethical categories. And because of this confusion there is always pressure to break down the differences between art and life, to confuse them, to see them as the same.

The Breaking Down of the Distinctions Between Art and Life

This process has really been going on for a good part of this century. It was the central intuition of Dadaism. It was implied in Duchamp's found objects. It was the dominant dramatic idea in Pirandello's theater, which in turn had a profound influence on the Theater of the Absurd. It was hinted at by the atonal composers and became manifest in aleatoric music. It was even one of the deaestheticizing premises of action painting. John Cage is probably its most articulate prophet, and over twenty-five years ago he said: "For too long art obscured the difference between life and art. Now let life obscure the difference between art and life."

But these were still minority views. The dominant tendency in the arts since World War I—and especially in the fifteen to twenty years after World War II—was to shrink the world to a rebellious gesture. The governing spirit during this time was one of protest and retreat and the work of most artists had become violent graphs of the cornered man. From such movements as the Theater of the Absurd or abstract expressionism in painting it is clear that man was defined by his estrangement and solitude and not by his participation in the life of his society. Then in the 1960s, when all art forms seemed to erupt into the spasms of a mad Saint Vitus's dance, things began to change. It was then that the idea that art was not about life but was a form of life itself came to be the predominant view of the avant-garde. This happened, I think, because of a major shift in the artist's attitude toward technology. Technology came to be seen not as a dehumanizing enemy but as a great new resource that could be used in both material *and* spiritual ways so as to enhance the present and its possibilities. However, whenever we embrace anything—an attitude, an idea, even another person—we must remember that we are acted upon by the object of our embrace every bit as much as we affect it. There is no such thing as embrace with impunity. Thus, when the artist came to embrace technology not only was his work affected; his whole sense of himself was changed.

Probably the first noticeable effect of the artist's embrace of technology is that it gives him a radically new sense of choice. This is the central theme of the reports of the Harvard Program on Technology and Society. We know that each one of us has opportunities for choice that were unthinkable a generation ago, and more important, we know that we had better keep on making them. We don't need to be locked into anything because the number of choices available to us is greater than ever before and the possibilities for continuing new choices are rapidly increasing. Now I happen to think that the possibility for choice is at the very heart of the creative process; but when you also believe that one need not be bound permanently by his choices because new choices are made available to us every day, then your attitude toward what you create invariably changes. And this accounts—at least in part—for the growing dominance of the spirit of improvization and impermanence in all of the arts.

Today our artists are less and less concerned with creating lasting works of art. Because each day brings with it new choices, the artist comes to find joy in the creative process itself—indeed, involvement in the process of creating has tended to replace concern for the project or object that is made. This being the case, it shouldn't surprise us that in the past couple of years some artists have carried this to even further extremes. Why bother making anything at all—especially since the marketing systems in all of the arts are so unashamedly corrupt? Rather than write plays, some playwrights give interviews before and after a performance no one has ever seen to explain the meaning of what hasn't occurred. In the visual arts—at least in some quarters—there has been a noticeable shift away from the creation of tangible objects to calling attention to the attitudes by which art has or can be made. In each of these instances execution has disappeared completely; philosophic attitude has taken precedence over unique form.

But there is probably a more meaningful explanation for this bizarre situation of an art world without art. In the past material objects were valuable because in an economy of scarcity what one made was more enduring than those who made them. Objects were sacred not only because they were unique and irreplaceable, but because they represented an ideal of mankind which would endure beyond the life of any individual man. Under such conditions man was as expendable as the materials were valuable. If the lives of a thousand more men had to be sacrificed in order to build a pyramid or a cathedral, so be it; such structures would last forever as eternal monuments to those ideals and aspirations by which men (or at least their monarchs) lived. But today we believe less and less in the permanence of matter, or, for that matter, in the stability of nature. After Hiroshima, how can we? Furthermore, in an economy of sufficiency, all materials are—theoretically, at least—expendable. Any object is replaceable, and our industrial technology has made it possible for us to replicate anything from a rare antique to the latest model automobile. In a society with such an economy, and with such a prodigal attitude toward human artifacts, the only unique and irreplaceable element is man. It is an awareness of this basic change that prompts the sociologist John McHale to write about the future of art as follows:

> The future of art seems no longer to lie with the creation of enduring masterworks but with defining alternative cultural strategies, through a series of communicative gestures in multimedia forms. An art and non-art become interchangeable, and the master work may only be a reel of punched or magnetic tape, the artist defines art less through any intrinsic value of the art object than by furnishing new conceptualities of life style and orientation. Generally, as the new cultural continuum underlines the expendability of the material artifact,

life is defined as art—as the only contrastingly permanent and continuously unique experience.

While I am horrified by such gobbledygook and jargon, I must admit that if one picked up any fairly recent issue of the *Drama Review* or *Artforum, Performance* or *New Sound,* he would find article after interview that will echo McHale's prognosis, even if they cannot match the lucidity of his style. But the fact is, that as the life of the individual comes to replace the object or the performance as the only unique and irreplaceable creation in the universe, then increasingly the artist comes to think of his own physical and psychic being as the material from which and the medium through which he will shape his most meaningful, if not his only, creations.

The effects of this conviction are most clearly manifest in the idea of life itself as a performance. Critics such as Richard Poirier and Richard Gilman have been the leading spokesmen for this view, and Norman Mailer is the supreme embodiment of it. In the mid-fifties Mailer had reached a creative impasse and the novel form was no longer working for him. As he turned his attention to the turbulent events going on in the world, he came to believe that the most interesting source of art was the interaction between himself and those events. He no longer thought of writing as a mimetic act but rather as a "kind of combative enterprise analogous to war." Form was not a pattern imposed on experience, it was an account of one's engagement and struggle with it. For Mailer there was no longer any separation between living and creating. The artist himself is the work of art. He said as much when he maintained that "the first art work in an artist is the shaping of his own personality." It is important to understand that Mailer's running for mayor in New York City was an aesthetic, not a political, act. We see the same thrust in the more recent films of Godard, and Dennis Hopper's *The Last Movie* is indeed the last because art and life get so confused that the whole idea of making a film is lost. The Theater of Fact is governed by the same impulse. Peter Weiss used the transcript of the Nazi trials because what went on in the concentration camps was more horrible than the human imagination could comprehend and, therefore, no artistic form was capable of expressing them or their meaning. In the visual arts we find the same phenomenon. The persona of Andy Warhol is probably more interesting to the art world than the works of art that he has created. He has, in fact, created his persona as an aesthetic object. There is something compelling about this idea, so long as it remains essentially theatrical. Warhol's performance is a match for Mailer's any time. But recently artists have become more literal in their thinking about themselves as the object of art. In speaking about his 1973 show at the Whitney, Bruce Nauman said: "I'm trying to explore how we experience things—occasions, spaces, situations. I use my body as an object, not autobiographically." I suppose this idea has already reached its ultimate—and I might add, absurd—expression in the work of the Viennese artist, Rudolf Schwarzkogler. Schwarzkogler's achievement—and there's no question about its being unique—consisted of amputating his own flesh, inch by inch, until he finally killed himself. This process was photographed and was reverently exhibited last summer at Documenta 5 in Kassel, Germany. To be sure this is an extreme expression of the idea that the artist's own self is both the subject and object of the art work, but in its gruesome madness it reveals how the politics of experience gives way to the poetics of impotence. John Cage has recently modified the statement I quoted earlier to read: "I wouldn't say that we are interested in destroying the barrier between art and life or even blurring it. I would say we are interested in observing that there is no barrier or distinction between the two." But if there is no difference between art and life, then there is finally no difference between the artist and his public. Instead of representing creative mysteries, the artist becomes a cross between a cocounselor, a recreation director, and a social worker.

The Challenge to the Mimetic Idea of Art

However, once the artist no longer believes that art and life are separate and distinct—albeit related—orders of experience, he must also question the mimetic nature of the artistic process. This is the most radical and profound challenge facing the arts today. Certainly the most widely held traditional belief of the artist's function is the one which asserts that the artist's main job is to take the chaos and complexity, the ambiguity, contradiction, and inconclusiveness of actual experience, and to impose on them a meaning and order by means of the unique powers of his temperament, the depth of his imagination, and his capacity to create form. That is, through words, tone, color, line, or image, he creates an object in which the inconsistencies of life experience are made whole and within the work are organically and coherently expressive. This view is based upon the essentially platonic premise that reality can never be directly or totally known and that our awareness of it will always be limited; that there is a realm between conceptual certitude and the chaos of sense data which can only be bridged by approximate realities and provisional truths. Hence the need for fictive possibilities, for only fictions can mediate between what men desire or hope reality to be and the way things actually are. I think one can safely maintain that this has been the dominant view in western thought and art from the time of the Greeks until the middle of the twentieth century.

But once you challenge the platonic view and replace it with the more existential belief that reality is whatever one experiences, then the relationship between art and life will begin to change. When Jackson Pollock says "Painting is a state of being," or when Mark Rothko insists "a painting is not a picture of an experience; it is an experience," each of them is indicating that his concern is no longer with the finished work so much as the *act* of painting, which is supposed to guide him in his quest for personal identity. Thus, art becomes the occasion for a more heightened kind of participation in a reality which can be directly known. Today's artists have, with increasing frequency, substituted the myth of immediate experience for that of derivative experience. And the aim of advanced art in all its forms is not to put reality at a remove through art, but to use art to remove barriers to reality by presenting the complexity and ambiguity of life as directly as possible. These artists are not interested in producing works of art for people to mull over, but making the arts an immediately experienced transaction. The Aristotelian aesthetic of improving the audience's moral well-being has been spurned in favor of professed involvement in social change. It is this shift of attitude which caught Herbert Marcuse's attention and which prompted him to observe in 1970 that the revolutions of the young were, in fact, aesthetic and not political. In their concern for life-style and the quality of life they were demanding that art and life, politics and education, be totally interrelated and that art be not apart from life just as education should not be preparation for it. However, it should be pointed out that whenever anything becomes totally at one with its environment we cease to notice it. Thus, if these artists succeed in making art and life one, they will also have to accept the possibility that they may no longer be thought of as artists.

But I don't think they'll care. The famous graffito inscribed upon the walls of the Sorbonne during the student revolt of 1968 which read "Art is dead, let's liberate our day-to-day life. Poetry is in the street," is a striking example of how the aesthetics of direct experience is deaestheticizing. Actually, I am coming to believe that those who would deny the mimetic nature of art do in fact want art to become religion. Hence, their attraction to Lévi-Strauss, Eliade, and some of the primitivists. Hence, also, the evangelistic stance of most of the leaders of the new actualist movements. They are not artists, but high priests, prophets, or voices crying in the wilderness shouting, "Prepare ye the way of the new lord!" And if not religion, then politics. Certainly the artists in the celebrated Judson Flag Show were testing a law, not the limits of art. The case of R. G. Davis is an even better, because it is more serious, example. Mr. Davis was the founder and director of the San Francisco Mime Troup. Over the years his company became increasingly radicalized, but they were never political enough for Mr. Davis. Indeed, he was correct in realizing that their work was not political at all, but only something aesthetic presenting itself as politics. It was all a pose, a masquerade, politics manqué. So in the summer of 1972 he left his own company to go into politics. Given his views toward art and life, Davis had the correct intuition. For him to satisfy his political concerns he would have to go outside of art altogether. Art has always been poor politics. And, I might add, artists have not been very good politicians either. Thus, the politicizing of the avant-garde is yet another example of its self-destructing nature. Harold Rosenberg made this point very forcefully in his latest book, *The De-definition of Art*, where he wrote:

> The notion that art is an obstacle to expanded creativity is an art-world notion. . . . In calling for the death of art for the sake of liberating mankind, art confronts not society, but the dilemma of its own existence in an epoch of new media that have assumed most of art's function.

The Collapse of Critical Judgment

I should like to touch upon one other aspect of the problem. When the distinctions between art and life have been removed, how do you know what a work of art is and how do you judge it? James Joyce had anticipated these questions in a delightful scene in *A Portrait of the Artist as a Young Man:*

> I have a book at home—said Stephen—in which I have written down questions which are more amusing than yours were. In finding the answers to them I found the theory of the esthetic which I am trying to explain. Here are some questions I set myself:
> *Is a chair finely made tragic or comic? Is the portrait of Mona Lisa good if I desire to see it? Is the bust of Sir Philip Crampton lyrical, epical or dramatic? If not, why not?*—
> —Why not, indeed?—said Lynch, laughing.
> —*If a man hacking in fury at a block of wood*—Stephen continued—*make there an image of a cow, is that image a work of art? If not, why not?*—
> —That's a lovely one—said Lynch, laughing again. That has the true scholastic stink.—

A scholastic stink, indeed. The source of this problem can be traced back to the attitude expressed by David Hume in the second half of the eighteenth century—we're back there again—when he asserted in his essay "Of the Standard of Taste" that "beauty is not a quality inherent in things: it only exists in the mind of the beholder." Once you shift the source of beauty from the object of art to those who behold it, the whole idea of beauty becomes so relative, personal, and idiosyncratic that it soon ceases to have any real significance. We must remember that all conceptual revolutions are defined by the questions that are asked. "What is the speed of light?" can be an intelligible question only when it is conceptually possible to think of light having velocity. In a similar way the shift from the question "What is the sublime?" to "What is beauty?" represented an enormous change. Today, the question of "What is beauty?" doesn't seem very relevant and is seldom asked. Santayana was the last person who discussed the question with any confidence. For most of us the more appropriate question, and the only one I ever hear being asked, is "What is art?" And the answer, of course, is that art is whatever someone who says he is an artist creates and calls art. Increasingly, our artists do not think of art as something reserved for the high holy days of the spirit; in fact, in their desire to make art and life more interrelated and mutually involved, the idea of "going" to a museum, a theater, or a concert hall has become repugnant to them. I remember going to a performance of Robert Whitman's *Prune Flat* a number of years ago. It was given in a loft and the work was a film but the actors in the film were acting live in front of the screen; it also had static visual images, strobe lights, and an electronic musical score. It all worked together, not in an additive but in a synthetic way, and I thought it was a very interesting and moving experience. Afterward, I went up to Mr. Whitman and in an old-fashioned way, I asked: "Wouldn't this have been better if it had been performed in a theater?" He replied, "That's just the point. We don't want it in theaters. We want it in the loft where we made it, where we do it, where we are all together, where you are a part of us, where you're totally involved with us, where we live, where we eat, where we make love, where we are related together. We want to break down the gulf that exists between the artist and the audience. We want, in effect, to destroy audiences." If art is a life experience, then at best it is a game and all that is required to make an object into art is, as Japser Johns put it, "its introduction into the art context." (Cage meant the same thing when he said: "So long as there is a concert situation there is a concert.")

To ask, "What is beauty?" implies the primacy of the art object and artists are simply those who create them. To ask, "What is art?" asserts the primacy of the artist and art is simply whatever he produces. The theory of beauty is centripetal in nature; it is concerned with those masterpieces at the center of culture which determine the standards by which all else is judged. The theory of art is centrifugal. It, of necessity, moves to the ambiguous peripheries of creation and is finally more concerned with the act of creation itself than with what is created. But if art is in fact a life experience and whatever an artist does is a work of art, then the qualities of art objects become irrelevant in judging it. Indeed, even the objects become irrelevant; the only irreducible remainder of the idea of art is the figure of the artist. Such a condition invalidates the whole idea of aesthetics, and hence redefines the critic's role. When, as Rosenberg observed, "art springs from ideas about art, rather than admired art objects, the evaluation of works cannot avoid being interpretative in a partisan way." It is no longer a question of aesthetics, but of ideology.

This explains one of the most remarkable characteristics of avant-garde art. When ideology is more important than objects, intention becomes more significant than results. This makes it possible to ignore, dislike, or hardly know the work of any given new movement in the arts and still comprehend it. I know a number of reputable critics—who shall remain nameless—who do not go to the theater or galleries, are not interested in the new music, dance, or film, and yet are highly regarded because they write so knowledgeably and intelligently about what is going on. The same can be said for most art educators. I have heard brilliant discussions of the avant-garde by deans who hardly knew the difference between a harpsichord and a synthesizer, or street theater and commedia dell'arte. At most schools the last person you would expect to see at performances or in studios and classrooms is the dean. When attitude and the zeitgeist are more important than the work of art itself, the critic does not need the capacity to judge so much as to be able to feel the process of history which is passing from potentiality into act. As Poggioli pointed out. "All one need to do to understand avant-garde art is to understand the starting point."

Without normative principles, the idea of criticism as a judicial act is impossible. And this is the situation we are in today. Our critics have ceased to be judges and have become guides and promoters. But there will be plenty of work for them, since, as Hilton Kramer observed, "the more minimal the art, the more maximal the explanation."

The Restoration of the Mimetic Nature of Art

However, enough of explanation and analysis. If my description of the present state of the arts is accurate, then it would appear that they have reached a kind of dead end. Not only does the emperor not have any clothes on, he isn't even an emperor. In a sense this is true, but I think it is more a case of our mapmakers having gotten lost. They are reading the territory wrong and hence producing the wrong charts not only for themselves but for the rest of us as well. Back in 1925, Bertolt Brecht observed that "when one sees that our world of today no longer fits into the drama, then it is merely that the drama no longer fits into the world." What he meant by this was that the theater had ceased to be meaningful to audiences because it was based upon outmoded premises. That is what is so clearly happening today. The reason the relation of art to life has become so askew is because the ideas governing our experience of works of art have become both inadequate and false.

The idea of antiformalism is as illusory as it is fraudulent—

fraudulent because the subversion of form cannot be established except by artistic means, that is through effects that are essentially formal; illusory because it is impossible for there to be any aesthetic which is not mimetic and hierarchical. Let's not forget that the conceptual and process artists still need some form of documentation. Those documents become the art object or the performance; they involve selection and choice; they are mimetic in nature. The same thing holds true for the so-called random art events. This is so because as long as I am I and you are you there can never be perfect communication or total participation. Even when we are most involved with another—say, in making love—we are always conscious of otherness. Indeed, given our divided nature, it is impossible for us to experience these things within ourselves. So long as this condition exists all experience will always be more or less real, true, or significant according to some standard of value. In short, separateness creates hierarchies and judgments based on hierarchies. To be sure, the nature of our hierarchies can and do change—sometimes quite radically—but no matter how they change, we will never be able to bridge the gulf between I and thou wihout some metaphoric "form."

What has really happened is that it is becoming increasingly apparent that the reigning paradigms of our modernist culture are not working or have already broken down. We certainly can no longer believe in an economy of limitless sufficiency when we know that the world's resources are being depleted at a faster rate than we can discover new ones. We are well aware of the energy and fuel crises, but who would ever have thought that in this "Plastic Age" we could have a shortage of plastics. But we do; just read the morning papers. Equal opportunity and other welfare programs may be noble ideas, but economists are telling us that no matter how we may alter our priorities our social needs and the cost of supporting them are growing at a rate that far exceeds that of the gross national product. Given the extent of pollution, the time-honored capitalistic idea of grow or stagnate doesn't bode well for industry. Already many are predicting that the future of the

Ralph Naders looks better than that of the Henry Fords. We have discovered that you can do away with kings and princes, but elitism somehow survives in new forms. And we didn't need happenings, chance music, and self-destructing artifacts— all strategic denials of the future tense—to convince us that the idea of progress is no longer tenable. In short, as those paradigmatic experiences which gave rise to the idea of avant-gardism in the arts cease to be operative, it is reasonable to assume that the end of modernism is at hand. There is plenty of evidence to support this view, the most persuasive being the avant-garde's almost mechanical determination to carry on its own processes in a vacuum. Today's vanguardism has become ritualized. It attacks nonexistent enemies and it heralds new advances when there is in fact nothing being advanced.

This condition doesn't worry me very much. For while it is true that our existing paradigms are collapsing, it is also clear that new paradigms are emerging to take their place. As and when they do, the hierarchies which are implicit in all paradigmatic structures will return and the mimetic nature of art can begin to function more easily. It is only during this time between reigning paradigms, when the principle of syntactically organized vision of necessity gives way to more paratactical ("to exist side by side") conventions, that the distinctions between art and life tend to dissolve.

No one can say with certainty what the new paradigms of our posturban consciousness will be. I agree with Arthur Clarke that "the real future is not logically foreseeable." But I cannot help but notice that increasing numbers of historians, scientists, and anthropologists are beginning to discuss the future in terms of a transformation of human consciousness. William Irwin Thompson, in his most important book, *At the Edge of History,* asserts that what we are experiencing is not just a technological revolution, but a cultural transformation. And he predicts that we are moving into a very hierarchical, mystical, Pythagorean and antidemocratic system. The recent work of Andrew Weill (*The Natural Mind*). Rene Dubos (*The God Within*), and Edward T. Hall (*The Hidden Dimension*) discuss psychic transformations of unbelievable dimensions. The mind-boggling work—not yet published—of the zoologist J. T. Robinson indicates that we are actually going through a fourth phase of evolution which is probably psychic in nature and is in no way comparable *or* related to the first three phases. How do you account for the increasing popularity of Castaneda? Maybe C. S. Lewis was right when he predicted thirty years ago that human travel in outer space would be an experience of spiritual conversion. Edgar Mitchell's research in healing, ESP, psychokinesis, and astral projection are as startling as Rusty Schweikart's embrace of the Maharishi's Transcendental Meditation is unexpected. I know Bishop Pike's family and many of his closest friends, and they insist that he was completely sane even as he believed he was communicating with departed spirits. The writings of Teilhard de Chardin, scientist and theologian, pointed in this direction. So do the recent works of George Leonard (*The Transformation*) and Theodore Roszak (*Where the Wasteland Ends*). The British philosopher/physicist, Sir James Jeans, adumbrates this new vision when he writes:

> Today there is a wide measure of agreement, which on the physical side of science approaches almost to unanimity, that the stream of knowledge is heading toward a non-mechanical reality; the universe begins to look more like a great thought than like a great machine. Mind no longer appears as an accidental intruder into the realm of matter; we are beginning to suspect that we ought rather to hail it as the creator and governor of the realm of matter.

All of these writers are arguing that what appears to be a breaking down of civilization is not an eruption of madness or self-destruction, but a process that is entirely natural and inevitable. It is simply a breaking up of old forms by life itself.

If new paradigms based on the transformation of consciousness are in fact emerging, then those hierarchies so essential to the making and judging of art will do so also. Thus, even as the once creative and now debilitated notion of the avant-garde is transformed, we will begin to discover a great new vitality.

Many cultural historians have pointed to the medieval nature of our times. This is probably a correct assessment. But if this is the case, I would add that it is also not too optimistic to think that there is a new renaissance on the way, a renaissance which in the arts will be based on the restoration of the mimetic, a restoration that will invalidate those hallmarks of our present collapse, especially the widespread attitude of dilettantism and the belief that "being into things" is the equivalent of creation. I believe that the rebirth, if it comes—and I have faith that it will—will celebrate the qualities of energy and stamina, discipline and commitment. It will make us aware once again, although I am sure in new ways, that renewal is as dependent upon our capacity to maintain—even through the most excruciating boredom—as it is upon our ability to discover. It will reaffirm for us that the ideas of art as creation and as increment, while they may be in tension, need not be in dialectic opposition. In short, I think we may be coming to realize that our most profound discoveries are almost always things we already knew.

The stolen fire of the Promethean myth is the capacity through intelligence and imagination for man to create constructs and metaphors which will enable him to better understand himself and his world. While these metaphors can never fully express reality, since the tongues of fallen men can only relate to reality as through a glass darkly, nonetheless, no metaphysic is speechless. Even Samuel Beckett, who has expressed the breakdown of the paradigms of modernism more powerfully than anybody, can still say "I look for the voice of my silence." Such a continuing commitment is the great hope of these otherwise bewildering times. It is this commitment which is being celebrated once again here by the Hopwood awards. Yeats said that the "Fiddles are tuning all over the world," and they are—on campuses and in coffeehouses, at cultural centers and in ghettos, in rural communes and in cosmopolitan capitols. What is being reaffirmed here tonight is what Thomas Mann referred to as the artist's "honorable sleeplessness." It is a search for the right and redeeming word, shape, image, or sound. Each of us has this "honorable sleeplessness" and we are here because we must go on working, giving form to truth, hoping darkly—sometimes even confidently—that truth and form will help set free the human spirit and prepare mankind for a better, lovelier, and worthier life.

1973

Moonshine and Sunny Beams: Ruminations on *A Midsummer Night's Dream*

W. D. Snodgrass

"*A Midsummer Night's Dream!*" exclaims one early editor. "Who is the dreamer? The poet, any of the characters of the drama, or the spectators?"

Well carped, critic! Let's go on from there. Not only who is dreaming; who gets dreamed? Surely a dream, or a play, must be "about" someone. In this dream, we find four separate groups of characters derived from different periods of history, far-flung areas of the world, diverse literary and mythological backgrounds, opposed levels of reality. Can we decide which group is central to the play's concern? Mightn't we even ask for a central character?

And is it really too much to ask what the dream means? What most critics tell us about this play would apply to the dreariest hackwork. No one would perform a play that means so little—neither Peter Brook, the Comédie Française, nor Podunk Junior High. Yet all those troupes *have* been performing this airy flummery for 350 years and with almost unmitigated success. What has this play been imparting to so many actors, so many audiences, all these years?

Until Jan Kott came along and said some really interesting things about this play, it seemed almost impossible to give a performance lacking in all interest. Should we not question this play's secret workings, lest some well-meaning director snap up our speculations, turn them into overt and conscious motifs for his production, and ruin the thing once and for all?

The Rulers

Scholars tell us that *A Midsummer Night's Dream* was probably first written and produced to celebrate a wedding in the British royal family. If there is little hard evidence for that, it does seem to fit our feeling about the play. Its first scene opens on just such a royal pair, Theseus of Athens and Hippolyta of the amazons, planning their own marriage. And if marriage implies a joining of opposites, Theseus and Hippolyta have assuredly been opposed:

> Hippolyta, I wooed thee with my sword
> And won thy love doing thee injuries;
> But I will wed thee in another key
> With pomp, with triumph, and with revelling.

Modern practice, of course, has changed all that. To have the fighting all settled before the wedding must have left them little to look forward to; we'd be bored.

And if that seems old-fashioned, it seems downright quaint for Theseus and Hippolyta, each of whom has quite a past, to forgo sex until after the ceremony. We moderns have reversed that, too. If we fail to stay chaste before the wedding, we frequently make up for that afterward.

Still, in most things, Theseus seems old-fashioned. He governs by right of conquest and by ability to rule. No wonder he seems half-mythical! He even obeys the laws he enforces on his subjects. No sooner has he announced his wedding plans and his determination to restrain his lusts until that time, than in rushes Egeus with his daughter Hermia, to accuse her and her two suitors of a willful desire to break Athens's marriage laws. Most of us sympathize with Hermia, yet we see a justice in Theseus's rule. Suppose we thought he and Hippolyta were slipping off now and then to make out on the sly?

All the better then, if Theseus is upright as well as erect; restraint is valuable, especially when it channels great force:

> .... but O, methinks how slow
> This old moon wanes; she lingers my desires
> Like to a step-dame, or a dowager,
> Long withering out a young man's revenue

His desires for Hippolyta, then, are strong; yet his telling of
them sounds strangely rancorous. Hippolyta's reply seems almost threatening:

> Four days will quickly steep themselves in night
> Four nights will quickly dream away the time;
> And then the moon, like to a silver bow
> New bent in heaven, shall behold the night
> Of our solemnities.

Even lusts so high-strung needn't be imaged as weaponry.
Both rulers seem to have slipped back into recollections of that
war between them which we had hoped was finished.

Who are these two we have come together to join? Surely,
Theseus stands for the model ruler and male, the man of conquest as of conquests, who is yet capable of noble commitment. If his rule is just and central, so is reason's rule in him.
When he later comes to the forest, his hounds baying musi-
cally, he gives an admirable picture of the animal forces
trained and held in harmonious order. The hunter's bow
(which elsewhere stood for Diana's chastity or for sexual attack) now is turned to useful sport. Such controlled sport, such
harmony, he must induce in himself as in the lovers, those
who look to him as their authority.

Hippolyta? She is an amazon. Spenser's Radigund makes
her role clear enough: the warrior woman whose single aim is
to defeat and enslave the male. As the story goes, all amazons
cut off one breast lest it be injured by the bowstring—that is,
partly defeminized themselves to better fight the male. Still,
we imagine amazons were thoroughly democratic; would as
readily subject the male to surgery. So the sexes would be
more equal, yet the woman would rule. Hippolyta, seen here
in defeat, has none of these fiercer qualities. True, she seems

to get the last word in arguments; yet she is both right and uninsistent, an engaging combination. She carries herself with such grace and dignity that we wonder if a woman might be as improved by defeat as some men can.

These two, then, have been fierce enemies; it would be a wonder if no bitterness remained. Their reconciliation, their coming marriage, is indeed a consummation devoutly to be wished. To them, the present moon seems a time of drained resources, of grudging tightfistedness. How shall we reach a new moon of generosity, of free spending and fulfilled desire—how shall we bring this couple to union? How but by airing and expiating, owning and healing those age-old grudges, the wounds of our long war?

Where better to do that than in our dreams—perhaps in just such a dream as this play? Midsummer Night, after all, was the night when a girl might dream about her future husband. A Midsummer Night's dream, then, tells the truth about our love. Dare we ask it not only to reveal, but also to reconcile us to our love?

The Fairies

OBERON   Ill met by moonlight, proud Titania.

TITANIA   What, jealous Oberon? Fairies, skip hence:
I have forsworn his bed and company.

OBERON   Tarry, rash wanton; am not I thy lord?

TITANIA   Then I must be thy lady; but I know
When thou hast stolen away from fairy land,
And in the shape of Corin sat all day,
Playing on pipes of corn, and versing love
To amorous Phillida.

Now *that* has a good modern sound—nothing restrained about the fairies' rage or their lust. Like Theseus and Hippolyta, they are chaste; theirs, however, is that spiteful abstinence many of us have found in marriage. These fairies fully display and act out those passions which compel all the couples—though Theseus tries to control them, though the lovers try to disguise them. The fairies could almost be a negative and all the other couples its various positive prints.

The fairies' war echoes another of the problems plaguing Theseus, not only the struggle for dominance between the sexes but also that between parents and children. He has just heard Egeus's claim that his daughter, Hermia, is his property to give in marriage as he wills. The fairies, too, are struggling for ownership of a child—a "little changeling boy" each wants as a page and follower.

Faced by such problems, Theseus defeated his woman in open conflict; Oberon uses subtlety, magic, stealth. It hardly seems cricket (even among lovers) to win the war by putting your woman to bed with the most bestial creature available:

> Be it ounce, or cat, or bear,
> Pard, or boar with bristled hair,
> In thy eye that shall appear,
> When thou wak'st, it is thy dear.
> Wake when something vile is near.

Bottom may not be all *that* vile; most wives would scarcely thank their husbands for so asinine a lover. Yet, the very queen of fairies, once her vision has cleared, does almost thank Oberon. How can her humiliation result, not in a deeper rejection of Oberon, but in acceptance? Can he, like Theseus, win his woman's love doing her injuries? Perhaps the ferocity of his strategy flatters her—he must love her very much to fight so fiercely. Or persuades her to surrender quickly before he does *worse*. More likely it shows her something about her own desires and her rejection of her lord—that she would be willingly embowered only with a man who could be made an ass. Or that her love is a love of the ass.

Anyway, Oberon's strategy works; who is to quarrel with success? The fairies' reconciliation is surely no less desirable than is the rulers'—do we imagine any love can be happy while these fairies rage? These are love's divinities, parental figures who have guided both Theseus and Hippolyta through all their past loves and must now assure their permanent union. By their own admission, they have caused the world's present coldness and sterility. The seasons are disordered, disease rampant, the rivers rebellious and uncontained; fields are barren, the folds empty, the flocks dying:

> And this same progeny of evils comes
> From our debate, from our dissension;
> We are their parents and original.

In the normal rounds of his practical business, Theseus encounters most of the other characters of the play. He judges and helps reconcile the lovers; their wedding becomes part of his. The artisans devise their play just to celebrate that same marriage. For all his hard-nosed narrow-mindedness, he seems a splendidly capable ruler; we expect him to be a good husband. Moreover he has had a considerable hand in straightening out the lovers, his subjects. On the one hand, he has made it clear to Hermia that he will maintain the laws of Athens; on the other, he has drawn both Egeus and Demetrius aside for "private schooling" in matters that concern them closely. We have seen that his rule is firm and effective.

Yet Theseus never meets the fairies, those who have guided his past and on whom his future totally depends. How strange that he should not even believe in forces which he has somehow successfully enlisted, and without whose help all his reason and power would be useless.

In act 5, Theseus issues various firm pronouncements on the unreality of love and lovers, plays and players, above all fairies:

> I never may believe
> These antique fables nor these fairy toys.
> Lovers and madmen have such seething brains,
> Such shaping fantasies, that apprehend
> More than cool reason ever comprehends.

No sooner has he left the stage, though, taking his bride to bed, than those same nonexistent fairies enter to bless his marriage and make that bed fruitful. Had their quarrel gone on, not only his bed but his household, his state, his world had been barren and fruitless.

No more than Theseus do we believe in fairies. Yet we see something that he cannot—you had better have them on your side. There is no Oberon. And Titania is his consort.

The Lovers

If you ask the romantic lovers—Hermia and Lysander, Helena and Demetrius—they don't want to rule each other, only to serve each other. "I am your spaniel." If you ask the lovers, they wouldn't think of hurting each other. (There's a fact— they do it without a thought.) If you ask the lovers, they want only to marry.

But who believes a lover? They are as full of passion as the fairies, as full of reason as the rulers. But they use reason not to channel passion, rather to disguise and license it. So they remain willfully chaste, willfully sexual. Yet, being so ready to fool themselves, they seldom fool anyone else:

> LYSANDER   O take the sense, sweet, of my innocence.
>   Love takes the meaning in love's conference....
>   Then by your side no bed-room me deny,
>   For lying so, Hermia, I do not lie.
>
> HERMIA   Lysander riddles very prettily;...
>   But, gentle friend, for love and courtesy
>   Lie further off, in human modesty.

At times their speeches have more truth than they yet recognize:

> Love looks not with the eyes, but with the mind,
> And therefore is winged Cupid painted blind.
> Nor hath Love's mind of any judgement taste;
> Wings, and no eyes, figure unheedy haste;
> And therefore is Love said to be a child,
> Because in choice he is so oft beguiled.

The lovers demand to choose love by their own sight, yet they obviously can't see who they are, what they want, or what they are doing. As the play later shows, they are running around lost in a fog. They think they are trying to get married; to us they seem to be doing the exact opposite.

The law will not let Hermia and Lysander marry, so they plan to run away to the home of his widow aunt. (A very moony aunt she seems, "a dowager of great revenue.") No sooner has Hermia joined him in the woods, eager to marry him, than Lysander becomes curiously unable to find that place where marriage will be so easy; within hours he has fallen desperately in love with someone else. Soon, he is plying Helena with all the frantic endearments he once gave Hermia, meantime treating Hermia as hatefully as Demetrius ever did Helena. Throughout the play the truly hurtful things are always said by someone to the person they most love— Titania to Oberon, Lysander to Hermia, Demetrius to Helena. We are told art imitates life.

Where did all these tangles start, these triangles among our four lovers? Apparently when Demetrius, having won Helena, turned from her to Hermia, obtaining her father's permission to marry her. Why did he suddenly desire the scornful Hermia, abandoning the willing Helena? Perhaps just because Helena *was* willing? Lysander certainly turned against Hermia precisely at the point he could marry her.

Consider the advantages for Demetrius in this "unhappy" unfulfilled love. Imagine saying to your true love:

> Hang off, thou cat, thou burr! Vile thing, let loose
> Or I will shake thee from me like a serpent!

and getting this answer:

> Why are you grown so rude? What change is this?
> Sweet love...

Or better yet, to say:

> I do not and I cannot love you

and then get this reply:

> And even for that do I love you the more...
> Use me but as your spaniel, spurn me, strike me,
> Neglect me, lose me; only give me leave,
> Unworthy as I am to follow you.
> What worser place can I beg in your love—
> And yet a place of high respect with me,—
> Than to be used as you use your dog.

What victory has either Oberon or Theseus compared to that? What has marriage compared to that? Suppose Demetrius won either Hermia or Helena—he would have to live with her. He would have to give up self-pity in being deprived of some imagined love, stop rejecting what love is convenient and available. He would have to become an adult; small wonder both he and Lysander postpone it as long as possible. Meantime, each is deeply indulging himself in injuries to the girl he loves:

> LYSANDER   What, should I hurt her, strike her, kill her dead?
>   Although I hate her, I'll not harm her so.
>
> HERMIA   What can you do me greater harm than hate?
>   Hate me? Wherefore? O me, what news, my love?

That is almost motive enough in itself.

But meantime, both girls are just as agile in preserving their "single blessedness." In the first scene, Helena hears that Hermia and Lysander are about to elope—that she will be relieved of her rival. Instead of bidding them a fond good riddance, she tells Demetrius of their plans:

> Then to the wood will he tomorrow night
> Pursue her; and for this intelligence,
> If I have thanks, it is a dear expense.
> But herein mean I to enrich my pain,
> To have his sight thither, and back again.

If she ever was as available as Demetrius thought, she must since have learned the pleasures of rejection and abandonment.

Earlier in this scene, she wished she might be translated into Hermia, who is pursued by both men. In the woods, she gets her wish; under Puck's enchantments both men turn gaga over her. How does she respond? By refusing both, starting a quarrel with Hermia, then running away. What else can you do if events threaten to impoverish your pain?

As to Hermia, when both men courted her, she chose the one forbidden. Listening to Egeus's long speech, we cannot quite make out whether Hermia wants Lysander because her father insists on Demetrius, or whether her father insists on Demetrius because she wants Lysander. Both may be true. It's worth noting, though, that in the companion play (I cannot think of them separately) Juliet fell in love with Romeo only just after her father gave her to Paris. That, surely, is part of the reason she fell in love with someone else, especially with an enemy of her family. In this play, we feel that one of Pyramus's greatest attractions is precisely that he is a family enemy and so forbidden to Thisby. As to Hermia's choice between Lysander and Demetrius, everyone concedes there is no difference between them. How does she tell them apart?—ideally they would be played by identical twins. Lysander has only two discernible advantages: he is not available to Hermia, and he gives her a way to oppose her father.

Only occasionally do we have glimpses of the girls' disdain for their lovers. Hermia gives only a hint:

> Before the time I did Lysander see,
> Seemed Athens as a paradise to me.
> O then, what graces in my love do dwell
> That he hath turned a heaven unto a hell!

Helena's slam against Demetrius is much nearer the surface:

> . . . as he errs, doting on Hermia's eyes,
> So I, admiring of his qualities.

> Things base and vile, holding no quantity,
> Love can transpose to form and dignity.

Except for Hermia's opposition to her father, neither girl shows much desire to directly assault the male. (There will be years and years for that.) On the other hand, before the young men are accepted as husbands, each has proved himself inconstant, trifling, and childish. Perhaps the girls need do nothing to humiliate their lovers; Lysander and Demetrius can be counted on to make asses of themselves.

The rulers then have already fought out their war and wish to be married; the fairies are married and fighting harder than ever. The lovers must keep up the pretense of wanting marriage but are actually doing everything to evade it—at least until they have carried their battle to a point where the final outcome is clearly indicated.

The Craftsmen

Like the lovers, the artisans live in Theseus's world and must seek resolution there; like the lovers, they can reach that only by first withdrawing into Oberon's world. The young lovers now must enter a world of adulthood, marriage, business, reason; in their revulsion, they regress even further into fantasy, childhood, magic. The artisans also go there, apparently sensing that's the place to learn a role, to discover one's part. So develops one of the major structures of the play—the general migration from the sunlit city into the moonlit forest, then back again.

Just as Theseus never had contact with the fairies, the world most comparable to his own, so the lovers have no contact with the artisans, the world that most reflects theirs. True, they watch the craftsmen perform "Pyramus and Thisby." But only after they have married—it is questionable whether they *are* lovers then. In any case that's small contact with a world which sheds such light on theirs.

From the first, "Pyramus and Thisby" has been a mockery of lovers:

FLUTE   (as Thisby) My love! thou art my love, I think.

BOTTOM   (as Pyramus) Think what thou wilt, I am thy lover's
          grace,
          And like Limander am I trusty still.

FLUTE   (as Thisby)
          And I like Helen, till the Fates me kill.

Like the lovers whose names they just echoed (Lysander and
Helena), Pyramus and Thisby ran away to meet far from the
constraints and divisions of society. There, they found much
what the lovers found, much what Romeo and Juliet found—
that they are certainly not "trusty still," that they are much
more likely to kill themselves than to be killed by Fate. All are
like the old joke about the spinster and the hen: "Poor dears,
they'd rather die!"

That old sexual pun (among a myriad others) is much in
evidence here. The artisans not only rehearse "obscenely and
courageously," they perform that way as well. Pyramus picks
up Thisby's mantle, bloodied by the lion's mouth, and
exclaims:

> O wherefore, Nature, didst thou lions frame?
> Since lion vile hath here deflowered my dear:
> Which is—no, no, which was—the fairest Dame
> That lived, that loved, that liked, that looked with cheer.
> Come tears, confound:
> Out sword, and wound
> The pap of Pyramus:
> Ay, that left pap,
> Where heart doth hop;
> Thus die I, thus, thus, thus.
>
> Now am I dead,
> Now am I fled, . . .
>
> Now die, die, die, die, die.

Demetrius sets out to cap the pun:

> No die, but an ace for him; for he is but one.

Then Theseus caps the cap:

> With the help of a surgeon he might yet recover, and prove an
> ass.

We are reminded, of course, of Bottom's earlier transformation. Yet, much as the court mocks the craftsmen's acting, this whole playlet remains a mockery of the hammier performances these lovers just gave with the very substance of their lives.

We are never allowed to forget that the playlet is only a way to pass the time till the lovers may and must bed each other for the first time. By the end of the play, even Hippolyta (who earlier had soothed Theseus's impatience) seems anxious to get on to bed:

> I am a-weary of this Moon; would he would change!
>
> THESEUS ... in courtesy, in all reason, we must stay the
> time.

The play's purpose is, in part, to make us more eager for marriage and for bed; it does this partly by its mockery of romantic love. At the same time, it helps reveal and expiate our fear of marriage, even of sex itself.

Demetrius calls Snug the Joiner (O sweetly fitting name!):

> The very best at a beast, my lord, that e'er I saw.

then says of Bottom and Flute:

> A mote will turn the balance, which Pyramus, which Thisby
> is the better, he for a man, God warrant us, she for a woman,
> God bless us.

Such ready criticism suggests that he is trying to rise to better performance himself but may be none too sure of his abilities. Still we must not be overcritical ourselves—he has had a courage lacking in Pyramus or Romeo, has come back from the world of fantasy and settled down to live with the woman he loves. No mean feat, that.

Yet it is not only in their playlet that the craftsmen provide an ironic view of love and lovers; they do that far more richly in their forest scenes. There, we watch Puck tangling and untangling the lovers; watch him first transform Bottom into an ass, then, with the same herb that charmed the lovers, put him into the cradle of Titania. Bottom went to the forest when the lovers did, was enchanted by the same magical powers, was released when they were. He of all people has known the quintessential love experience, has been embraced by the queen of love, gone to the very bottom of the world of passion and imagination. And he was an ass. And he is an ass. Watching Titania coo and gurgle over him, we see as nowhere else how

> Things base and vile, holding no quantity,
> Love can transpose to form and dignity.

In some sense, then, all the lovers have proven an ass in the bower of divinity.

Bottom, above all, has had the power (a very passive power it must be) to reenter the world of the child's, even the baby's, sexuality—the world of Mustardseed and Cobweb, of Mother Squash, Father Peascod, and Baby Peaseblossom. There, without the faintest qualm, he replaces the "King of shadows." If he does not actually cuckold that king (we cannot be sure), it is only because he is more interested in eating. The queen has made every amorous advance to him and he has come back safe and sound to tell of it. Well, not perhaps to tell of it:

Man is but an ass if he go about to expound this dream. . . . Methought I was, and methought I had. . . . I will get Peter Quince to write a ballad of this dream; it shall be called "Bottom's Dream," because it hath no bottom and I will sing it in the latter end of the play, before the Duke.

He never does but the clear implication is that it is this experience which is not only the basic love experience but also the material which must be translated into the work of art, the experience which makes "Pyramus and Thisby" possible. In the play's last act, the artisans bring back to the city their forest experience; there they wield (however awkwardly) the powers of transformation which they must have gathered from the fairies who had transformed them in the woods.

All along, we have seen that the artisans making their play to further Athenian royal wedding clearly image Shakespeare and his company making *their* play to celebrate an English noble wedding. Who knows better than Shakespeare what goes into the making of a play?

The Firmament

You could scarcely imagine, unless you had looked into the Furness *Variorum,* what energy critics have spent arguing for the centrality of some one or another of these four worlds. The lovers, the fairies, the rulers—each has its partisans heatedly arguing that their candidate holds the central place while the others only revolve around it, reflecting and illuminating its meaning.

No critic (excepting Dr. Gui, whose penetrating and eccentric analysis appears in the *American Imago*) sees the artisans as central. Yet actors and directors often make them so. We surely remember their scenes most vividly—the enchanted Bottom in Titania's bower; the hilarious "Pyramus and Thisby"—and those scenes are often extracted to play separately.

I certainly don't intend to take sides here. The mere existence of the dispute lends force to my view—that *none* of these worlds is central. As I see it, all four worlds exist only in their balanced relationship to one another. Just as four dancers, or four groups of dancers, might all be part of a larger pattern, each maintaining relation with the others, none more important than the others, our four lovers did, in fact, create just such a dance pattern in their shifting and alternating triangulations. Or to return to the astronomical figure, the play's firmament holds four worlds, one of which has created its own moon—the play within the play. These four worlds form a circle, as twinned stars might in *our* universe, holding each other in orbit around a center which no one of them may permanently occupy. Each world has close narrative contact with two of the others; each remains apart from a fourth. Each, as it passes through the center, gives and takes illumination from all the others—often most strongly from that fourth world opposite to and separate from itself.

This play was written, after all, at a time when centrality was being broken down in all areas—I take as my authority here Hiram Haydn's *The Counter-Renaissance*. There, we may trace the rise of individualistic philosophies and religions, of capitalist economies, democratic ideas of government; of the child's rights against his parents, the subject's rights against his sovereign, of relativistic views of the world, of reality, of astronomy. Giordano Bruno, that most daringly relativistic of thinkers, had been in England only about ten years before the writing of this play. Haydn quotes Bruno:

> Since the horizon forms itself anew around every place occupied by the spectator as its central point, every determination of place must be relative. The universe looks different according to whether we conceive it from the earth, the moon, Venus, the sun, etc. . . .
>
> Why, indeed, may not all the stars be themselves suns, and each new sun appear to itself the center of the universe? Where then are its limits? . . . There must be hundreds of thousands of suns, and about them planets rolling, each one, perhaps, inhabited. . . . Throughout, Nature must be the same, everywhere worlds, everywhere the center, everywhere and nowhere.

From this amazingly modern view, Bruno advances directly to relativity of motion, of time, even of weight.

It is Montaigne, however, who can show us a comparable

relativity of manners, morals, of levels of reality. First he points out that such relativity of place and judgment makes all agreement between men impossible:

> Men are in agreement about nothing. I mean even the most gifted and ablest scholars, not even that the sky is over our heads.

Yet even if only one man had ever existed, that one could not truly know reality:

> The conception and semblance we form is not the object, but only the impression and the impression and the object are different things. . . .
>
> Now if anyone should want to judge by appearances anyway, to judge by all appearances is impossible, for they clash with one another by their contradictions and discrepancies. . . . Shall some selected appearances rule the others? . . .
>
> Finally, there is no existence that is constant, either of our being or of that of objects. And we, and our judgement and all mortal things go on flowing and rolling ceaselessly. Thus nothing certain can be established about one thing by another, both the judging and the judged being in continual change and motion.

Such men as Bruno and Montaigne had moved into a world of limitless change, of rolling and flowing, boundaries shifting and reforming, realities dissolving and illusions becoming real. Shakespeare was a man of his time; not the man least sensitive to forces which were driving others to create and explore new areas of thought and feeling. Most readers would grant that the play implies that all illusions have their reality, all realities their illusion. It is only a step further (though a dangerous one, as Bruno found at the stake) to suggest that no reality is more important, more real, that no one appearance may be selected to rule the others.

One of the peculiar triumphs of Shakespeare's art is to have taken an artistic convention common to his time—the use of subplot—and let it grow until it quite broke down the whole principle of central plot. What is for lesser writers only a useful device, a way to relieve and vary their central story, is for Shakespeare a way to suggest a whole new view of the world.

Such tendencies must have been very deep in Shakespeare's nature. We see it in every aspect of his work—for instance, his use of imagery. In the sonnet cycle we can watch his technique growing into something that reflects his own psyche, his peculiar vision. In the earlier pieces, imagery tends to be confined to rather low-powered metaphors and similes; we always know what is real and what merely compared to it. As Shakespeare's art grows, the components of an image will be drawn from ever more bafflingly diverse areas of experience, ever more complex structures of reality:

> Not marble, nor the gilded monuments
> Of princes, shall outlive this powerful rhyme
> ... you shall shine more bright in these contents
> Than unswept stone, besmeared with sluttish time.

Not only is metaphor added to metaphor; the vehicle of the first may be snapped up as the tenor of a second, mounted metaphor:

> That time of year thou may'st in me behold
> When yellow leaves, or none, or few, do hang
> Upon those boughs which shake against the cold,
> Bare ruined choirs where late the sweet birds sang.

until we can scarcely say which term is "real" and which only a reflection of it.

In *Rehabilitations*, C. S. Lewis sees a similar urge in Shakespeare's rhetorical practice, contrasting that with Milton's. Milton normally tries to sum up the meaning of his subject in some one description or definitive statement, then lets that stand for better or worse. Shakespeare, on the contrary, tends to come back to his subject again and again—or rather, his characters do. They say things quite as brilliant, as definitive, as anything in Milton. Yet they say them only in the rush and fumble of trying to grasp a reality that seems always elusive, always too broad for summing up. However wonderful their words may be, they never seem to feel them adequate to experience. Again, we find this same drive toward variousness, toward turbulent diversity, in that violent mixing of genres which so disturbed continental critics: realistic scenes collide with highly fanciful stylized scenes; prose rubs shoulders with blank verse or even with tight rhyme; high wit mixes with buffoonery, high tragedy with melodrama. Shakespeare's plays may not, like the artisans', be "tedious and brief"; they are surely "very tragical mirth. . . hot ice, and wondrous strange snow." In their despair of imitating this life, they become downright "tragical-comical-historical-pastoral." All conventions are seized on; none is admitted to yield final truth.

And this, of course, is intimately part of what makes Shakespeare so bafflingly great. Stepping into the universe of his plays, we are surrounded with characters, with situations, with meanings, various and far-flung as stars on a summer night. We can no more locate the center of this universe than we can fathom its edges. We cannot define the creator from within his creation. We cannot sum up Shakespeare; we only set up housekeeping there.

Translations

In the play's first scene, when Hermia is being pursued by both Demetrius and Lysander, Helena says to her:

> Sickness is catching; O were favour so,
> Yours would I catch, fair Hermia, ere I go. . . .
> Were the world mine, Demetrius being bated,
> The rest I'd give to be to you translated.

Soon, she gets her wish: she becomes Hermia; both men pursue her. That, of course, is even less satisfying.

In that same process, Hermia is translated into Helena and

finds herself abandoned. Weary from wandering in the forest, she and Lysander had lain down to rest. First, however, she has had to persuade him to lie at a more modest distance. Then, with vows of eternal constancy, they fell asleep. Suddenly Hermia wakes with a nightmare-vision, a dream-within-the-*Dream:*

> Help me, Lysander, help me! do thy best
> To pluck this crawling serpent from my breast!
> Aye me, for pity! what a dream was here!
> Lysander, look how I do quake with fear.
> Methought a serpent eat my heart away,
> And you sat smiling at his cruel prey.

Lysander has already abandoned her, chasing after Helena. The dream has shown her her own plight, both in this abandonment where Lysander enjoys her pain, and also in her fear of being preyed upon—a fear which Lysander must have activated by his sly and subtle attempt to seduce her.

Sickness is indeed catching. During the lovers' near-epidemic Lysander, too, suffers a translation: not into what he wished to be, but into what Egeus said he already was. In the opening scene, it was ironic that Egeus should try to take Hermia from the constant Lysander on the grounds that he was inconstant and feigning, giving her instead to Demetrius, whom we know to be faithless. Yet no sooner have the lovers fled to the woods than Lysander becomes all Egeus said he was. He even goes Egeus and the fairies one better: Puck's enchantment may force him to love Helena; to hate and mistreat Hermia is an improvement supplied from his own nature.

Puck's final enchantment, the curing of Demetrius's vision, straightens out all the tangles at once—shows Demetrius that he has always loved Helena and that his pursuit of Hermia was

> . . . an idle gaud
> which in my childhood I did dote upon;
> And all the faith, the virtue of my heart,

> The object and the pleasure of mine eye,
> Is only Helena...
> ... like in sickness did I loathe this food
> But, as in health, come to my natural taste,
> Now I do wish it, love it, long for it,
> And will for evermore be true to it.

This brings the lovers back where they started before the play began. Except that they may be a little more mature after an experience which reveals so much about themselves. Demetrius is shown who his love is; Lysander, what. He, once so ready to call others "spotted and inconstant," is full of inconstancy. Even more, full of hate and venom which he, like Theseus, must recognize and control. The aim of all these translations, then, is to change something so we can see how it always was.

All the lovers are shown lost in a fog where they cannot find, cannot recognize each other or themselves. They declare a deathless love for another person, without whom their lives will be desolate; an hour later, they feel exactly the same thing for someone else. As wild beasts wake famished and devour the first prey at hand, so the lovers wake enchanted and fall in love. It is love-in-idleness that enchants them; being of the leisure class, they can indulge their fantasies, can grieve and blame, can enrich their pain. Hardworking people like Peter Quince may dabble with such loves as they dabble in the arts; they haven't the leftover energy or time to let it control their lives.

I have earlier touched on some of the ways that the enchanted Bottom in Titania's bower reveals the truth about Bottom and about the rebellious Titania as well. Those same scenes also show much about the lovers who undergo a similar enchantment in the same time and place. What happens to Titania and Bottom is obviously related to what happens to the lovers, and not only in the asininity all display.

If the two young men seem almost identical to each other, the two girls are only slightly more differentiated. They cherish, moreover, a vision of their union in infancy:

> We, Hermia, like two artificial gods,
> Have with our needles created both one flower
> Both on one sampler, sitting on one cushion,
> Both warbling of one song, both in one key;
> As if our hands, our sides, voices and minds
> Had been incorporate. So we grew together,
> Like to a double cherry.

This vision, of which Helena prates so ecstatically, is close kin to that of Bottom in Titania's bower. It is an imagined bower of bliss where, above all, the pains of individuality and separateness are turned to ecstacy in a dream of childish, even babyish, union.

Moving toward maturity and marriage, the lovers must give up the narcissistic dream of being one with those identical to themselves. As individuals they must learn not only to accept what is different, but even what is opposite. They are growing into a world where things are separate and self-willed, yet where union is still possible:

HERMIA   Methinks I see these things with parted eye
            Where everything seems double.

HELENA   So methinks. And I have found Demetrius like a
             jewel
            Mine own and not mine own. . . .

DEMETRIUS   . . . . Do you not think
            The Duke was here, and bid us follow him? . . .

LYSANDER   And he did bid us follow to the temple.

DEMETRIUS   Why then, we are awake.

The lovers, then, are waking from their dream of blissful union (essentially Bottom's dream) and going to the temple and to marriage—a world of differences, of separations, of walls, yet walls that can be penetrated.

The lovers, making this painful change, have the help of the artisans who shared their forest experience. In the last act, the artisans take over from the fairies the power to transform things so they may be truly seen. Performing "Pyramus and Thisby" they mock their own and the lovers' flight into moonshine and so help them emerge into the raw and difficult light of day. Truly, Bottom and his friends do not "stand upon points," are poor enough actors. Fearing lest the lion terrorize the ladies, or that everyone be shocked by Pyramus's suicide, they seem not to discern what in their art is reality and what illusion. Yet, in effect, they perform very well indeed. Theseus does well to honor them, not because of their supposed good will to him (their *real* aim, of course, is self-advancement), but because their play has a salutary effect on the lovers, helps lead them into reality.

In the play, the lovers leave the world of Bottom's dream to enter the world of marriage. Outside the play, lovers made Bottom's dream the aim of marriage. Alas and alack for us all.

The Fundament

Bottom was translated into an ass. Like all good translators, Puck must have been quick to leap to a pun. And as any good analyst must be quick to hear a pun, Dr. Gui finds Bottom the central character of the play.

Bottom has a strong urge to take over all roles—not just the lover and the lady, but the lion's part as well. He wants to play the tyrant; if there is to be no tyrant, the next best thing is to be the director. While directing the playlet, Peter Quince— whose name echoes Penis Cunt—has continual trouble keeping Bottom in his place.

Bottom himself, almost like a baby, has trouble keeping straight the parts of the body and *their* proper roles:

> The eye of man hath not heard, the ear of man hath not seen, man's hand is not able to taste, his tongue to conceive, nor his heart to report, what my dream was.

Playing Pyramus, he says:

> I see a voice; now will I to the chink
> To spy an I can hear my Thisby's face.

He does not let many things keep their assigned function:

> Sweet moon, I thank thee for thy sunny beams.

He is not just undiscriminating; he seems determined to break down all distinctions. He dissolves the meaning of words, often saying the exact opposite of what he means:

> You were best to call them generally, man by man.

> There may we rehearse most obscenely and courageously.

> I will aggravate my voice so, that I will roar you as gently as any sucking dove.

In our world, doves have voices neither grave nor aggravated; they seldom roar and never suck; in Bottom's world, fish, flesh, and fowl are all one.

> There is not a more fearful wild fowl than your lion living.

Bottom so longs to equalize everything that when Quince proposes to write a prologue in eight and six syllable verse (the "fourteeners" then so common), Bottom will not hear of it:

> No, make it two more; let it be written in eight and eight.

Loving equality, he tends to break down social distinctions, too. He never hesitates to correct Demetrius or even Theseus. Unlike other characters of the play, he addresses everyone he meets with a complete democracy of courtesy. In Titania's bower, he has no sense that he is out of place, addressing Titania's pages with the absurdly patronizing familiarity of le bourgeois gentilhomme. There, in the bower of the fairy queen, he realizes what must be his dearest dream: the blissful union of the asinine with the sublime, the beastly with the ethereal, the great with the small, the ugly with the beautiful.

This is all thoroughly apt, for in the world of the emotions, anality is the direct counterpart of relativism in philosophy. At bottom, we can scarcely tell male from female; it is the great equalizer which yearns to break down the hierarchies, discredit the phallic or superior. Taking over both male and female roles, it is impatient to assume the world.

Theseus and Bottom, then, stand for diametrically opposed ways of life, not only in their social stance but in the whole bases of their natures. Theseus, the phallic male, always of the elite, holds his position simply because he has more (more anything) than others have. Bottom is the Common Man; he has what we all have.

Theseus takes for granted the artisans' goodwill toward him. To us, he may seem absurdly complacent. Kaiser Wilhelm, after all, was replaced by a saddlemaker; King Alexander by a mill mechanic. Nowadays, Bottom has not only taken over the throne; Theseus could not even get into the legislature—every chair already has an ass. Theseus is no longer Theseus when he seeks the masses' vote; besides, they wouldn't give it to him.

Not believing in fairies, in the overwhelming powers of the unconscious, Theseus could scarcely suspect what powers Bottom has lain beside. Theseus is very much of the past—a past so ancient it may never have existed.

Yet, as far back as the Bronze Age, perhaps we *can* see a bit of Theseus after all—a hunting society demands the direct and powerful rule of one man; bronze weapons could only be owned by an aristocracy. Bottom is of a time when artisans, working in a poorer but commoner metal, iron, would give the farmer tools and so a surplus, letting him turn sedentary, anarchic, indulge himself in dreams, would give the masses weapons and so control of the battlefield and ballot box. Bottom directs the present and the future.

One day, I was talking about all this with a dear old friend, Donald Hall. By now, I don't know which ideas came from him and which from me. Suddenly he burst out laughing: "But how predictive! Where did our modern collective and democratic states come from? From the asshole of society; where else?"

Poets and Parents

Romantic love, of course, has no very ancient history; it is open to dispute whether even the Romans were romantic. The first time we can isolate and firmly identify this strange virus in the western world is in the courtly love lyrics of the twelfth-century renaissance in Provence. Oddly enough, there, too, it is involved with a historical movement which helped break down centrality of rule.

We are only now beginning to suspect that neither the troubadour's music nor his sentiments were as "pretty" as we had been told. With some justice, we could say that the troubadour song has only two obsessions: let's go crusading and kill Moors, or let's go seducing and lay the boss's wife.

After many centuries of terrifying upheaval, the twelfth century was a time when men could once again afford unhappy love, self-pity, betrayal, envy of authority. After all, the local strong-arm chief, the feudal equivalent of Theseus, was no longer so desperately needed for protection against invaders, had become in fact a considerable threat himself. It has been seriously argued that one real purpose of the crusades was to keep the turbulent and idle aristocracy out of trouble nearer home. Meantime, the lower orders were beginning to envy their power, their freedom, their women.

The courtly love object is always a married woman, usually the wife of the singer's overlord. Most troubadour songs are much less interested in that lady's excellences (which are praised in habitual, desultory fashion) than in the desire to humiliate, annoy, or deceive her husband. Thus, the singer might satisfy two illicit cravings at once: to get a forbidden woman and, at the same time, exercise a good deal of homosexual fascination. Beyond this were the pleasures of a dual betrayal—offering to the lady that loyalty the singer owed her husband and the Christian deities, then using this false "loyalty" to convince her that she, too, should betray her husband, her feudal lord, her religion. Throughout these songs the husband is known as the jealous one, the thief, the liar.

What else can you call a man of whom you are jealous, whose wife you are stealing, to whom you must continually lie?

As prosperity filtered downward during the next two centuries, this tradition spread through the *trouvères* and *minnesänger*, the French *chansons de toile*, and into the folk ballad which apparently began among the French peasantry of the fourteenth century. Throughout this process, the effects of a growing prosperity and security are seen in a growing concern with human wishes and aspirations (not merely actions), with personal psychology, with self-expression, with love.

No doubt the spread of romantic love was hastened by the Albigensian Crusade in which the French obliterated Provence—ostensibly to clean up the vice down there; actually to bring it all back home. One of the chief effects of this crusade, like most earlier ones, was that a little of Arabic high culture rubbed off on the barbarous Franks and Europeans. Likely enough, the Provençals themselves had picked up romantic love (with most of their musical and poetical practices) from brushes with the Moors in earlier crusades. Those who survived the Albigensian Crusade were scattered all across Europe; no doubt this helped disseminate their type of song, their type of love. Yet surely any tradition that offered such lively music, together with so many opportunities for betrayal, was bound to catch on.

By the seventeenth century, the time of *A Midsummer Night's Dream*, the forces of church and state had managed to change romantic love—it had been, in every sense, housebroken. It had moved from the aristocratic warrior classes of the court (which it had helped undermine) into the households of the triumphant middle class. (We should not be surprised that capitalism, value through scarcity, first expressed itself in love.) It remains essential that the lady be unattainable—what's romantic about a woman you can have? But now the lady is single; the obstacle is not her husband, but her father. The aim is not seduction but marriage against opposition. No doubt it must have seemed to the church and state—the initial targets of romantic love—that this was a less dangerous line of attack. Indeed, for a time it probably had a salutary effect: it may be argued that the sudden dramatic rise of western culture over its neighbors was very much furthered and fueled by the tensions romantic love fostered between fathers and sons. When this tension could not be directly expressed, one result would be an increase of competition with other males and so a generally higher level of achievement. You can no more write a great play alone than you can run a great mile. You can only have Shakespeare *with* Marlowe and Jonson; Bannister *with* Landy and Chattaway. Such accomplishment usually demands a kind of admiring competition—and so is often more available to those not entirely comfortable with themselves or their loved ones.

In any case, the art form leading this attack against the father as center of authority was no longer the love lyric, but rather the drama. One often feels that half the surviving renaissance plays portray the struggle of two young people to marry against their parents' opposition. If they can defeat, trick, or thwart those parents, it is automatically assumed they will settle down to love each other forever, all their dreams fulfilled. The play ends in confident assurance that this may be called "a happy ending."

This is one of the reasons it is so fitting that Bottom be an actor—consider the loss if the craftsmen had decided to form a chorus and sing for Theseus's wedding! Beyond this, to be an actor, a role player, fits in perfectly with the anality, the antisexuality of his nature. The driving aim of an actor has always been to escape his own definition in a borrowed role, above all to escape sexual definition. Theater was greatest when only men played (renaissance England, ancient Greece); the crowning achievement has always been to play the opposite sex.

This is to say that while actors and dramatists were among the first to demand freedom to control their own sexuality, what they really sought was either the transformation or the obliteration of that sexuality. Thus we can clearly see in them those self-deceptive drives toward freedom which have proved so superbly productive in the hands of the gifted men who could sublimate them into areas such as the creative arts. We can also see the underlying passivity which would make these drives so destructive in the hands of the mob.

Bottom seems to have known all along where fashions in the arts were running, both in our greatest creative geniuses and in our popular travesties of art. The poem did not stop at eight and eight—it finally lost its erect shape altogether, falling into a soft and pliable (at worst, doughy) shape. Music overthrew the phallic hierarchy of the dominant seventh for the artificial communism, the unisex, of the tone row. The same tendencies could be followed out in any of the arts.

No doubt, most of our greatest artistic creations derive a part of their force from profoundly antisexual drives. The phallic artist whom D. H. Lawrence demanded was, after all, only a figment of his fantasies—above all, fantasies of becoming something diametrically opposed to the artist he was. Who can be sure that if he had become as phallic as he wished, he mightn't have stopped all artistic work? Knowing such achievements as Lawrence's or Whitman's, we can only be grateful for those less phallic forces which fostered them. At the same time, we may be horrified at the results of those drives as acted out directly by ordinary men: modern government and modern marriage, glamour and sexlessness, mediocrity and conformity, drugs and television, the paintings everyone can paint, the songs everyone can write.

Who says poetry makes nothing happen? The artist's open rendering of his emotions may have such unpredictable effects on the public that totalitarians from Plato to Stalin have been willing (with some justice) to muzzle or exterminate these unacknowledged and unconscious legislators. Poets and playwrights helped bequeath us a society where we could choose our own mates and settle down to lives of unmatchable wretchedness. A psychoanalyst recently commented that domestic troubles, unhappy love lives, have cost us more misery than all history's wars and famines together. Who can say him nay? It is only one of the ways we are now at the mercy of our pitiless fantasy lives.

Clearly, Egeus is a vengeful old cur, ill-equipped to pick a mate for Hermia. The only person less well equipped is Hermia. No more than anyone else am I willing to give up the right to pick my mate. No more than any other of the freedoms I habitually demand is this likely to make me happy or (unless I am uncommonly lucky) more creative or useful. My personal experience—and I have had too much—has been the exact opposite. To the best of my knowledge, no sensible person has ever tried to show that we westerners have become either happier or more useful since we started picking our own mates.

Neither do I think renaissance dramatists are responsible for the wretchedness of our families, the uselessness of our women, the emptiness of our men, the loneliness of our children. The artist's only business, after all, is to depict his passions honestly; the citizen must decide what to do about them. Artists, in fact, showed perfectly clearly how self-deceptive and dangerous those passions were; we preferred not to hear. We at least need not go on feeding ourselves the old lie that what is good for the artist is good for the citizen, or that what either one wants (or thinks he wants) is likely to be good for him. Both might recall what the Athenians knew: if the gods really hate you, they give you just what you're asking for.

Weavers and Revolutionaries

If it is strangely apt that Bottom be an actor, how much more so that he be a weaver. Who can imagine him as anything else—Bottom the Butcher, Bottom the Greengrocer, Bottom the Hostler?

It's not just the name—that a bottom is the spool or base on which weavers wound thread. Not only that it is a sedentary trade, demanding a good deal of *sitzfleisch*, leaving its practitioner time for mooning and fantasizing (even as the lovers were enchanted by "love-in-idleness"). So, as Hazlitt commented, it is right that Bottom be "accordingly represented as conceited, serious and fantastical."

It goes far deeper into our past. Weaving is a craft basal to our history, ingrained to our oldest thinking; it takes us even into our prehumanity—birds can do it, some with surprising skill. It has come to image some of life's most fundamental processes. We say a man's life is spun or woven by the weaving goddesses until his thread is finally cut. As Pyramus, Bottom rants:

> O Fates! come, come:
> Cut thread and thrum,
> Quail, crush, conclude and quell!

In northern mythology, the Norns weave the loom of war, whose threads are weighted by human skulls. A man and a woman, in marriage and in sex, are seen as weaving the fabric of our life; Theseus says:

> in the temple, by and by, with us
> These couples shall eternally be knit.

We have long used weaving, or related crafts, to represent the building of the body through digestion, or the building of the mind in its cross-lamination, layer on layer. We image the products of that mind, too, as a woven fabric. The radio announcer who late at night (when no one else would buy the time) read sentimental poems to sentimental music was called, of course, "The Dream Weaver." There is probably no creative art (unless it be weaving) for which we do not use weaving as a habitual metaphor.

If weaving is so involved with our ancient history, it is no less entangled with the building of our peculiar modern society. It was among the artisans, and especially among weavers, that the revolutionary religious ideas of the Albigensi took firmest root. Perhaps no single invention was more crucial in developing our special way of living than was the power loom. In this primeval skill, free craftsmen had to work as only slaves or manual laborers had worked before, not for fulfillment in their work but rather to get the money and free time to buy other enjoyments outside their work. Work became a burden, an imprisonment; the modern itch for fun was born. How much of good and of ill came there into our world! Throughout Europe, the early inventors of power weaving equipment were drowned, hanged, stoned, driven out—as if men knew what a Pandora's box was opening before them. But no use; modern society was not to be escaped.

One of the first plays involved with the revolutionary history of our modern democratic and communistic states is *The Weavers* by Gerhart Hauptmann, a play even more relativistic than is *A Midsummer Night's Dream*. It has no central character, no central group of characters, not even a central theme beyond a never-ending complaint: "It ain't fair!"

The most memorable representation of weavers in modern art, however, is rather to be found in the marvelous early drawings of Vincent van Gogh. In those rough, monumental scribbles I find something oddly bisexual: weaving is an art we always associated with the mother who nourishes, shelters, and comforts, yet it is most often practiced by men—and, in Vincent's drawings, men who are specially square-cut and rough-looking. Watching someone weave, I have always been impressed how satisfying the craft seems to its practitioners. Yet I have to be amused, too: it is as if the weaver had his own built-in sex act where he is both male and female; meantime, he rocks soothingly back and forward not only like the rhythm of sex but like the baby rocked by its mother or calmed by the rhythm of her heartbeat.

In van Gogh's drawings, the weaver sits encased in his enormous loom like a man in the stocks, a child in his pen, the baby in the womb. Meantime, his own creation grows before him like an artificial belly or pregnancy. (It is a creation, too, embodying fundamental patterns, but usually centerless.) Like the fat man Auden mentions in *The Dyer's Hand*, he has a built-in image of the mother he would join once more. (In the play, he rejoins her in the body of Titania. In the playlet he does not; he perishes.) The weaver, then, is symbolically self-sufficient; has taken over all roles. He has rid himself not only of the sex difference but of the size and generation difference—he is not only the contained baby, but also the containing and nourishing mother.

Vincent's weavers seem to me like the devotees of some goddess of fertility and motherhood—say Cybele, whose priests castrated themselves in consecration to her. They sit self-imprisoned in the loom as if in the stocks, totally absorbed in the fabric of their rites. The goddess of their devotion is bodied forth by the almost ever-present lamp hanging over the loom—in his letters, Vincent writes with near ecstasy of finding one of those lamps. We may trace that lamp and its symbolic relatives all through Vincent's work, beginning with the cradle scenes. The lamp (in my mind, it resembles that "lanthorn" Starveling carries into the Duke's chamber as Moon) represents that light which announces to the baby that he will soon be fed and is, ever after, associated in his mind with all that is warm and comforting. It glows over the world of these trapped and shackled weavers just the way the moon glimmers above the world of changeling and Starveling, the enchanted world of *A Midsummer Night's Dream*.

Moonshine

In almost every overt way, the play gives victory to the male, hands the child to its father. The little changeling boy is awarded to Oberon—presumably to be trained and follow in his image. True, Theseus tempers Egeus's vengeful severity against his daughter, even helps her escape a full confrontation with the law by his "private schooling" of Demetrius. Yet he also makes it clear she cannot flout that law: had Demetrius not relented, she apparently would still have to choose between her father's will and chastity or death. Although neither the father's will nor Athenian law, then, are left as immutable or inescapable forces, both remain operant powers which must at least be successfully evaded. That evasion will probably require help from the Duke, a male ordering authority or father-surrogate.

Yet the male's victory, like so much else here, may well be

illusory. Theseus seems very much in control; he is, in fact, completely dependent on unrecognized forces. Oberon is awarded the child; his triumph never pervades the mind as does the recollection of the imperious Titania, supreme in her bower.

From our vantage in time, it is easy to see that Theseus's and Egeus's days are numbered; Bottom, who has lain beside darker powers, will soon oust both of them. It is astonishing for Shakespeare, so near this culture's first greatness, to render so clearly the drives which first produced that greatness, and now draw us toward decay. He could hardly have imagined that the machine and the bomb would make Theseus, if not obsolete, expendable. He could not imagine a people so luxurious and leisurely they could dispose of Theseus's strength, authority, aggressiveness, ability; that mediocrity *could* drive out superiority. He did see, only too clearly, the complex of emotions which, once this became possible, would make it inevitable. As a tree or animal contains, in the structures of its growth, the principles of its limits and death, cultures seem to hold, in the very form of their successes, the forces which eventually destroy them. To have attacked so successfully the centers of direct and conscious authority seems to have left us at the mercy of unconscious powers whose despotism may be much more far-reaching.

The play's most powerful image—Bottom in Titania's cradle—holds both the constructive and the decadent side of this complex. On the one hand, we usually think of creative work in strongly phallic terms, and without considerable phallic drive, the creative man can scarcely perform. On the other hand, it must also be noted that most of our truly creative men have had very strong mothers and have been deeply attached to them, even directly imitative of them. We have already noted that the experience of Titania's bower may be quintessential to the creative act; we have also noted what incredible energies we have tapped in the boy's desire to replace his father in that bower, or in the opposing desire to lose his own sexuality in becoming his mother. Yet those desires are only valuable so long as they are frustrated, unfulfilled—so long as the child embodies the unresolved struggle of his parents. Naturally, we all would see that conflict resolved; to resolve it through the evisceration of either power may be to eviscerate the child and perhaps, also, that civilization built partly upon the tensions of that struggle. Detente implies that both opposed powers *remain* powers; for all the dangers of antagonism, we would not lose the enormous energies it has given us.

If the father is successfully castrated or driven out, or if one's own sex is successfully obliterated, then all that tension—the source of energy—is dissipated. How quickly all that phallicism turns anal and passive, all that invention turns sluggish, static, aimless. We fight our way, with what vigor, to the throne, to Titania's bower. Once there, we just can't seem to think of anything to do.

How imperceptibly competition turns to betrayal. Given our special circumstances, the boy's attachment to his mother can be used to enlist him in the general weakening of the male—ultimately, himself. The baby's fear of abandonment has always given the mother immense powers over the imagination. This makes her less subject to our natural compulsion to betray whomever we love. But add to this the industrial revolution which makes the male seem dispensable, romantic love with all its castrative possibilities, individualistic philosophies with all their self-deception; it scarcely bodes well for the male. What can the too successful young man do? He has helped undermine the forces that might have sustained and directed him in this surplus of power. Now there is no one left to betray but himself.

Or he can betray the active ideals he used to reach the seat of power. Why not settle down to be babied, soothed and pampered, lied to, fed, and cajoled?

> Be kind and courteous to this gentleman:
> Hop in his walks and gambol in his eyes;
> Feed him with apricocks and dewberries,
> With purple grapes, green figs, and mulberries;
> The honey-bags steal from the humblebees,

> And for night-tapers crop their waxen thighs,
> And light them at the firey glow-worm's eyes.
> To have my love to bed and to arise; . . .
> Tie up my love's tongue, bring him silently.

Or, better still, feed him on endless beer and potato chips, plant his ever-widening buttocks before an inextinguishable television set, all channels of which play various episodes from an endless soap opera called "Bottom's Dream." We are not ruled by those who have an idea of what the state should do, nor even of what they want from it. We are ruled by any who can contact and control the dream life of the masses. It is not bread and circuses; it is ice cream and revolutions, equal pay and concentration camps. If I speak of Hitler and Stalin, it is only to avoid mentioning anyone closer home.

Nowhere is the mother's dominion over the unconscious world of the play more evident than in the omnipresence of the moon. No doubt Dr. Gui is right to see it as the symbol of the mother's breast, of that nourishment the child must have or die. Titania, her earthly avatar, echoes that breast in her very name; Hippolyta, so closely kin to her, must lack one teat, thus already suggesting the possibility of starvation. Who is it, after all, that carried the moon's lanthorn and thornbush?—none but Starveling. The moon, then, is indeed "governess of floods," the tides of liquid in our world. But the moon is also goddess of virginity and of marriage, of barrenness and of birth, of grudging coldness and of warm affection. She shines on the lovers as on the raging, hate-filled fairies. She is patroness of art, of illusion, of dreaming, of lunacy—of all those forces that control the wide-awake, sunlit, reasonable, paternalistic city of Theseus.

Dr. Gui reminds us that if Theseus's first speech is true, then throughout the whole time of the play there is no moon shining at all. The moon, then, the symbol of illusion, may itself be an illusion. Why talk so much about it, if one were sure that it was really there? Why weave so cunning a web as this play, so circular, so delicately filigreed, so glimmering with dew, if one were really able to catch the thing itself?

No one of the worlds of this play can be truly understood or located until we know its relation to the moon. And, after all, in so relativistic a play as this one, all worlds may very well revolve around the moon.

1974

The Hopwood lecture for 1975 was delivered by film critic Pauline Kael, who spoke without notes. After reading a transcription of her remarks, Miss Kael declined to have them published.

The Word on Film

John Simon

Let me begin by explaining my title, "The Word on Film." It is not to be taken as meaning the lowdown on cinema, but as an attempt to assess the role of dialogue in the movies, where it has been generally miscast. Often it has been given a stellar part in a film that could not support it; at other times it has been assigned a mere supporting role in films that could have greatly profited from more extensive use of its talent. The result appears to have been that people who ought to know better have viewed the spoken word in movies with suspicion, condescension, indeed hostility; while other people have been pleased to regard the film as an infant that has learned to talk in the natural process of growing older—what the child is saying, however, as long as it makes rudimentary sense, is of no great import. My own point is that the word in the cinema—contrary to the opinion of those who consider it ancillary or downright negligible, if not indeed subversive of the true powers of the art—is, in fact, of primary importance, and must be nurtured and developed rather than subordinated and downgraded. I insist that film as it has or will come to be is a fully audiovisual medium rather than a visual one like painting, sculpture, or silent movies; and that, as such, its voice has to be as good as its movements and vision.

If I now turn to an attack on my film criticism by Professor Edward Murray in his book, *Nine American Film Critics: A Study in Theory and Practice*, it is not because I consider either my criticism or Professor Murray that important. But it was his remarks that spurred me on to compose this essay, and Mr. Murray, as only begetter, is entitled to his place on the threshold of my discussion. He writes:

It is doubtful whether any responsible film critic or theorist would agree with Simon that the word is equal in significance to the image. Sound has greatly extended the reach of film as art; speech allows the filmmaker to reveal character in greater depth and to explore theme in more detail than was possible in the silent-film period. But to say that sound is now an integral part of film is not to argue that word and image are of equal importance. Film is still . . . a basically pictorial medium. If this were not so, then why does Simon himself say that "dialogue conveys only a fragment of what happens in a film"?

Here let me interject that fragments come in all sizes and degrees of importance: the Venus de Milo and the Victory of Samothrace are also fragments, but rather more important and satisfying to the Louvre than the missing parts would be to the institution that might acquire them.

But to return to Mr. Murray, who, as one would have guessed, proceeds to agree with those "opponents" of mine who have "charged" that I am "more of a literary critic than a film critic," and offers as evidence that I seldom or never cite film theorists, whereas literary references are "such a conspicuous feature" of my writing. I could answer that the literary figures I am apt to quote write immeasurably better than the film theorists Mr. Murray lists as unquoted by me: what is more relevant, though, is that I abhor most theorists and take a dim view of theory itself, which is why I implore you to take what follows also with an appropriate number of grains of salt.

The pejorative *literary,* as applied to a film or film critic of a supposedly literary bent, is one of the keys to our problem. This hostile use of *literary* antedates questions of film and has been hotly debated in the realm of the fine arts, which, according to most modernist painters, sculptors, and art critics, had to be freed of "literary" content. It is probably from this source that film inherited its antiliterary—and, by extension, antiverbal—bias, yet what may apply to the fine arts is irrelevant to film. For a painting, clearly, is not based on a script; films, however, even those preconized by the most antiliterary elements, are so based. The screenplay may be a very poor piece of literature—as it frequently is—nonetheless, a piece of literature it is. Hence *literary* seems like a highly self-destructive term of opprobrium.

But similar accusations are hurled from other embattled positions as well. One of them is the historical or, better, historicist position. This view is based on the fact that film was for a long time silent, which resulted in the early film theorists' concerning themselves with silent films. But even some of the later and still very influential ones, like Arnheim, Panofsky, and others, grew up in the silent-film era, formed their cinematic tastes from silent pictures, became sentimentally involved with them, and resented the coming of talkies almost as much as did silent-screen stars with squeaky voices. Thus the concept of film as a visual medium was formulated and accepted at a time when it could not have been any other kind of medium, any more than a carriage could have been horse-less before the invention of the automobile. So if Rudolf Arnheim speaks of the sound film as a "radical aesthetic im-poverishment," the real reason for this discontent may be nothing more than psychological: in his youth, films were si-lent, and both his older years and his attitude toward film in them may have been less glowing—hence the alleged im-poverishment.

There is, again, the so-called purist position. Thus Erwin Panofsky, the distinguished art scholar whose essay, "Style and Medium in the Motion Pictures," is still a much an-thologized and revered landmark of film theory, argued:

> A moving picture, even when it has learned to talk, remains a picture that moves and does not convert itself into a piece of writing that is enacted. Its substance remains a series of visual sequences held together by an uninterrupted flow of move-ment in space . . . and not a sustained study in human character and destiny transmitted by effective, let alone "beautiful" dic-tion.

And, Panofsky continues, "the sound, articulate or not, cannot express any more than is expressed, at the same time, by

visible movement; and in a good film it does not even attempt
to do so." This position is by no means a forgotten curiosity
dating back to the 1930s. Panofsky himself revised the essay
several times over the years without taking out these remarks;
the very same ideas—or should we properly call them
sentiments?—are still echoed in important quarters today.
Only quite recently I had an argument with Maximilian Schell
in which he insisted that not for nothing was the medium
called motion pictures, and that what we remembered, what
we carried with us from a film, was certain images, not bits of
dialogue. As he kept reiterating his point, I could not help
thinking, "Play it again, Sam!"—the line that, with the song
that goes with it, is what I remember most vividly from
Casablanca—even if it does not occur quite like that in the
film.

To make a fetish out of the term *motion* or *moving picture*
strikes me as an oversimplification. It is a term that describes
the type of pictures a kind of camera could take as opposed to
those of an earlier type of camera; it does not pretend to define
or limit the uses to which film can be put. Even if you are
stupid, arrogant, and untalented enough to mount your camera on a tripod in front of the Empire State Building and keep
shooting for several hours, the result is a motion picture,
though the building does not make the slightest attempt to
compensate for the stationary camera by dancing a jig. More to
the point, Susan Sontag, in her essay, "Theatre and Film," has
answered Panofsky with a question, a very pertinent question:
"What then of the films of Bresson and Godard, with their
allusive, thoughtful texts and their characteristic refusal to be
primarily a visual experience? How could one explain the extraordinary rightness of Ozu's relatively immobilized camera?"

What, we must ask ourselves, are the purists bemoaning?
The great director, René Clair, wrote in 1950 that "speech and
sound, adding the element of reality to the film presentation,
have made the viewer lose the feeling of dream that the sight
of the silent shadows created in him." The theme of regret at
the coming of sound runs through Clair's entire book, *Cinema
Yesterday and Today*, and, because this collection of texts

spans more than half a century, through Clair's entire creative life. It is evident that the director of such masterpieces as *Le Million* and *A Nous la Liberté*, which might have worked as well without their minimal verbal content, was concerned with the claim of the dream on us, with making life, or at least that part of it that could be captured between the beginning and end of one of his films, as idiosyncratic and whimsical as a dream. Harsh realities are not totally absent from Clair's work, but the aim is to transform them into something lyrical and palliative like a happy reverie. Not necessarily a bad aim, but not one to which all cinema can or should subscribe.

If what lurks behind Clair's championing of wordless cinema is the dream, what hides behind Panofsky's position is something slightly different and comes out in praise for "early melodramas [that] had a highly gratifying and soothing quality in that events took shape, without the complications of individual psychology, according to a pure Aristotelian logic so badly missed in real life." And when he goes on to praise various types of genre films, Panofsky makes clear to me that he speaks for those intellectuals, often but not always associated with the academy, for whom the movies are a mode of escape from intellect, from the rigorous forms of daily mental discipline—an escape abundantly provided by melodramas, farces, Westerns, thrillers, and the rest. To invoke Aristotelian logic, or any other prestigious or modish nomenclature, is only a way of legitimizing, of making respectable, that "soothing and gratifying quality" associated with movies as a flight from "the complications of individual psychology."

It is well to consider here that one's sociopolitical and philosophical views may also cause one to opt for a cinema in which words are subordinate. Thus Panofsky writes, "It is the movies, and only the movies, that do justice to that materialistic interpretation of the universe which, whether we like it or not, pervades contemporary civilization." How sharply this tone of resignation to materialism contrasts with that of the Italian essayist and critic, Nicola Chiaromonte, who wrote in a 1965 essay entitled "Theater in Utopia," from an idealist-elitist point of view, "The tendency to underestimate inner life and moral phenomena is one of the salient characteristics of modern barbarity, as well as one of the most obvious effects of the cinema on the psychology of the masses." The problem with the cinematic image, for Chiaromonte, is that "it cannot render thought, consciousness, or ideas, for the simple reason that the camera cannot catch these modes of reality, but, rather, their material and external aspects."

The interesting thing to note here is that both the reluctant advocate of materialism and its aristocratic opponent perceive the cinema as essentially visual, but draw from its visualness different conclusions. This agreement within opposition becomes even more arresting when we consider the following pair of statements. First, Chiaromonte again, denying the validity of the word on film:

> What is certain is that the spoken word cannot be replaced. The recorded word, the word of the cinema, the word of radio, the word of television not only lack a living presence, but are not real words; they are something else, something entirely different. They are artificial words, part of an artificial language valid for everybody and for nobody at the same time. The word accompanied by a living presence, on the other hand, is not only a clear word, which reaches us free of mechanical diaphragms; it is also, above all, an authentic word, addressed to us in particular and in the concrete, not in the general and the abstract. It is addressed not only to our ear but to our spirit, to our mind, to our consciousness, and it is therefore the only word capable of conveying a fullness of meaning.

By now, we see, Chiaromonte has conceded a verbal facility to the film, but only to deny its vitality and trenchancy vis-à-vis the theater. This strikes me as only a more sophisticated version of the old theater person's argument against the movies—that what people want to see is flesh and blood, not celluloid—a theory that gets its conclusive refutation by the simple comparison of box office takes at cinemas and so-called legitimate theaters.

While Chiaromonte chastises the film for trying to talk yet being inherently unable to do it well, René Clair exults in the film's ability to talk superlatively without recourse to words: "I believe," he wrote in 1923,

> that the film is only at the beginning of its conquest of the inner world. The succession of images, infinitely supple, now as precise as a phrase in literature and now as vague as a phrase in music, will make possible the expression of the most complex feelings and the remotest sensations. Will not the film be able to suggest to the general public more easily than the word the things they cannot understand or accept in the theories of Freud or the novels of Proust?

As opposed to film as a barbarous demotic art form that, even with words, cannot speak profoundly, we encounter here film as a blessedly democratic genre speaking with simple, wordless directness to the general public. Since it can be argued that children, aborigines, and the mentally retarded can deal with pictures more easily than with words, those who want film to be a mass art naturally espouse its pictorial and kinetic, rather than verbal and intellectual, aspects.

Yet in all this I smell that to me rather malodrous creature, the inveterate theoretician. For whereas it is indisputable that simple images are easier than complex words, and probable that simple images are easier than simple words, who says that filmmakers can, or want to, deal only with simple images? The images in a film like *Persona* are as complex, allusive, and elusive, as arduous to explicate as the words in any modern novel or poem, let alone movie. The general public would much sooner embrace the words in most movies, no matter how thick and fast they might come off the soundtrack, than the often arcane or abstruse imagery of Bergman's film. Furthermore, there are poetically pregnant utterances in certain films that may function satisfactorily on the lower level of general comprehension, and sublimely on the higher one of minds equipped to deal with symbol, metaphor, double entendre, irony, and the like. And for all that the great age of American film comedy may have been a nonverbal one, it would be precarious to argue that the verbal comedy of Fields, the Marx brothers, and the rest was very far behind.

But there is yet another source of hostility to words on film that is the exact opposite of that of the weary intellectual eager to get away from his daily discursiveness. I refer to the position of the anti- or nonintellectual, the person who is defeated by words, fears and abominates them, and looks to the movies as an alternative to verbalization. I do not wish to put the blame for the new antiverbalism on the movies alone; it is a tremendous symptom of the general falling off of our culture on levels as diverse as language study in the universities and the ability of people, students or others, to express themselves in speech or writing, indeed, to comprehend what they read. If one compares the lyrics of popular songs of the twenties, thirties, and forties with those of the fifties and beyond—or, roughly speaking, the pre- and postrock lyrics—one will experience fully the recession of the word. Similarly in the avant-garde theater, the word has faded into the background; more revealingly perhaps, the comparison of boulevard plays by Behrman and Barry with those of Neil Simon and his ilk epitomizes the waning of verbal proficiency.

It would be an oversimplification to trace this general deverbalization to a single cause, cultural, social, economic, or political. But its effects are felt across the board; in the cinema, which doubtless is one of the many culprits, no less than elsewhere. And, of course, there is a vicious circle: if the movies contribute to the hebetude of those who absorb them, they, in turn, will become stultifying filmmakers in an ever-worsening progression. And with the coming into existence and growing popularity of underground cinema with its very limited budgets, the silent film with perhaps a little pop music, as it were, taped onto it has once again come into favor.

Moreover, the overwhelming preponderance of abstract art, as well as certain trends in "serious" music, deemphasizing representational or "human" elements, have spilled over into film to the further detriment of the word—at least as coherent dialogue. In this respect it is worth noting that even a big-budget, more or less establishment filmmaker like Robert Altman has tended to conceive of dialogue as a kind of verbal wallpaper of which one is supposed to be only generally or subliminally aware, without actually deciphering more than a modest fraction of it. It seems to me that abstract art of almost all kinds partakes of anti-intellectualism or game playing, whether practiced by disenchanted intellectuals or enchanting ignoramuses, and so we are back to the question of the debasement of cinematic dialogue as part of the overarching disrepute and desuetude of the Word. When Alexandre Astruc coined his famous definition of a personal cinema as the product of a *caméra-stylo*, a camera functioning as a fountain pen, he prophesied even more than he described: what the pen used to be in the hands of occasional illiterates, the camera, often literally handheld, has become in hordes of illiterate hands—a gobbledygook of images with or without words.

It is time, however, to return to Edward Murray's original charge, that according to me the word on film is equal in significance to the image. He bases his accusation on the following passage from my book *Ingmar Bergman Directs:*

> I take film to be a totally visual and totally aural medium—in this ambidextrousness lies its glory—and I consider utterly mistaken and nostalgic the sentimentality of those exalters of time past who would put the silent film above the sound, or in any other way minimize the importance of the ear in the enjoyment of film. Although I would not slight the functions of the other senses, I do think vision and audition are the ones by which we communicate best and the most. To the extent that film can make untrammeled use of both those avenues of communication, it can absorb us more masterfully and variously (though not, therefore, more importantly) than any other art, including the theater, whose visual discourse is somewhat more limited. Now, though a filmmaker who masters the visual possibilities of cinema is to be admired, the true lord of the medium is he who controls equally sight and sound, whose word is as good as his image, and, above all, who can manipulate the two in such a way that they reinforce each other and perform in unison or harmony, contrast or counterpoint, at the filmmaker's beck.

All right, then, I plead guilty: I did and do say that image and sound are equally important to the film. But to evaluate this statement, we must first try to reach a fuller understanding of what is meant by the words *equally important*. Let me say it right out: I am not a statistician, and I cannot reduce film to 50 percent images and 50 percent sounds, which latter would then have to be further subdivided into words and other kinds of sound. Nor am I a horse trader, with the horrible gift of haggling attributed to that profession; so, if someone were to say, "How about images 60 percent, and words 40 percent?" I might go along with him, although I could not settle for less. And even then two questions would immediately present themselves. First, how do you arrive at those figures? And, secondly, can you determine actual importance by any such mathematical means?

Let me illustrate with a hypothetical example. Suppose we had a film in which an adolescent girl obediently and more or less mutely performed everything her father demanded, odious or onerous as some of the tasks were. Suppose, furthermore, that her face never betrayed any hostile feelings. This goes on for perhaps thirty minutes; then, quite unexpectedly, the girl confronts her father and says, "I hate you!" Only she does not say that exactly; she says it in a few more highly original words, well chosen but not beyond the vocabulary of an adolescent, and not out of proportion to what she has been subjected. She says it forthrightly and compellingly. The words would take some thirty seconds of painfully sobering screen time. How would one reckon the half hour of dismal experiences *shown* versus the thirty seconds of cathartic outburst *spoken?* Surely you cannot say that thirty seconds goes into thirty minutes sixty times, and that our stretch of film is therefore sixty parts visuals to one part words. Yet no more could you say that the actions of the thirty minutes merely lead up to that climactic ejaculation, merely set it up, and are thus quite unimportant compared to it.

Someone shrewd or perverse enough might, of course, claim that if the filmmaker were truly gifted, he would not need to make the girl say anything; he could suggest it more powerfully through certain looks and gestures. But is this true? In the notes to Jean-Paul Sartre's lecture, "Theater and

Cinema" (for which, as with Aristotle, only the notes are available), we read: "Speech is the clearest gesture; that is, the clearest representation of the act is speech." I am not quite sure what Sartre meant by this, but I take it to mean that our fictitious bit of film can express through words just how long, to what degree, and against what inner and outer pressures the girl's hatred for her father has been welling up, and what she now proposes to do about it, or what compensation, if any, she is willing to settle for. Her words can then be assessed in the light of the events that precede and follow them, but we need this "clearest gesture" or "clearest representation" to understand fully and evaluate what the actions permitted us only to sense and sympathize with. Then, too, the girl may do nothing about it; everything may go on as before, even though the relationship may be utterly changed after the full awareness that torrent of words swept out into the open. To quote that sensible book by Stephenson and Debrix, *The Cinema as Art*, it is a case of "visuals and sound . . . reinforc[ing] one another. The combination can be more powerful than the sum of the two would be."

If I say then that I would not want my supposititious film to have lacked either the incidents preceding the outburst or the outburst itself, what can I honestly conclude from that? Only that images and words are, for all practical purposes, equally important. And we must bear in mind that if the happenings before the verbal eruption were badly shown, the words, however excellent, could not redeem half an hour of ineffectual film. Likewise, if the words were banal, derivative, verbose, or out of character, the most graphic or suggestive action would be marred by them. Still, the captious defender of visuals *über alles* might contend that if the girl had just uttered a simple and searing "I hate you!" accompanied by good acting, camera work, background music, and what have you, those plain, unliterary words would suffice to yield first-class filmmaking. Not so, I say. Unless the girl is a halfwit or an utter simpleton—which could also be quite moving, but does not happen to be the case in my scenario, or, for that matter, in most scenarios—we are going to judge her sensibility, her

sensitivity and humanity, by her ability to express herself in
words that have freshness, flavor, poetry in them; whether we
like it or not, a hero or heroine has to appeal to us physically
and verbally, which is to say erotically and intellectually, thus
affirming the simultaneous importance of the seen and the
heard.

Here let me explain my view of the place of film in the
context of the performing arts. I perceive these arts as a scale
extending from poetry (which, we tend to forget, was meant to
be recited), the most verbal and least kinetic, all the way to the
dance, the most kinetic and least verbal. Bunched together at
the center between these extremes are two middle arts: theater, which is somewhat nearer to poetry; and cinema, which is
closer to dance. I mean by this that the more obvious emphasis
in theater is on words, because the stage restricts the possibilities of movement and action; and that the more immediate emphasis in films is on such movement and action,
because the camera can go everywhere, move in every conceivable way—and what it cannot do, the film lab can. Nevertheless, I wish to underline my contention that these different
stresses, however significant, are only external differences between theater and film, determining what type of situation or
story is best suited to each genre, but not meaning that the
theater can dispense with action or that the film can afford to
be cavalier about dialogue. Let the theater forget to put actions on stage, and it becomes a kind of poetry recital, a nice
enough thing in itself, but not theater; let the film forget about
the expressive power of words, and it becomes a kind of pan-
tomime or dance, with much of the dancing done by the camera and editing. That, too, may be nice to watch, but it does
not live up to the highest potential of film.

To put it another way, we are proceeding along a scale of
arts where, at one end, the flesh has become totally word,
while at the other, the word has become totally flesh; that is,
poetry and dance. But the peculiar greatness of theater and
film lies in the fact that they are jugglers with both these
techniques or strategies—that they can make deed and word,
action and comment, image and idea flow into each other,

merge and separate again, proceed parallelly or alternatingly, and reflect on each other in a variety of ways, from overlapping to counterpoint. Both have a chance at what Wagner wanted opera to be: a *gesamtkunstwerk* or total work of art, subsuming all the other arts. Film, though, has the best chance of all three to be all-encompassing, but only if it remembers the importance of words and allows them their due.

In this context, it is useful to quote Orson Welles's remarks to Francis Koval in a 1950 interview for *Sight and Sound.*

> You all seem to start from the article of faith that a silent picture is necessarily better than a sound one. . . . What I mean to say is that you always overstress the value of images. You judge films by their visual impact instead of looking for content. This is a great disservice to cinema. It is like judging a novel only by the quality of its prose. I was guilty of the same sin when I first started writing about the cinema. It was the experience of filmmaking that changed my outlook.

Koval, who admits to being startled by such opinions from the man who made *Citizen Kane,* a film of extraordinary visual impact, reports these further Wellesian comments:

> Take a picture that has become a classic, and deservedly so: *La Femme du boulanger.* What have you got there? Bad photography, inadequate cutting and a lot of happenings which are told instead of shown. But there is a story and an actor—both superb—which makes it a perfect movie. The story is not even particularly "cinema." I think I could make a play out of it in one evening, if I wanted to.

And Welles concludes, "It is really more a combination of human factors and basic ideas that makes a subject worth putting on the screen."

While one need not agree with every syllable of this—very probably Welles relished being a counterirritant to the critical consensus—there is much common sense in these observations, and I only wish their maker had borne them in mind when he went to work on some of his subsequent films. It is certainly instructive to note how many of the world's influential, and often great, filmmakers were theater people before, and frequently even after, they came to the movies: Sergei Eisenstein in Russia; Welles and Kazan in the United States; Sir Carol Reed in England; Abel Gance, Marcel Pagnol, and Jean Cocteau in France; Pabst and Murnau in Germany; Sjöström, Stiller, Sjöberg, and Ingmar Bergman in Sweden; Luchino Visconti and Lina Wertmüller in Italy—to name only the most salient. So it might be wise to bear this in mind before writing essays on the differences between theater and cinema, real though some of them may be. Let me add a further name to my list: that of a man who, though he did not come to the movies from the theater, was always a devotee of it, later directed stage productions, wrote plays, used great stage actors in his films, and indeed made the theater, or theatricality, the main theme of a number of his pictures. You will have guessed that I refer to Jean Renoir.

What theater and film have in common is the bisensory approach: reaching us neither just through the eye, like painting or architecture, nor just through the ear, like music or, to a large extent, poetry, but through both senses. To be sure, this presents certain risks. Nothing is more loathsome about that less than prepossessing medium, television, than certain commercials in which a voice declaims in stentorian tones the very same message that is written out on the screen, as if the sponsors were terrified of missing out on the deaf and blind segments of the audience. This redundancy is the archetypal trap into which the sound film can fall: making what is heard an unnecessary duplication of what is seen. Clearly it is tautological to have a man fumbling for a keyhole in the dark declare how hard it is to find a keyhole in the dark—unless the point is that he is a crashing bore—yet much filmmaking is just that dedicated to supererogation. Or, perhaps, just that boring. But dialogue can achieve wonders if the man complains in a well-lighted hall: we realize with a pang that he is going blind. Or the man may complain about the difficulty of finding the keyhole even as his key slips almost instantaneously into the lock, and we realize with amusement that he is a petty malcontent. Or he may start complaining before he has even reached the door, in which case we recognize him in a flash as an inveterate pessimist, always assuming the worst. These, then, are a few of the ways in which words and visuals become more powerful in combination than either of them could be alone.

Yet the interplay between visual and verbal elements need not always be as trickily out of sync as that. Let me cite some other examples of interaction between sight and sound from recent movies, not even particularly great ones. In Dino Risi's *Profumo di donna* (rather badly Englished as *Scent of a Woman*), there is the following sequence. The blinded ex-officer hero who abominates the pity people show for his infirmity sits on a restaurant terrace and awaits the return of his seeing-eye boy, whom he sent off to find him a suitable prostitute. While the boy is away looking, our hero pretends to be reading the newspapers. The boy finally settles on a woman in a run-down café; as the prostitute rises to go home and wait for her client, a shabby old man in the café looks up from his paper and jovially exclaims, *"Buon lavoro!"*—good work! Risi now cuts to the hero on the terrace reading a socialist-labor publication— we can make out the banner: *IL LAVORO*. We have here a complex audiovisual pun: the socialist-labor orientation of the paper is contrasted with the dubious, capitalist-oriented labor of the whore. Nevertheless, even a down-at-heel old-timer, both biologically and economically out of the running, smilingly approves her kind of work, gives it his vicariously pleased benediction. Meanwhile the socialist workers' notions are wasted on the blind aristocrat who, even if he could read them, could not appreciate them. What the film seems to be saying here is that one person's work is another's pleasure; that grave notions of the nature and rights of labor may fall on blind eyes not only among sightless aristocrats but also among sighted proletarians.

Now, it may be pointed out in opposition that *"Buon lavoro!"* is not great dialogue (true), and that its place could have been taken just as well by an intertitle (false). An intertitle would have been a visual element, no different from the name

of the newspaper in the hero's hand. But it is precisely by
going from a spoken and heard *lavoro* to a printed and seen
(or, in the hero's case, unseen) *lavoro* that we are tipped off
about the difference between kinds of labor, and all the sad,
funny, of simply matter-of-fact implications of that difference.
The old man's comment could, of course, have been omitted
altogether, but only to the appreciable impoverishment of the
film.

Let us advert now to another example of a quite dissimilar
nature: two consecutive scenes from *Salut, l'Artiste!*, a film by
Yves Robert. The hero, played by Marcello Mastroianni, is an
Italian bit player eking out a humdrum existence in French
theater, movies, television, commercials, nightclubs, and still
more peripheral regions of show business. Besides troubles
with his finances and children, he has perennial problems with
women: his ex-wife, his mistress, and a passing parade of all
the others he lusts for. In one of this fine but by no means
extraordinary film's loveliest scenes, Mastroianni and his mistress, played by the incomparable Françoise Fabian, are walking along the sandy seaside of Cabourg. It was supposed to
have been a weekend of reconciliation and rekindling of a love
our hero has been foolishly jeopardizing. The sky, however, is
overcast; the beach, cold, gray, deserted. The man tries to
blame his accumulated failures on the Italian accent that
makes him a sempiternal stranger in France, but his companion points out that he would be a stranger anywhere, even in
Rome. Certain actors are said to have a presence, but what he
has, fundamentally, is an absence: *"Quelle absence tu as!"* she
tells him. *"Tu n'es personne pour personne!"* ("What absence
you have! You are nobody for nobody!" Ungrammatical, but
wonderfully right.) The hero's anguished face and oversolici-
tous tone convey both his awareness that he is prevaricating
and his histrionic inadequacy; the woman's tormented gaze
and her leaning toward him suggest how much she still loves
the man she must leave. Sight—the cheerless surroundings,
moody camera angles, nervous cutting—and sound—the exchange of words between a sadly mendacious lover and still
more sadly truthful mistress—combine into a sovereign vision

of despair. But the clinching effect is achieved by the next shot, in which the disaffected lovers are seen brunching in a deserted hotel dining room. Outside, the beach is as drained of color as before. In the foreground, at an open glass-paneled door, a middle-aged waitress, with her back to the camera, is gazing out at the sea. Farther back, at an ideal lovers' table by the plate-glass window, sit our hero and heroine. They, too, look bleached out; neither of them speaks nor stirs. The only movement is that of the drapes straining in the breeze at the open door. The waitress and the drapes seem full of yearning; the lovers, empty. It is a devastating image that scores largely through its silence after all those heated or weary or remonstrating words of the preceding scene. This is the reverse of Yeats's "Speech after long silence"—silence after long speech—and it took a speaking cinema to make silence become eloquent in the movies.

In the introduction to his Hitchcock book, François Truffaut enunciated what he calls "the cardinal rule of the cinema: Whatever is *said* instead of being *shown* is lost upon the viewer." This and similar notions are based on the assumption that word and image are two separate entities, a concept at least as fallacious in my opinion as the debunked old notion that form and content are discrete aspects of a work of art. I think it is mandatory for us to comprehend that sight and sound, image and word, function as two eyes do in our head, giving us the kind of depth perception we would not have with a single Cyclops eye. Nevertheless, Truffaut's statement oversimplifies even the concept of "shown." Take the nurse's account of a summertime orgy on the beach from Bergman's *Persona;* Pauline Kael has rightly recognized that it is "one of the rare, truly erotic sequences on film." This is a case of no flashbacks intruding on pure narration: nothing is shown except the excitement of the nurse as she tells the story, and the slightly insidious savoring of it by the listening actress. There is a strange, unstated erotic bond between the two women held together by the shared narrative. You do indeed see something on screen, only it is not an enactment of what the words describe. The orgy becomes real enough through the aptly written and delivered words, but what is *shown* is the effect of the words on these two women in their resembling nightgowns: a naive nurse spilling her secrets to her uncannily silent patient who takes it all in like a cat—a cat not so much lapping up milk as swallowing a canary. We are made to perceive subtle, indirect connections between the narrative and the relationship of the two women.

It should be obvious, though it isn't to many people, that the word, by being put on screen, becomes something more than, or at any rate different from, a word on paper, or even a word on the stage. The printed word may be highly evocative, but its evocativeness functions solely in terms of what the reader brings to it. The word in the theater is accompanied by some gestures and trappings, but these gestures are limited by the distance between the actor and the audience, just as the trappings are modest compared to what the cinema can surround the speakers with. On screen, the word performs, as it were, in concert with faces in closeup that can be exceedingly, even unbearably, near to the viewer; or with backgrounds that can be an actual jungle full of assorted perils; or with a convincing piece of trick photography that can make everything from deeply hidden private fantasies to the farthest reaches of outer space come palpitantly alive. The word gains unprecedented richness from its context, but it pays back the debt by interpreting the images with poetic or psychological, historical or philosophic insights such as no image in painting or still photography can benefit from.

In a recent book by Professor Frank D. McConnell of Northwestern University, *The Spoken Seen: Film and the Romantic Imagination*, we find among much that is pretentious, windy, even absurd, some perfectly sensible descriptions of the profound and necessary interaction of image and word on film. "No other art," McConnell writes, "is able to register with quite the same immediacy the solidity and the clutter of the human universe, and at the same time the awful fragility of the words we speak to each other amid that clutter." Except for the solecism "each other" where "one another" is meant, this is a very good evocation of one aspect of the relation of words to their on-screen ambience. But the obverse is equally true and important: the ability of the right words to triumph over the surrounding clutter and give meaning to the universe. In film's greatest moments, however, both ends are achieved simultaneously: the awareness of our verbal, indeed existential, fragility; and the revelation of the strength that comes from understanding and acceptance.

Take the final words of *The Seven Samurai,* one of the masterpieces of Akira Kurosawa and world cinema. Of the seven samurai defending the farmers, only three have survived. Standing on a bridge and looking down at the peasants blithely back at work in their rice paddies, Kambei, the wise leader of the samurai, remarks, "We've lost again." Shichoriji, the jolly extrovert, looks puzzled. Kambei explains: "Those farmers are the winners. Not we." As he turns and looks up, the camera tilts with his gaze up the burial hill and comes to rest on the four mounds with the dead men's swords stuck into them. I quote from the screenplay: "The samurai theme comes in over the planting music, as the wind blows up the dust among the mounds." Kambei's head movements are symbolic: when he says that *we,* i.e., the aristocratic samurai, have lost again, he looks literally and figuratively down at the farmers. When he explains that it is they who have won—in the sense that they have survived, that their kind will always survive—he turns to the four warrior graves and looks up at them. The glorious fighters can be looked up to even in death. Yet all the samurai, dead or alive, are losers: the heroic age yields to the age of the common man. Though the spirit of those noble dead is more exalted than the very flesh of these living nonentities, it is for the nonentities that the heroes gave their lives. Even if the last words proclaim the defeat and passage of grandeur from the earth, the samurai's music—their spirit, their memory—supersedes that of the peasants. It is a deeply ambivalent ending across which, significantly, the wind blows up dust. The wind, the cosmos, continues indifferent to peasant and samurai, survivor and casualty, human life and death. Is the end all bleakness then, or is there hope in that wind stirring among the graves? Remember Paul Valéry's *Le Cimetière marin:* "*Le vent se lève!... Il faut tenter de vivre!*"

This ambivalence, or ambiguity, created by the interplay of word and image can occur just as easily in a great comic film. Consider the ending of Fellini's *The White Sheik*. The newlyweds, Ivan and Wanda, have become reconciled and are about to be rushed off with a large group of tourists to a quick audience with the pope. Wanda assures Ivan that her dalliance with her dream hero, the White Sheik, was platonic; she has remained "pure and innocent." Ivan is vastly relieved, and both young simpletons cry for joy. Through her sobs, Wanda tells Ivan: "Now... *you* are my White Sheik." All would be well if Ivan did not catch his bride's face lighting up as she looks in another direction. But Ivan's worry is allayed when he sees what Wanda is looking at: the statue of an angel atop the colonnade. As the pair are marched off on the double, there is a closing long shot of the piazza in front of St. Peter's, the procession climbing up the steps to the papal audience, and the statue of the angel. What, then, do Wanda's last words mean: "Now ... *you* are my White Sheik"? Has Wanda given up her romantic fantasies to accept her funny-looking husband as her hero? Then why, as she says them, does she look up beatifically at another creature of fantasy? Perhaps Wanda's schoolgirl romanticism is incurable—even the fact that she clings to the term "White Shiek" may substantiate this. But perhaps the angel is only a symbol of Wanda's childlike innocence; and calling a homely husband "White Sheik," the sincerest tribute of love.

Suggestive ambiguity, however, is only one of many ways in which the word, the literate word, makes its contribution to the cinema. Let us recall that desideratum on which Alexandre Astruc put his finger in the already mentioned "Caméra-Stylo" essay: "The fundamental problem of the cinema is how to express thought." And so I ask you to consider that in becoming talkies, the movies did not merely learn how to speak, they also began to learn how to think. No doubt, certain simple ideas could be expressed through images alone, but let us not fool ourselves into believing that the thought content of, for example, *Intolerance* or *The Battleship Potemkin* even approaches that of, say, *The Rules of the Game*, *The Children of Paradise*, *L'Avventura*, or *Winter Light*. Still, the spoken language of the cinema need not be of a highly intellectual or belletristic sort; what is certain, though, is that it is the best means of expressing thought. Words are, in fact, the appropriate accompaniment for one of the finest and most important things the film has to offer: the closeup. A closeup, to be sure, can be accompanied by mere silence, or just background music, or certain significant sounds, and still be enormously effective. But the most natural, expressive, and profound coupling available to film is the expressions of the human face seen in infinitesimal detail combined with what that face, or head, is saying. Or, if the lips are not moving as we hear the words, what that head is thinking. Yet even before cinematic words acquire meaning, they are a human voice, and, as Jean Renoir asked in *My Life and My Films*, "Is not the human voice the best means of conveying the personality of a human being?" It is a two-way street: not only does the voice combined with what it is saying comment on the face, but also, as Béla Balázs long ago reminded us in his *Theory of the Film*, "the mute play of the features" can make us realize in the middle of a character's discourse "the difference between this [mute] soliloquy and the audible conversation."

It is a well-known fact that most silent-screen acting was exaggerated: excessive gesturing and mugging, indeed posturing, in an attempt to compensate for the missing words. This became particularly offensive in the closeup, when delicate, subtle, or nascent and inchoate feelings had to be conveyed by overexplicitness. Such overstatement obviously worked best in farce, melodrama, and spectacle, and that may well be why these genres came to dominate the silent screen. Even the best attempts to get beyond these genres—for example, Murnau's *Sunrise*—were doomed to look like farce and sentimental melodrama, partly because the acting style dictated the basic characterizations of the actors, and partly because silent scriptwriters had to deal in broad, sweeping strokes and simple, elemental themes. It is highly probable that what makes film suspect in certain quarters to this day, what makes even certain film reviewers wonder whether it is really an art, has to do with its having begun as a medium condemned to primitivism by its lack of sound. Today's prejudice was yesterday a plausible judgment.

Still, most contemporary advocates of pure cinema would not go so far as to wish to throw out sound altogether. Even a film like Antonioni's lamentable *The Passenger*, whose climactic sequences have either no dialogue or the barest minimum, contains other scenes full of verbiage, highflown and ludicrous as it may be. So I wonder what measures they have in mind when they insist on the lesser importance of dialogue: how would they want to delimit its scope and keep it in its subservient role? The two manifest ways in which you can keep dialogue down are to make it sparse or to make it worse. By worse, as I see it, they would mean less literary, less noticeable. This is plainly correct in some cases. In Stanley Kubrick's *2001*, where one of the points is the contrast between mankind's tremendously expanded horizons and its obsolete, bureaucratic and constricting vocabulary, the flattening out of language is a legitimate—though still, I insist, literary—device. Again, a film about very simple folk or taciturn professional soldiers rightly eschews Jamesian or Wildean dialogue. But even films about tight-lipped private eyes, for instance, profit appreciably when the tight-lipped dialogue comes out of Raymond Chandler or Dashiell Hammett.

I must content myself here with one example of the difference the quality of language can make when all other elements are as nearly as possible alike. There is a moment in Ingmar Bergman's latest film, *Face to Face*, when the young woman psychiatrist, played by Liv Ullmann, who has been hospitalized after an unsuccessful suicide attempt, exclaims from her bed to her solicitous doctor friend and quasi-lover, played by Erland Josephson: "Do you think I'm crippled for the rest of my life? Do you think we're a vast army of emotionally crippled wretches wandering about calling to one another with words we don't understand and which only make us even more afraid?" The switch from the first person singular to the first person plural in this *de profundis* constitutes the simplest way of showing the uncertain boundaries between personal failure and universal collapse. In Bergman's preceding film, *Scenes from a Marriage*, the closing sequence has Ullmann and Josephson married and in bed together. Only they are no longer married to each other, as they once were, but to new partners; and even this bed they share as sporadic lovers belongs to some distant acquaintance. A nightmare has awakened Marianne in the middle of the night and leads to an intimate conversation with her ex-husband: "Johan!—Yes, my dear.—Do you think we're living in utter confusion?—You and I?—No, the whole lot of us." The conversation gropes along in the dark for a while, then Marianne asks again: "Johan . . . —Yes?—Have we missed something important?— All of us?—You and I." The scene is incomparably more affecting than its counterpart in *Face to Face*, yet the device used in the dialogue is a distinctly literary one: incremental repetition, derived from poetry and consisting of a refrain that is not repeated verbatim, but with some small yet significant variation. Here the refrain is reversed: a universal *we* is first mistaken for a personal one; then, with almost identical diction, a private *we* is mistaken for a generalization. The effect—call it literary or cinematic—is a powerful rapprochement of the problems of the principal characters with those of people everywhere.

And what about the question of quantity? Is dialogue, in the interest of good filmmaking, to be used only sparingly? The dialogue in some of the world's great films is not only highly literate but also profuse. The just quoted *Scenes from a Marriage* is a case in point; mind you, the English subtitles, copious as they are, represent extensive and not always judicious pruning of the Swedish. But almost all of Bergman's films have at least long sequences brimful of words; take only the magnificent scene in *Winter Light* where Ingrid Thulin speaks the letter Gunnar Björnstrand is reading. The camera is stationary, Thulin barely moves her face, and there is only one cutaway from the relentless closeup. But there are torrents of words. Yet, for me, this is one of the most moving scenes in cinema, closely followed by other Bergmanian monologues delivered by his marvelous actresses.

And what of the burstingly verbal screenplays of Jacques Prévert (notably that for *The Children of Paradise*), rightly adduced by Orson Welles, in the already quoted interview, as pinnacles of French filmmaking; or of the other extremely "talky" French films, like those of Pagnol, Duvivier, and many others? Consider a film like *Monsieur Vincent*, the only successful filmed hagiography, which owes so much more to Jean Anouilh's prodigally articulate scenario than to Maurice Cloche's decent but conventional direction. In eastern Europe especially, words often seem to tumble off the screen in heaps; I mention only three emblematic directors: the Hungarian István Szabó, the Pole Andrzej Wajda, the Czechoslovak Hynek Bočan. The American screwball comedies of the thirties, one of Hollywood's most satisfying achievements, depended as much on the nonstop verbal wit of their writers as on the charm of their actors. What, for instance, do we remember of *The Philadelphia Story?* Certainly not the mise-en-scène, but Hepburn and Grant and the bright rataplan of their crackling exchanges. Yet good, abundant dialogue works not only in comedy; though atmosphere, acting, and direction were all exquisite in David Lean's *Brief Encounter*, it is the eminently verbal screenplay of Noel Coward that kept the sentimental story on its consistently dignified level.

But rather than multiply examples let me close with one last remark from Ingmar Bergman to the editors of *Chaplin:* "Whatever is visible or audible—image and sound—that's what affects me most." And that, I think, when combined artfully by a master filmmaker, is also what affects us most.

1976

The State of the Novel: Dying Art or New Science?

Walker Percy

The novel is regularly said to be dying—and now it is said with perhaps more justification than at any other time. In fact it is difficult now even to speak of the novel as a generic art form. If one uses as a criterion the familiar features of the traditional novel—plot, scene, characterization, action, denouement, development of character, and so on—it is hard to find a worthy example of the ancient art. Anything can and does pass for a novel now. A novel is what you call something that won't sell if you call it poems or short stories. Autobiography is novel. History is novel. Sociology is novel. Tirade is novel. I am not complaining. For the undeniable fact is that nonnovels which pass as novels now are usually better than novels which look like novels. *Love Story* and *Oliver's Story,* which look like novels—have characters, good people, bad people, love, action, and so forth—are not very good. In fact the less said about them, the better. Celine's novel, *Castle to Castle,* which has no nice people at all and resembles a novel less than it does a cobra striking repeatedly, one venomous assault after another, is memorable and somehow astringent. After reading it, one feels revolted perhaps but also purged. After reading *Love Story* and such memorable lines as "Love means never having to say you're sorry," the reader *needs* a purge. He certainly doesn't need an emetic. Maybe there are times when an honest hatred serves us better than love corrupted by sentimentality, meretriciousness, sententiousness, cuteness. Beckett's novels where nothing much happens, people say very little, and what they say is usually misunderstood, are

more honest, bracing, less depressing than eventful good-
story Harold Robbins novels. In Joseph Heller's *Something
Happened* nothing happens, yet it is somehow more eventful
than a Jacqueline Susanne novel where everything happens.
The last great conventional novel may have been *War and
Peace* or perhaps *Middlemarch. Gone with the Wind* bears a
certain resemblance to a great novel but what it really is is
very good soap opera.

Here I am making a couple of assumptions which I shall not
bother to defend, since they seem to me self-evident. One is
that if we take the novel seriously, it follows that it is an art
form just as a poem or a painting or a symphony is an art form.
And if this is the case, it follows that while it is true that a novel
should have an action, it does not suffice for it to be "a good
story." That is to say, it is a good thing to tell a good story or to
hear a good story, but it doesn't necessarily follow that a good
story is good art. Good art tells some home truths about the
way things are, the way we are, about the movement or lack of
movement of the human heart. In great ages, when people
understood each other and held a belief in common, great
stories like the *Iliad* or *War and Peace* were also great art
because they affirmed the unspoken values which a people
held in common and made it possible for a people to recognize
themselves and to know who they are. But there are other
times when people don't know who they are or where they are
going. At such times storytelling can become a form of diversion,. perhaps even a waste of time—like the prisoners facing
execution Pascal talks about who spend their time crapshoot-
ing instead of trying to figure out how they got in such a fix and
what is going to happen to them.

So my main assumption is that art is cognitive, that is, it
discovers and knows and tells, tells the reader how things are,
how we are, in a way that the reader can confirm with as much
certitude as a scientist taking a pointer-reading.

A corollary to the proposition that art in general and the
novel in particular is cognitive is that the stance of the novelist
in the late twentieth century is also diagnostic. The implica-

tion is that something has gone wrong, which it certainly has, and that the usual experts cannot tell us what it is—and indeed that they may be part of the problem.

Something, it appears, has gone wrong with the western world, and gone wrong in a sense far more radical than, say, the evils of industrial England which engaged Dickens. It did not take a diagnostician to locate the evils of the sweatshops of the nineteenth-century Midlands. But now it seems that whatever has gone wrong strikes to the heart and core of meaning itself, the very ways people see and understand themselves. What is called into question in novels *now* is the very enterprise of human life itself. Instead of writing about this or that social evil from a posture of consensus from which we agree to deplore social evils, it is now the consensus itself and the posture which are called into question. This state of affairs creates problems for the novelist. For in order to create a literature, whether of celebration or dissent, a certain shared universe of discourse is required. It is now these very shared assumptions which are called into question. Forty years ago Steinbeck had an easy job writing about the Okies and the dustbowl. It is a different matter now when the novelist confronts third-generation Okies in California who have won, who seem to have everything they want—and yet who seem ready any minute to slide physically and spiritually into the Pacific Ocean.

So the novelist today is less like the Tolstoy or Fielding or Jane Austen who set forth and celebrated a still intact society, than he is like a somewhat bemused psychiatrist gazing at a patient who in one sense lives in the best of all possible worlds and yet is suffering from a depression and anxiety which he doesn't understand.

There are similarities, I think, between these two branches of art and science, that is, novel writing and psychiatry. There is also an intriguing difference between the points of view of the two professions. The issue between science and art is of perennial interest to me since I started off in science in college, in medicine, was headed for psychiatry and ended up writing novels—and so I hope it will also have general interest as an example of culture crossing and perhaps as an occasion also of shedding some light on what the two cultures of art and science have to do with each other.

It is all the more intriguing in this case because at first sight it would appear that the two points of view are directly opposed. If the novelist is right, the psychiatrist is deceiving himself. If the psychiatrist is right, the novelist is crazy.

If the latter is the case, then novelists stand in need of psychiatrists—as in fact they often do. But it may also be the case that psychiatrists and other nonnovelists stand in need of novelists and that it is the novelist who is peculiarly equipped to locate such elusive phenomena and answer such odd questions as: what is pathological and what is "normal" in the last quarter of the twentieth century?

More often than not, however, novelists and psychiatrists find themselves either talking at cross purposes or upstaging each other from carefully prepared vantage points. Some psychologists and psychiatrists profess to understand such things as creativity which I do not understand. Novelists on the other hand often find psychiatrists easy prey in their novels. The long-term goals which psychology erects, such large abstractions as emotional maturity, meaningful intersubjective relations, and so on, do invite a certain satirical treatment.

This is all in good fun. But what is important to notice is that the hero or antihero of the contemporary novel hardly qualifies under any of these conventional mental health canons—emotional maturity, autonomy, and so forth. Indeed he, and more recently she, is more often than not a solitary, disenchanted person who is radically estranged from his or her society, who has generally rejected the goals of his family and his peers, and whose encounters with other people, friendships and love affairs, are regularly attended by misunderstandings, misperceptions, breakdowns in communication, aggressions, and withdrawals, all occurring in a general climate of deflated meaning. People in novels meet, talk, make love, and go their separate ways without noticeable joy or sorrow. Indeed the main emotion one encounters in contemporary fiction is a sense of unreality, a grayness and flatness, a diminished sense of significance. Relations between people take the form of silences, misunderstandings, impersonal sexual encounters.

If someone were to propose to the hero of modern fiction that he undergo psychotherapy to make his life more meaningful and to improve his interpersonal relations, one can imagine his response.

Now of course the issue can be settled very quickly in favor of psychology if we make the obvious inference—that the hero of the contemporary novel is the way he is because that's the way the novelist is, a difficult, unhappy, cutoff sort of person. Might it not indeed be the case that the novelist writes novels precisely because of his sombre view of the world and his own difficulties with people? Like the poet in Allen Tate's definition, is he not a shaky man who steadies and affirms himself by the creative process?

To a degree this diagnosis is probably correct. We are dealing here with several half-truths. Most novelists and those poets who have not yet suicided would probably agree—with an important reservation. The poet may admit to being a wounded man, yet point out that the wounded man often has the best view of the battle. The novelist or poet may in his own perverse way be a modern version of the Old Testament prophet who, like Hosea, may have a bad home life, yet who nevertheless and despite himself finds himself stuck with the unpleasant assignment of pointing out to his fellow citizens that something is wrong, that they are on the wrong track.

What I am suggesting is that art and science, in this case the novel and psychology, have different ways of approaching the truth and different truths to tell. Contradictions appear only when one discipline invades the territory of another.

But let me get down to cases. Perhaps one example from current fiction will suffice to convey the special flavor of a commonly encountered fictional view of the dislocation of modern American life.

In the novel *Something Happened* Joseph Heller writes about Bob Slocum and his family. Slocum is a successful middle-aged executive who works in New York and lives in

Connecticut. He is the current version of the John Marquand character a generation ago who suffered a kind of gentle disenchantment with life. But things seem to have gotten worse since. None of the Slocums is noticeably neurotic. On the contrary, they are a gifted, attractive, and intelligent lot, the best of an affluent, upwardly mobile, upper-middle-class northeast exurban society. But Bob Slocum is unhappy, his wife is unhappy, his son is unhappy, his daughter is unhappy. Everyone is afraid of at least one other person. When the family assembles at mealtime, the traditional social celebration of all past civilizations, the occasion is a disaster of misunderstandings, sarcasms, put-downs, and uproar. "Can't we get through one meal in peace?" somebody asks. No, they can't.

Bob's wife drinks. Bob chases office girls and prostitutes without enthusiasm. Yet he succeeds in his profession. Like Marquand's hero, he gets his promotion, buys a new house in Connecticut. This is how he feels about the new house:

> All of us live now—we are well off—in luxury . . . in a gorgeous two-story wood colonial house with white shutters on a choice country acre in Connecticut off a winding picturesque asphalt road called Peapod Lane—*and I hate it*. There are rose bushes, zinnias and chrysanthemums rooted about, and I hate them too. I have sycamores and chestnut trees in my glade and my glen, and pots of glue in my garage. I have an electric drill with sixteen attachments which I never use. Grass grows under my feet in back and in front, and flowers come into bloom when they're supposed to. . . . Families with horses for pets do live nearby, and I hate them too, the families *and* the horses. . . . I hate my neighbor and he hates me.

Something Happened is the title of Heller's novel. Something has happened all right. Actually nothing much happens in the novel but something must have happened before, something dreadful, but what is it? How did these good people get in such a fix? What happened? We are not sure, but whatever it was, it was not a single event in the usual sense of events in traditional novels, like the fatal wounding of Prince Andrey in *War and Peace*, or even a tragic historical event like America importing slaves from Africa. It is more like some aboriginal disaster, the original sin of the twentieth century. But where do we locate the disaster? What was the nature of the Fall? Has something dreadful happened to Bob Slocum or to the society in which he lives? Or both?

Fictional examples could be multiplied. Indeed the twentieth-century novel might be set forth as one or another aspect of disenchantment ranging from the gentle disillusion of the Marquand character to the derisive wiseacre disgust of Bob Slocum, with stopovers at the restiveness of the Hemingway expatriate, the metaphysical anxiety of the European existentialists, the apathy of Camus's Meersault, the rampaging gallows humor of a Portnoy.

Someone has in fact characterized the change in direction of the great body of poetry and fiction for the past hundred years as the Great Literary Secession, meaning that poets and novelists have, for whatever reason, registered a massive dissent from the modern proposition that with the advance of science and technology and education, life gets better too.

This issue, I would suppose, must sooner or later be confronted by anyone, scientist or artist or layman, interested in trying to figure out how things are and how to make life more tolerable both for oneself and for other people. Do we not indeed have the sense that the question grows daily more urgent, that there is a cumulative sense of crisis which allows us less and less room for temporizing? Something has happened all right. But perhaps something worse is about to happen.

Perhaps the issue can be clarified by making it both more concrete and more hypothetical. Given the unhappiness of Bob Slocum, let us assume the added circumstance, admittedly unlikely in this case, that Bob Slocum has submitted himself to science to diagnose and correct his pathology. Since he is unhappy, he goes like many Americans to the expert of unhappiness to find out what is wrong. He goes to a psychiatrist. Now what kind of therapeutic goals do we envision for him? How would we like to see him change? Or would he like to change? Suppose we imagine his future in terms of the conventional abstractions used to define such goals, namely, that he become more creative, autonomous, productive, and so forth; that he become more integrated in the life of his community. These goals seem worthy and unexceptionable, but do we not have a sense of misgiving when we picture such a Bob Slocum in the future, no longer unhappy and derisive, but, as they say nowadays, being "into" this or that, into ceramics or folk dancing, or working for the political party of his choice? And if we secretly like him better the way he is, how do we articulate and justify a preference for his unhappiness?

The possibility I want to raise is whether from the novelist's point of view there may be at least two kinds of distresses to which people fall prey.

One is a distress with which one can surely deal as straightforwardly as a surgeon dealing with abdominal pain. It too is pain pure and simple, that is, suffering without referent or redeeming qualities, anguish, sadness, conflict, terror which cripples and paralyzes. People hurt and come for relief to friends and experts who specialize in this kind of hurt, and friends and experts try to help them.

Such distress, in short, can be understood as a malfunction of the psyche which can be addressed from the traditional posture of the medical sciences, that of an observer who recognizes a class of disorders to which he applies a class of techniques.

But another kind of distress engages us, that is, us novelists. It is the ironic disaffection of Bob Slocum in *Something Happened*, the suicide of Quentin Compson in Faulkner's *The Sound and the Fury*, the loneliness of Ivan Karamazov, the anxiety of Roquentin in Sartre's novel, the flatness and banality experienced by J. Alfred Prufrock, the bemusement of Joan Didion's solitary heroine cruising the freeways of Los Angeles.

As different as are these fictional disorders, they share certain features in common. They are manifested by characters who are not only not portrayed as sick people but who rather are put forward by their creators, the novelists and poets, precisely because they are held to possess certain insights into the way things are, insights not yet shared or perhaps only dimly shared by most of their fellow denizens of the western world. Yet it is these latter who by virtue of their freedom from symptoms, it would seem, would be judged by all the traditional criteria of mental health to be better off, happier, and healthier than the dislocated fictional hero.

It appears indeed that science and art are taking here directly opposed views, that what science regards as normal, art regards as somehow the failure or coming short of the *self*, and that what art regards as an appropriate response to the age we live in, science sees as antisocial or aberrant behavior.

Insights, I suggest, are what the novelist has in mind, insights into the way things are. But what things? And where? Certainly we are talking about a pathology. Something has happened all right, something has gone wrong, but what? Is it a psychic disorder which can be diagnosed from a scientific, therapeutic stance? Or is it something else? Is it the final passing of the age of faith? Are we talking about a post-Christian malaise, the sense of disorientation which presumably always comes whenever the symbols and beliefs of one age are no longer taken seriously by people in a new age?

Clearly we are talking about a species of alienation, the traditional subject matter of psychiatrists, the original alienists. But notice that the novelist is raising a Copernican issue and standing the question on its head. Who is alienated? And from what? And is one better off nowadays alienated or unalienated?

Toward the end of identifying what the novelist is up to, I would like to go a bit deeper into this matter of literary alienation, deeper than Heller's character, Bob Slocum, who after all might be put down as yet another projection of yet another novelist, American novelists in particular being by the very nature of their calling and their peculiar place or nonplace in the culture of a perverse and dislocated lot. Bob Slocum, like Alexander Portnoy, can after all be read as a convenient satirical vehicle by means of which the novelist practices a kind of double-edged therapy, on the one hand flailing away at all those features of United States society he doesn't like, and on the other hand exposing and, he hopes, exorcizing his own personal demons. And has a good time doing both. Both novels are very funny, funny enough to give the reader leave not to be too seriously challenged and engaged.

Other novels are not so easily disposed of. I'll choose one, a classic of sorts, though not necessarily the best, toward the end of shedding some light on what I consider the peculiar diagnostic role of the novel in this century.

I have in mind Sartre's *Nausea*. It is germane to our purpose, I think, not because it somewhat self-consciously sets forward certain of Sartre's philosophical theses, which do not directly concern us here, but as an onslaught on the "normal" or what is ordinarily taken for the normal. Unlike Sartre's later political novels, it is interesting because the attack is phenomenological, not political, an examination, that is, of the way things are.

What interests us about Roquentin, the protagonist of *Nausea*, in the present context is his conscious and deliberate alienation from those very aspects of French culture which by ordinary standards one would judge as eminently normal, for example, the apparently contented lives of the provincial bourgeoisie and the successful lives of the savants of the academy of science.

Roquentin is a historian. He lives a quiet life in the provincial city of Bouville, a routine existence consisting of research in the local library, solitary walks, eavesdropping on conversations between strangers, a mechanical sexual relation with the patron of a cafe.

"I live alone, entirely alone," Roquentin tells us. "I never speak to anyone, never. I receive nothing, I give nothing."

Yet he observes objects and people in the minutest detail, a scrap of newspaper in the gutter, people sitting in cafes, people strolling in the street, people who seem to fit into the world, who talk and listen to each other and give every appearance of understanding themselves and the world.

His favorite diversion is walking downtown on Sunday morning and watching whole families dressed in their Sunday best promenade and greet each other after Mass.

> A gentleman holding his wife by the arm, has just whispered a few words into her ear and has started to smile. She immediately wipes all expression from her chalky, cream-colored face and blindly takes a few steps. There is no mistaking these signs: they are going to greet somebody. Indeed, after a moment the gentleman throws his hand up. When his fingers reach his felt hat, they hesitate a second before coming down deliberately on the crown. While he slowly raises his hat, bowing his head a little to help its removal, his wife gives a little start then forces a young smile on her face. A bowing shadow passes them: but their twin smiles do not disappear immediately; they stay on their lips a few instants by a sort of magnetism. The lady and gentleman have regained their impassibility by the time they pass me, but a certain air of gaiety still lingers around their mouths.

Sartre's point seems to be the paradox that although the bourgeoisie seem happy and all together, there is nevertheless something wrong with them. Their lives are a kind of masquerade, an impersonation; they are not themselves. Sartre calls it bad faith. Roquentin with all his dislocation appears to know something they don't know—yet seems worse off for his knowledge, at first simply out of it, isolated, then at length overtaken by attacks of anxiety and nausea at what he takes to be a revelation of the true nature of things, a highly unpleasant glimpse into being itself.

It is important to notice that *Nausea* is no ordinary freethinking rationalistic-skeptical assault on the Catholic bourgeoisie. For Roquentin (and Sartre) have as little use for the opposition, the other triumphant sector of French society, the anticlerical members of the academy, famous doctors, generals, and politicians. Roquentin is equally repelled by the rational believer and the rational unbeliever like Renan.

Roquentin visits the Bouville museum where there are displayed a hundred and fifty portraits of the famous. He stops at the portrait of Dr. Parottin, member of the Academy of Science.

> Now I stood before him and he was smiling at me. What intelligence and affability in his smile! His plump body rested leisurely in the hollow of a great leather armchair. This unpretentious wise man put people at their ease immediately. . . .
>
> It did not take long to guess the reason for his prestige: he was loved because he understood everything; you could tell him everything. He looked a little like Renan, all in all with more distinction.

Now what are we to make of Sartre's and Roquentin's alienation? Can we lay it to the literary acrobatics of French intellectuals who ever since Descartes are well known for their ability to hit on a single philosophical thesis and use it for a yardstick to measure the whole world? Or shall we trace it to the social malaise of the French between two great wars?

Or is Sartre saying something of value about the condition of western man in the twentieth century or perhaps about the human condition itself?

Or is Sartre's existentialism to be understood as only a way station in his transit from a bourgeois intellectual to a Marxist ideologue?

If Sartre is correct, then things have indeed been turned upside down. For in his novel the apparently well are sick and the apparently sick are onto the truth. But is the truth an unpleasant business we would do well to avoid? Roquentin thinks he knows something other people don't know, that he has made an unpleasant discovery which scarcely makes for happiness but allows him to live with an authenticity not attained by the happy bourgeoisie and the triumphant scientists. Anxiety, a sense of unreality, solitariness, loss of meaning, the very traits which we ordinarily think of as symptoms and signs of such and such a disorder are here set forth as appropriate responses to a revelation of the way things are and the way people really are.

If this were the case and things are indeed turned upside

down, there is nothing much that psychiatrists could do about it—or would want to. It is hardly feasible for therapists to treat people who don't think they are sick, whether they are the happy bourgeoisie or the unhappy existentialist.

What I have in mind, however, is the intermediate case, someone located, as perhaps most of us are, between the intact bourgeoisie and the triumphant scientists on the one hand and the alienated hero of the novel on the other—a character who, let us say, falls somewhere between Roquentin and his existential despair and Bob Slocum and his comic disgust.

What, in short, are we to make of the widespread sense of malaise experienced by a great many people in these times and of the diametrically opposed views of this malaise taken by scientists and artists?

I'm afraid I cannot give a clear-cut answer to the question, who is crazy, novelists or scientists? Rather will I content myself with a more modest yet, I think, significant goal. It is to return to my original assumption, that art is cognitive, as cognitive and affirmable in its own way as science, and that in the case of the current novel what it cognizes, discerns, knows, and tells is of a unique order which cannot be grasped by the scientific method. It is an elementary axiom that the truth which science tells about things and events is a general truth. The scientist is only interested in a molecule of sodium chloride or a supernova or an amoeba or even a patient insofar as it resembles other molecules, other supernova, other amoebae, and even other patients sharing the same disorder. But the peculiar fate of the human being is that he is stuck with the consciousness of himself as a self, as a unique individual, or at least with the possibility of becoming such a self. The paradox of the triumph of science and technology is that to the degree that a person perceives himself as an example of, a specimen of, this or that type of social creature or biological genotype, to precisely this same degree does he come short of being himself. The great gap in human knowledge to which science cannot address itself by the very nature of the scientific method is, to paraphrase Kierkegaard, nothing less than this: what it is like to be an individual, to be born, live, and die in the twentieth century. If we assume, consciously or unconsciously, that science can answer such questions, we will never even be able to ask the questions, let alone answer them. Who then can address himself to the question? The individual person of course, who while accepting the truth and beauty of science, retains his sovereignty over himself. But someone else also speaks to the same issue: it is of course the artist who finds himself in league with the individual, with his need to have himself confirmed in his predicament. It is the artist who at his best reverses the alienating process by the very act of seeing it clearly for what it is and naming it, and who in this same act establishes a kind of community. It is a paradoxical community whose members are both alone yet not alone, who strive to become themselves and discover that there are others who, however tentatively, have undertaken the same quest.

There is, I would think, a puzzle here for many American readers in the so-called novel of alienation. I know from experience that many young readers find themselves put off and perhaps with good reason by the sombre view of life portrayed by so many novelists, both European and American, and I never argue with the reader who tells me that he is happy and that things are, after all, not so bad. But if the novelist is correct in his apparent dissent from the traditional American proposition and if it is true, as I suggest, that the contemporary novel at its best is cognitive and exploratory, in its own way as scientific as nuclear physics, perhaps some light can be shed on our confusion by taking note of the more familiar dilemmas of science in general and psychiatry in particular. We are all aware, I think, of the dangers of the passive consumership of technology, confronted as we are by the dazzling credentials of science. A certain loss of personal sovereignty occurs when a person comes to believe that his happiness depends on his exposure to this or that psychology or this or that group encounter or technique.

There is a similar danger attendant upon literature and art—what Kierkegaard might have called the perils of the aesthetic sphere. If it is true that the poet and novelist are in the vanguard in their foreboding that something has gone badly wrong and in their sketching out of the nature of the pathology, let the reader both rejoice and beware, rejoice that the good novelist has the skill to point out the specters which he, the reader, had been only dimly aware of, but beware in doing so of surrendering the slightest sovereignty over himself. If one happens to be a writer or a scientist and lucky enough occasionally to hit on the truth, or if one is a reader or a consumer and lucky enough to benefit from a great medical discovery or a novelistic breakthrough which excites him— well and good. Well and good, that is, as long as one never forgets that the living of one's life is not to be found in books, either the reading of them or the writing of them.

1977

Literary Technique in the Last Quarter of the Twentieth Century

Tom Wolfe

I just want to make a few remarks about a side of literary technique that is never written about and seldom talked about. It is one that most writers begin to understand only late in the game, if ever. If ever, as I say . . . for here I think we may have the answer to why this, the last quarter of the twentieth century, is the dreariest period of the century for such major forms as the novel and the play.

I think most writers go through the same stages, in terms of technique. The first I think of as the musical stage, in which the young writer is mainly fascinated by his ability to put pleasing, sonorous, rhythmical, or strange strings of words together. At about age thirteen, as I recall, I became intrigued by words that began with *j*. They looked marvelous to me . . . *jaded* . . . *jejune* . . . I didn't even know how to pronounce "jejune"—in fact, to this day I have never heard anyone use the word in conversation—but I put it in writing every chance I had. This one word began to take over entire passages, entire narratives. I wrote a short story in which everything was jejune and everybody was jejune . . . Pretty soon it became a noun as well as an adjective . . . "The jaded jejune of his hopes," that sort of thing . . . and finally it became a verb as well. People were jejuning each other all over the place and were in turn being ruthlessly jejuned by the jasmine jugate jinn of their own fantasies, and so forth and so on. It was not long after that I wrote my first poem. It was called "Owed to an Aesthete" . . . o-w-e-d . . . I considered that word play and a half . . . and it went:

Your only faintly saffron suns
Your nicely nipponesian nudes
Your limply purslane slyped-up dung
From your exema'd face exudes.

Nevertheless!—that example notwithstanding!—I think
that this early musical stage of technique accounts for the fact
that so many outstanding poets have done their best work
while quite young. Poetry is the music of literature . . . in that
like music it can have a nonrational but very sudden and powerful effect upon the mind. You will find a poet such as Shelley
at the height of his powers, writing *Alastor* by day . . . and in
the evenings sneaking hunks of bread off the table and rolling
them into doughballs and flicking them surreptitiously into
the face of his father-in-law. Nothing very strange about
that . . . they just happen to occur at the same time, the two
things, the marvelous surge of musical talent and the season of
the rising sap.

The second stage comes when the young writer discovers
that, for better or worse, the main arena in literature is prose.
It is here that the greatest status is to be attained; that is what
he finds out. This has been so for about 120 years, I would say.
At this point many young writers are attracted to "poetic"
prose or else to prose written after the manner of myths or
fables. I can remember that I decided at this stage to write
what I thought of as "crystalline" prose, prose that would
shimmer like crystals. It would ring in your ears like the music
of Richard Strauss. It would be timeless. It would seem as
ethereal in the twenty-fifth century as in the twentieth. I considered that an advantage if one intended to become one of
literature's immortals. Unfortunately, I can recite to you none
of my timeless prose. I abandoned most of these efforts on the
morning after. Today I see young writers, at this stage, tremendously attracted to the work of writers such as Tolkien,
Hermann Hesse, Kafka, Borges, Garcia Marquez, and
Zamyatin. All of them write modern fables, although
Zamyatin's range goes far beyond the fable.

What is the appeal of the fable to the young writer? I think it's this: the fable form avoids the problems of realism.

When you're at that age, when you're in your late teens or early twenties and you want to write, you want to feel that the only thing that matters is your genius. The material, the content of the writer's work, is merely the clay, the wax, that Himself is going to use. It is very hard for a young writer to come to grips with the realization that the material he finds— the subject matter—may account for 50 percent or more of his success . . . and of what comes to be known as his talent. A young writer does not want to believe that. He is apt to find that he is simply not very good at analyzing the world around him and selecting material from it. He doesn't know much about it. It becomes far more convenient to write a sort of cynical or ironic whimsy patterned after Borges or Kafka. It becomes quite easy to discount realism, if there is any way to justify doing so.

In the late 1940s and early 1950s, when I was in college, it was hard to avoid realism, because it was still so much in vogue in the literary world generally. So practically everyone was forced to enter stage three—writing realistic prose—fairly early on. The typical and natural solution was to write about your own life, poignantly if possible. This became more than just a solution, however. It was an article of faith at that time: namely, that the *only* genuine, legitimate, and truly profound material for the great novelist was the substance of his own life. Practically every highly praised first novel of the period was autobiographical: whether it was a war novel, such as *From Here to Eternity* or *The Naked and the Dead*, or a novel of school life, such as *End as a Man*, or the great picaresque novel of the fifties, Jack Kerouac's *On the Road*. When I was doing research on *The Electric Kool-Aid Acid Test*, I met Neal Cassady, who was the hero, under the name Dean Moriarty, of *On the Road*. "It used to amaze us," he told me.

Jack and me and everybody would take these wild rides back and forth across the United States, in these '46 Chryslers with the kickdown gears and whatever, and we'd start drinking and smoking and swallowing everything we could get our hands on, and when we got through everything we'd ever heard of, like we'd smoke Oriental rugs and eat dried creosote and swallow mildewed jute pellets, and end up absolutely wrecked and vomiting and Jack would crawl off into some flophouse, and we'd figure he was just sleeping it off, but in fact he would be in there with a typewriter, writing down everything that had happened, everything we had done. These things came out as his novels, and insofar as any of us could tell, he changed absolutely not one thing except the names.

Such was the mental atmosphere of the realistic novel fifteen or twenty years ago. In many cases it was nonfiction with the names changed. And I think this was the chief cause of what was notorious at the time as the "curse of the second novel." Without realizing what the process was, many talented first novelists had ransacked the first twenty years or so of their lives for material for one novel. When it came time for the second novel, they had lived only two or three years in the meantime and were absolutely baffled as to what to write about. Norman Mailer and James Jones were two in a long line of novelists of the period who had this problem and never really found a way out of it. Today we see something of the same thing plaguing Philip Roth, who I happen to think is the most naturally gifted novelist in the country. Roth has wound up continually ransacking and reransacking the material of his early life. *Portnoy's Complaint* was a brilliant book, in my opinion, but *My Life as a Man* and *The Professor of Desire* are rewrites of the same material. They are brilliant rewrites, for that matter—but here we run into the fact that, as I mentioned earlier, content is a big part of what we think of as talent or genius, and the material becomes thinner and less fresh, less novel, with each reuse.

When you think about it, it's a bit uneconomical to have to spend twenty years of your life to get material for one novel or even to spend five years of daily living to get new material for a second book. It reminds me of the marvelous Charles Lamb story called "A Dissertation on Roast Pig." A Chinese lout by accident burns down his house. In the ruins he finds the roasted carcass of a pig. It's delicious; it's the first roast pig he has ever had. When the passion for roast pig overcomes him again, he burns down his new house, first putting a pig inside, of course. Well, there I see the novelists of the forties and fifties trying to get tasty material out of their own lives.

In the 1960s a tremendous change in literary fashion seemed to solve the problem for the young writers of that period. The modern fable came into vogue. It became quite all right—quite desirable, in fact—for the young writer to remain in stage two, the "timeless" stage, and ignore the problems of realism altogether. The New Fabulism, exemplified by writers such as John Barth, Donald Barthelme, Thomas Pynchon, Richard Brautigan, and John Gardner, was the reigning form. The typical New Fable was a short story by Raymond Kennedy entitled "Room Temperature." It concerned a man named Jack who was living as a hermit in a shack in the woods in the dead of winter without plumbing, electricity, or any other apparatus of modern civilization. He is evidently happy to be removed from society, but we are told nothing of his background. Nothing in what he says or thinks betrays any ethnic, national, or class origin. We don't even know what part of the earth he is in, except that there is a lot of snow. Jack is possessed by a nameless dread. Soon an Inexplicable Visitor shows up, a man named Dick who has been beaten up in the city and dumped out here in the snow with no clothes on except for one shoe. Not the least bit dismayed by the way they stomped him in the city, Dick wants to return as soon as possible. Hermit Jack has just saved Dick from freezing to death, but Dick has an inexplicable attitude toward him. He orders Jack about his own shack and tells him he wants him to return to the city with him, apparently as a servant. Hermit Jack doesn't want to, but he finds himself inexplicably tagging along behind Dick out in the snowy wastes. The extreme cold is too much for him, and he slumps into the snow and begins to freeze to death . . . as Dick heads on back to civilization without so much as offering him a warm goodbye. As the story ends, Hermit Jack is alone in the snow, frozen stiff and dying.

These elements—the Hermit or Isolated Character, the Elemental Terrain (woods, snowy wastes, sea, desert, swamps), Lack of Background, Lack of Realistic Dialogue, Inexplicable Visitors, Inexplicable Attitudes, Inexplicable Forces, Frozen Death (or Paralysis)—plus an atmosphere of futility, meaninglessness, imminent and pointless disaster— these elements recurred continually in the New Fabulism. Not merely solitude, but Catatonic Solitude, became extremely fashionable, culminating in a story by Robert Coover that began: "In order to get started, he went to live alone on an island and shot himself."

So this century—this century which has seen wars so all-involving that they are known as world wars, this century in which man has perfected the means with which to obliterate himself but also the means with which to reach the stars, this century which has seen the growth of huge metropolises, tumultuous collisions of the races, and such crazy pileups of wealth that by 1968 every forty-eight-year-old vinyl-wallet manufacturer in America was out on the discotheque floor with his shirt unbuttoned down to his sternum and a lot of brutal chainwork around his neck and his red eyes beaming out of his walnut-shell eyelids, doing the Watusi, the Hully-Gully, and the New Boogaloo until the onset of dawn or saline depletion, whichever came first—this is the century that our most ambitious young writers chose to treat, in the words of the title of Gabriel Garcia Marquez's book, as *One Hundred Years of Solitude*. In all the publishing houses they were waiting for the great novels that the rising generation of writers would write about the war in Vietnam, the protest movements, the hippie world, race, class, sex, the new ways of life in America—and these novels were never written. Not a single first-rate novel has come out of the war in Vietnam; and precious few of any sort. The rising generation the publishers were waiting for never rose.

A parallel development occurred in the theater. It was illustrated most strikingly by the career of Edward Albee. Albee became famous through the success of *Who's Afraid of Virginia Woolf?*, which was in most respects quite a realistic slice of life among American intellectuals in the 1950s. Just then the fashion in the American theater changed from realism of this, the Tennessee Williams sort, to the European fabulist style of Pinter and Beckett. Albee became determined to write "timeless" plays like theirs. Starting with *Tiny Alice* and *A Delicate Balance* his work became increasingly abstract and fablelike . . . and windier and emptier and less and less successful, even among critics. The fashion was so strong, however, that Albee was unable to break out of it.

Supporting the new fashion for fables was a body of theory that had two main arguments. One was that realism was an approach that had been done to death and was now exhausted. The other was summed up by William Phillips, the editor of the *Partisan Review:* "Realism is just another formal device, not a permanent method for dealing with experience." In my opinion precisely the opposite is true. The introduction of realism into literature by writers such as Richardson, Fielding, and Smollett in the eighteenth century was like the introduction of electricity into machine technology. It was not just another device; it raised the state of the art to a new plateau. The effect of realism on the emotions was something that had never been conceived of before. No one was ever moved to tears by reading about the unhappy fates of heroes and heroines in Homer, Sophocles, Molière, Racine, Sydney, Spenser, or Shakespeare. But even the impeccable Lord Jeffrey, editor of the *Edinburgh Review*, had confessed to weeping, blubbering, snuffling, boohooing, over the death of Dickens's Little Nell in *The Old Curiosity Shop*. One doesn't have to admire Dickens, or any of the other writers who first demonstrated this power, in order to appreciate the point. For writers to abandon this unique power simply because it had already been used—this was one of the more intriguing literary follies of the 1960s.

Publishers began to give up on the New Fabulism in the early 1970s for the simple reason that it did not sell. It bored readers to the point of skull implosions. Now you began to see the New Fabulists backing into realism . . . while paying homage to fabulism. E. L. Doctorow started the trend with his

book *Ragtime,* in which he writes a typical modern fable but
populates it with real people from recent history. The
aforementioned Robert Coover then tried the same thing in *A
Public Burning,* a rather naive and amateurish fable populated
with real figures from the era of the Rosenberg spy case. In
October Light Gardner starts off with a typical modern fable of
solitude in the wilds. It's a story of a brother and sister who
hate each other. They're shut up in a farmhouse. One—the
sister, I believe—locks herself in a room, where she discovers
a paperback novel. Gardner now prints the novel she finds: a
book in which the rules and conventions of the New Fabulism
are freely transgressed. It was by far the most popular thing he
had ever written.

Today critical standards and theories in the literary world
are rather gloriously confused. In the fog I see writers sneaking toward realism in greater numbers. And I see playwrights
beginning to discover the value of *reporting* as a means of
gathering material for serious literature. Playwrights are actually following the lead of screenwriters, who have found that in
a medium so dependent upon dialogue it is often necessary to
go out and listen to the real thing in order to make it work;
i.e., it becomes necessary to do reporting. Novelists have
been slower in discovering how this works, and it is ironic. To
the great nineteenth-century novelists, reporting was a standard technique. They adopted procedures that today are
associated only with "investigative reporting" by news-
papermen. Dickens wanted to gain an inside look at the infa-
mous Yorkshire boarding schools, where families farmed out
their children for years at a time so as not to have to bother
with them. So he presented himself as the agent for a father
trying to park one of his sons in this manner, toured the
schools, and wrote down his findings each night in a notebook,
like any good reporter. When Balzac came to a point in a novel
where he needed to write, say, a scene about a socially correct
funeral in the countryside . . . he would stop writing and go
seek out a socially correct funeral in the countryside . . . and
take notes on it and then come back and write the scene. Zola
wrote many of his books serially, just as Dickens did. Often he

would spend two weeks of the month in reporting and two weeks on writing the installment. He would decide—in *Nana*—that he wanted a scene at the races. So he would head off to Longchamps and take notes. The result—as you will remember, if you have read *Nana*—is something far richer than simply convincing detail, although that is there. The detail itself, obtained through reporting, enables Zola to take off on flights of extraordinary technical virtuosity. But let me give you an example from another part of *Nana*. Nana, of course, is a courtesan, and Zola wanted to have authentic information about such a woman. So he obtained an introduction to a famous Paris courtesan of his day and went to her house. He found, to his disappointment, that she was far too sophisticated, too urbane a woman to be used as a model for Nana. But while in her house he had a look at her bed. It had been created by goldsmiths at a cost of about $75,000 in today's terms. Out of its four golden posts came marvelous priapic figures with shanks akimbo. The sight of that bed became for Zola a metaphor for the entire Second Empire in France and resulted in one of the most powerful images in French literature.

What I am saying is that it was *through reporting* that the great writers of the nineteenth century were able to come up not only with slices of life but also with the most important insights, the most arresting symbols, the most powerful material in prose literature. They did not labor under the illusion that profundity was to be found only in the inspection of one's own immediate existence. They seemed, rather, to believe the opposite: profound knowledge was to be obtained only through moving out from one's own circle and reporting on the world beyond. We are in a period today in which there is seldom a major novel with more than one interesting character portrayed, and this one character is usually the alter ego of the author himself. This is the great limitation of Saul Bellow's work. His books are filled up with the swollen figure of the protagonist in the foreground—obviously himself under another name—with little stick figures dotted around in the small space that is left. The challenge that Zola, Balzac,

Dickens, Thackeray, Dostoevski, Tolstoy, Gogol—and Faulkner—routinely accepted was that of entering into the hides of characters utterly unlike themselves and bringing them alive, a full cast, in each novel. The key—this they understood as something obvious, as a matter of routine—was reporting.

Actually, I suppose I should keep quiet about this business of reporting. It is partly due to the general obtuseness of novelists and playwrights in this area that journalists have had such a field day in American writing over the past fifteen years. This has been perhaps the first period since the 1830s in England when the literary history of any major country has been dominated by journalists, aesthetically as well as in popular appeal—and the difference has been in the least understood side of literary technique, which is the use and the necessity of reporting. Ah, but this brings me dangerously close to a topic which I swore five years ago I would never publicly expound upon again... the New Something-or-other... and so I will stop now.

1978

Making Up Stories

Joan Didion

Let me present you with a chain of associations.

I am delivering the 1979 Hopwood lecture at the University of Michigan in Ann Arbor, Michigan, near the city of Detroit.

When Detroit is mentioned I think reflexively of my father. I have never before yesterday been in Detroit but my father was stationed there, the last year of World War II. When he came home to California from Detroit he brought me three handkerchiefs of a very heavy silk twill, one brown, one orange, the third a quite brilliant emerald green. He had bought these handkerchiefs at the J. L. Hudson Company and the saleswoman had told him that "all the young girls" were wearing them, knotted around the neck.

I was undone by this present, for several reasons: one was that I was only ten, and overcome that my father should consider me a "young girl," should buy me a grown-up present, a present of something "in fashion." The pieces of silk seemed to me incredibly glamorous and beautiful, and they were rendered even more so by the fact that this was the first time my father had ever had occasion to buy me—all by myself, without my mother—a present.

I remember that we sat down to lunch.

I remember that we had cracked crab, although there remains some question about this. I may have invented the crab, you never know.

I definitely remember that we had iced tea, in a silver pitcher, because I picked up this pitcher to pour myself some tea—more evidence that I was grown up, a "young girl" instead of a little girl—and I spilled it.

This spilling of the tea was a very fraught moment—anyone old enough to wear silk handkerchiefs knotted around her neck and drink iced tea was too old to drop the pitcher—and I remember bolting from the table, running to my room, and locking the door.

We can call that story "Homecoming," or we can call it "Family Life," or we can call it "Detroit and Other Sorrows."

It is not a story I will ever write.

Similarly: When the Hopwood awards are mentioned I think reflexively of being an undergraduate at Berkeley and wishing that Avery Hopwood had left that famous one-fifth of his estate to the University of California instead of the University of Michigan. I wanted to win a Hopwood award. I wanted to win one not only because the very word *Hopwood* had a big-time national sound to it, a kind of certification that the winner was on the right track, but also because the prize was money, cash, and I needed it.

I hear the word *Hopwood* and I think of Corinne Benson, who was my roommate one year at Berkeley. Corinne was from Marin County and she turned on the radio to a certain station every night at midnight in order to hear the sign-off, which was a male tenor singing "The Bluebird of Happiness." She had blonde hair and blue eyes and many, many powder blue sweaters to match her eyes, many sweaters and many dresses and many different-sized bottles of the particular perfume she always wore.

She lent me one of her dresses one night, to wear on a date to San Francisco.

This date was with someone I had met in a writing class. In other words he was "literary," as I wanted desperately to be, and had no car. We went from Berkeley to San Francisco on the F train and we ate the inevitable coq au vin at the inevitable French family restaurant and we saw a play, the inevitable Restoration comedy.

I do not now remember the play but I remember the dress and I remember this boy reading Dylan Thomas out loud to me on the F train back to Berkeley. He gave me a gloss on every line he read. For example:

"*It was my thirtieth year to heaven,*" he would read.

And then he would turn to me and say: "It was his thirtieth birthday."

And I would nod.

He liked the dress, and asked why I never wore it, and I was too embarrassed to say that it was not mine. I was so young that I imagined it shameful to let anyone know that you cared enough about him to borrow a dress.

"*Altarwise by owl-light in the half-way house*," he would read, and then interpret it. I recall thinking that if we only had Hopwood awards at Berkeley we might each win one, this boy and I, and winning a Hopwood award would give me enough money to buy a dress exactly like Corinne's, and give him enough certification, enough confidence, to ride across San Francisco Bay without feeling impelled to improve the moment by giving me an interlinear translation of Dylan Thomas. Had he known what I was thinking he would have called me bourgeois. This is another story I will never write.

This kind of associating never stops.

Corinne Benson, the trace of her perfume in the borrowed dress, the particular brilliant colors of those silk handkerchiefs from J. L. Hudson, the flicker of the lights on the F train at night, coq au vin, iced tea, and the way the moisture condenses on the outside of a silver pitcher: these are only the skim off the top of all that floods through my mind when I hear the words *Detroit* or *Hopwood awards*.

For example, by a chain of associations too tedious to reconstruct, Corinne Benson leads me directly to watching *Splendor in the Grass* on television, with a drunk psychiatrist from Louisville, in the Faculty Club at Berkeley on the night Saigon fell in 1975. The Faculty Club at Berkeley leads me to the stone tower Robinson Jeffers built at Carmel. Carmel leads me to the ordination of a Jesuit priest, a summer afternoon in Sacramento, and the ordination leads me to Sante Fe and to New Haven and to the murders in Beverly Hills of Sharon Tate Polanski, Jay Sebring, Voitek Frykowski, Steven Parent, and Abigail Folger.

To give you the connections that take me from Detroit to

those five murders in California would be to give you a story of my whole life, and I say "a story" rather than "the story" deliberately.

I say "a story" because only part of that story would be true. Some of the story would be a trick of memory.

Elizabeth Hardwick has written a novel, *Sleepless Nights*, in which the subject is memory, and in this novel she wrote: "Sometimes I resent the glossary, the concordance of truth, many have about my real life . . . I mean that such fact is to be a hindrance to memory."

Some of what all of us remember is automatic improvisation, a scenario invented to link puzzling and contradictory scenes. When we tell someone a dream we try, in spite of ourselves, for a certain coherence, a dramatic shape: we interpret the dream, as we tell it, and filter out those details which seem to lead nowhere. We think of our dreams as stories, but they are not, at least until we tell them.

In fact the way we think in dreams is also the way we think when we are awake, all of these images occurring simultaneously, images opening up new images, charging and recharging, until we have a whole field of image, an electric field pulsing and blazing and taking on the exact character of a migraine aura.

All of us have this going on in our heads, all the time, this incessant clatter, this charging and recharging.

Usually we sedate ourselves to keep the clatter down.

And when I say that we sedate ourselves, I don't necessarily mean with drugs, not at all. Work is a sedative. The love of children can be a sedative. Planting a garden, locking the doors, cooking dinner, arranging the tulips in a certain glass and placing the glass so that the water catches the light: anything that successfully focuses our attention is sedative in effect.

Another way we keep the clatter down is by trying to make it coherent, trying to give it the same dramatic shape we give to our dreams; in other words by making up stories.

All of us make up stories.

Some of us, if we are writers, write these stories down,

concentrate on them, worry them, revise them, throw them away and retrieve them and revise them again, focus on them all of our attention, all of our emotion, render them into objects.

It is very common for writers to think of their work as a collection of objects. A novel, to a writer, is an object. A story or an essay is an object. Every piece of work has its own shape, its own texture, its own specific gravity. This perception of the work as an object is not usually shared by the reader of it, and seems to be one of the principal differences between writers and people in other lines of sedation.

The point of making the object is to give the clatter a shape, to find the figure in the carpet, the order in the disorder.

Robert Penn Warren once described fiction as "an attempt, however modest and limited, to make sense of experience, to understand how things hang meaningfully together."

Joseph Heller described the conception of *Catch-22* this way: "I was lying in bed when suddenly this line came to me: 'It was love at first sight. The first time he saw the chaplain X fell madly in love with him.'" The "X" turned out to be Yossarian, but Heller didn't have the name, didn't even know that this "X" was in the Army. "The chaplain wasn't necessarily an Army chaplain," he said. "He could have been a prison chaplain. I don't understand the process of imagination though I know that I am very much at its mercy. The ideas come to me in the course of a controlled daydream, a directed reverie."

Cocteau described his work as deriving from "a profound indolence, a somnolence in which we indulge ourselves like invalids who try to prolong dreams."

Saul Bellow said, when someone asked him what he thought about winning the Nobel prize, "I don't know, I haven't written about it."

There you are. I have never heard a more succinct statement of the way writers think. The act of writing is for a writer the process of thinking, of plugging into that electrical field of image and making an object out of the flash and the clatter.

I don't mean at all that this object comes "naturally," any more than a piece of sculpture comes "naturally." You don't find a novel or a story lying around in your unconscious like a piece of driftwood. You have to hammer it, work it, find the particular grain of it.

Nor do I mean to say that we write out of our "experience," whatever that means. Someone is always saying to young writers that they should "write from experience." As it happens I get copies of a lot of composition textbooks, and the worst of them feature sample "themes," sample papers written on "The Night Fresno Beat Bakersfield" or "The Day I Learned I Made All-State Tackle."

These textbooks present the sample theme, and then they show ways the theme might be improved, usually be inventing some kind of "action" lead, something along the lines of "The clock was running. The ball was arcing into Fresno territory."

The trouble with this is that it is based on a very limited and literal view of experience. The advice that a writer write from experience is obviously good advice, but it is advice devoid of real meaning, since it does not define experience, or defines it as something that happened, as having actually been on the fifty-yard line on the night Fresno beat Bakersfield.

Experience is something quite different. Joseph Conrad wrote his great South American novel, *Nostromo*, out of "experience," and yet he had never in his life set foot in South America. He had once, as a very young man, shipped on a freighter that called at a few ports on the west coast of Mexico, had been told a story in one of them, and—out of those few hours ashore in Mexico twenty or twenty-five years before— he had made that novel that remains today all anyone needs to know in order to apprehend South America.

Henry James addressed himself to this question of experience. He answers a contemporary who advised that "a young lady brought up in a quiet country village should avoid descriptions of garrison life" by saying, in effect, no, not at all, you have it wrong. A young lady brought up in a quiet country village can apprehend everything about garrison life by glancing once through a window of Knightsbridge Barracks in London. If—and this was of course James's famous phrase—she is "one of the people on whom nothing is lost." Let me quote James:

> I remember an English novelist... telling me that she was much commended for the impression she had managed to give in one of her tales of the nature and way of life of French Protestant youth. She had been asked where she learned so much about this recondite being, she had been congratulated on her peculiar opportunities. These opportunities consisted of her having once, in Paris, as she ascended a staircase, passed an open door where some of the young Protestants were seated at a table round a finished meal. The glimpse made a picture; it lasted only a moment, but that moment was experience.

"That moment was experience."

We have all had such moments.

We retrieve them from that field of image that assaults us every day we live.

In the spring of 1975 I was teaching at Berkeley, just for a month and just one class, which met two days a week from four to six in the afternoon. I was in the middle of writing a novel that spring, and all day I would sit in my room at the Faculty Club. This room was just a room: twin beds, a desk, a straight-backed chair and a rented typewriter. I would get up very early and go out for breakfast and then I would come back to this room and sit at the desk and make up the novel. Tell myself the story. Entrance myself, in the literal sense of the word *entrance*.

Then at night a curious thing would happen. I would go out to dinner, or to a lecture, and I would listen to people talk about novels.

Everywhere I went, people were talking about novels.

Finished novels. Famous novels.

Just on the face of it, this was intimidating in the extreme: the main thing a writer wants to keep out of his or her mind is the idea that anybody else has ever written a novel.

But it was intimidating for another reason as well.

Everyone to whom I was listening at Berkeley that spring

talked about novels as if the novelist—whether it was Dickens or George Eliot or Scott Fitzgerald—had known precisely what he or she was doing before setting out, as if the novel were schematic, and entirely planned.

If this was true, then I was in bad trouble.

I particularly remember a kind of amiable argument I was having one night with some people from the English Department. Someone had mentioned *The Last Tycoon,* and everyone was pointing out ways in which it didn't work, ways in which it seemed to them a flagrantly bad novel.

There was the "imbalance" of it.

There was the rather creaking deux ex machina aspect to the plot.

I didn't disagree with anything they said, but I still thought that *The Last Tycoon* was a brilliant piece of work, and they didn't.

Finally I realized what the argument was about, what the difference in our thinking was, and it was quite a radical difference. They were looking at *The Last Tycoon* not as a fragment of a novel in progress but as the first third of a novel for which we were simply missing the last two-thirds. In other words they saw that first third as completed, frozen, closed—the interrupted execution of a fully articulated plan on Fitzgerald's part—and I saw it as something fluid, something that would change as he discovered where the book was taking him.

They saw a novel as a plan carried out.

I saw a novel as an object discovered.

They saw the process as an act of intelligence.

I saw it as a mystery.

They saw the writer as someone who has a story to tell and writes it down.

I saw the writer as someone who discovers the story only in the act of making it up.

The novel I was working on during that spring in Berkeley had begun in 1971 as a book about a woman who was traveling through Mississippi and Louisiana with her ex-husband, who was dying. The novel was to take place entirely in motel rooms off interstate highways.

In Holiday Inns, in Ramada Inns. In Howard Johnson's.

It was to be a novel without event.

It was to be told in a flat third person.

By the time I was working on this novel in Berkeley in 1975—the novel was *A Book of Common Prayer*—it had taken quite a different shape. It had become a novel which took place largely in a Central American republic named Boca Grande and—far from being without event—involved bombings, a highjacking, a revolution and a number of other theatrical—not to say melodramatic—events. And it was told not in that "flat third person" but in the first person, by a sixty-year-old woman named Grace Strasser-Mendana, born Grace Tabor in Denver, Colorado. Grace Tabor went down to Latin America as an anthropologist. Grace Tabor retired as an anthropologist and married into the Strasser-Mendana family, which ran Boca Grande. Grace Tabor was dying of pancreatic cancer, and she was to tell us the story of the woman who traveled with her ex-husband through Mississippi and Louisiana.

You could call this telling the story the hard way. I would call it telling myself a story that incorporated all of the images I was getting at the time.

Once in the late sixties I took a series of psychiatric tests, one of which was the Thematic Apperception Test. The Thematic Apperception Test, or "TAT," is the one in which the subject is shown a series of drawings and asked to make up a story based on each drawing. I recall resisting this test. I remember telling the doctor that of course I could make up stories, but he would be misguided to think that he knew more about what the stories revealed than I did, because I made up stories for a living.

He persisted, and I took the test.

One of the pictures was of a woman, not smiling, standing on some kind of raised ground—alone—and gazing down to where a group of men were very busy building a bridge or a culvert or maybe just tilling a field, some kind of basic physical work.

I remember that the story I made up to "go" with this drawing had to do with an American woman who had become involved with the revolutionary forces in Cuba during the early days of the revolution, and had since become disillusioned, and isolated in Cuba.

The doctor of course wanted to know "why" she was disillusioned, and I remember saying quite sharply "because that's the story I'm telling you."

We didn't get much further than that—we were proceeding, after all, from radically different points of view—but in fact I was more interested in this story than in any of the other stories I made up that day, and it occurred to me some years later, when I was making up the story that had begun as a trip through Mississippi and Louisiana and had evolved into a revolution in Central America, that the story had actually been in my mind for all that time.

I am going to read you some of the notes I made during the time that this novel about the trip through the South was in the process of evolving into *A Book of Common Prayer*. These notes were all in certain notebooks I had, and I am going to give them to you in the order in which they were made.

> She goes out to the airport and watches the planes take off. Arousing uneasy glances in the Panama airport, out there in the morning when the midnight Avianca from Mexico comes in. Drinking tea in the coffee shop at the Cartagena airport, making them boil the water before she will put the tea bag in.

> Arrival of mail, magazines, seed catalogues. Projects to make money and fame. Correspondents. Walking downtown in Cartagena in the midday blaze. Cracks and ruts in the sidewalk. Dinner alone in the Capilla del Mar.

> Unfitted for the heat. Frequent fevers, illness, occasional unsatisfactory liaisons with locals, who misapprehend her.

> IF THIS IS THE FRAME FOR THE SOUTHERN STORY THEN THE SOUTH MUST HAVE UNHINGED HER IN CERTAIN KEY WAYS.

During the troubles in Boca Grande she dreamwalks her way into danger. Incapable of believing that it can touch her. Una norteamericana. Self-delusion. Herded into the bull ring.

Argument with local druggist or doctor during bout of fever. Paregorina.

The Miami Herald is what she reads.

Official functions, rum and quinine. Whenever the USIS man is invited, so is she.

SOUTH AMERICAN PART IN PRESENT TENSE, SOUTH IN PAST? MAYBE TWO NOVELLAS, PUBLISHED TO-GETHER?

Death very casual.

FIRST LINE: HERE IS WHAT HAPPENED.

FIRST CHAPTER HARD THIRD SUMMARY. THEN AL-TERNATING CHAPTERS. LAST CHAPTER SOUTH AMERICAN BUT BEGINS: "WHEN IT HAPPENED... " VERY HARD LINE THIRD PERSON.

WHO IS THE THIRD PERSON? MAYBE YOU DON'T KNOW WHO IT IS UNTIL 2/3 THROUGH?

"HERE IS WHAT HAPPENED: SHE LEFT THE FIRST MAN, SHE LEFT THE FIRST CHILD, SHE WENT TO THE SECOND MAN, SHE LOST THE SECOND CHILD, SHE DIED. IN SUMMARY. SO YOU KNOW THE STORY. IN FACT THE STORY HAD COMPLICATIONS, BUT ONLY FOR THE LIVING. IF YOU HAVE EVER MADE THEM BOIL THE WATER TWENTY MINUTES BEFORE YOU PUT THE TEABAG IN YOU WILL KNOW WHAT I MEAN. FEVER IS RAMPANT."

Cataloguing the flora and fauna. Writing to the British resident in Honiara, Guadalcanal. Reading the Pacific Islands Monthly. Devising a scheme to ship Christmas trees to Caracas.

When the ice melted in the Thermos bottles in the hotel rooms it left flecks of white in the water. She imagined as she drank it that the flecks were the salmonella typhosa, salmonella paratyphosa, salmonella shigella, but of course she knew that you could not see bacteria with the naked eye. Unless your eyes were very good.

She is always planning to go home. She takes lessons in Spanish, Castilian Spanish, from a very old woman.

Since the inception of the Nobel Prize in science there has been only one given to a South American. This was given to an Argentinian doctor in 1947. Later, under Peronist charges of incompetence, he resigned from the university.

The Argentinian neurosurgeon who cannot practice in New York or Buenos Aires. At the family compounds his wife is stopped at the gate by his brother, with a machine gun. Kidnapping insurance. His brother tries on military helmets all day, and on visits to New York tries to sell vicuna blankets.

The illuminated Christ on the hillside had been the idea, but there was no hillside in Boca Grande, was no hill. The Opera, the Botanical Garden, the race track, the Jockey Club. The sentries with tommy guns patrolling the presidential palace.

Asylum was available in Boca Grande, but no deposed president had ever availed himself of it.

The preference for speaking French among Boca Grande's three or four first families. The money in European banks. American oil, the National City Bank, Brown Brothers Harriman, United Fruit.

American covers. Americans come down to do "research," come in "study groups," to study "behavioral patterns."

There had once been a railroad line built in Boca Grande but the contracts for its construction had been let to two competing companies, and upon completion it was found that they had built track of different gauges, so the track went unused and grew over.

The prescription for depression is "removal to a hill station," but we have no hill stations in Boca Grande.

LA REPUBLICA DE BOCA GRANDE: a Spanish colony from 1525 to 1823. Independent since 1942. 28 constitutions as an independent nation. When Boca Grande was a Spanish colony it was governed from Guatemala City or Colombia by a captaincy general. Brief period as one of the United Provinces of Central America. A member of the United Nations, the OAS, and the Central American Common Market. Myriad aid offices with acronyms, all the American ones plus the International Bank for Reconstruction and Development and the Central American Bank for Economic Integration. In the early nineteenth century Boca Grande resisted an annexation attempt by Mexico. Gastrointestinal infection is the leading natural cause of death. Rainy season from June to October. There is nothing left of Boca Grande's colonial period because of an earthquake in 1900.

Let me describe Charlotte's appearance. Find the character clues here. A woman of medium height, extreme and volatile thinness, a pronounced pallor, and pale red hair which curled in the damp heat and stands out around her face. She has a tendency to drop her head slightly, as if the weight of her hair is more than she can carry. Her body has a tendency to retain water and since adolescence she has taken a diuretic, but has been told not to take it in the tropics, so that when she is tired her ankles seem thick. Her expression startles by its openness, as if she sees someone about to hit her. She is 40 years old but this naked and rather unfinished expression gives the impression of a somewhat younger woman. She wears expensive shoes and the careless observer might take her to be vain about her feet, but this is not so: in fact she believes her feet ugly and tries to hide them when she is seated. She has for 15 years carried the same Hermes handbag, day and evening, now in need of repair but the lifetime guarantee is useless in Boca Grande and she will not spend money to have it repaired, because it is guaranteed. This is the kind of conundrum she frets over. She wears expensive discreet clothes which on her manage to look flamboyant, and there is always something slightly askew: a hem about to come out, a seam with a quarter-inch split, a minute stubborn stain, a trace of powder on the chiffon blouse. What is this woman doing in Boca Grande?

Well, of course, there it was: there was the question I had to answer. There was the "story." What was this woman doing in Boca Grande?

During the time I spent answering that question, making up the story, I lived in Boca Grande. Everything I heard or saw or thought about—all the clatter, all the images—was framed by this imaginary country, by the light there, the weather there.

For a long time after I finished that novel, I continued living in Boca Grande. I couldn't let it go. I knew too much about it. I knew for example how to run a copra plantation, I had taught myself how. I knew that if you try to crowd 200 palms to the acre you are going to get a low yield, I knew not to plant near salt water, I knew about the particular varieties of scale and fungus that afflict coconut palms.

In other words I had, for a while, made the world hang meaningfully together, made all the images coherent, and it was hard to give that up.

It is still.

So I am making up another story.

And teaching myself the economics of the sugar business.

1979

The Myth of the Artist

Al Alvarez

Let me begin with a fragment of partial and potted history. In the first quarter of this century certain influential, "advanced" literary people were arguing that Romanticism was finally dead and a new period of classicism had begun. T. E. Hulme wrote a brilliant essay on the theme and T. S. Eliot worried away at it off and on for years. By Romanticism they meant poetry that was intensely subjective, yearned for the infinite, distrusted the intellect, and paid rather cursory attention to detail. Classicism, in contrast, meant impersonality, intelligence, lucidity, control. The message was: too much whining, too many roses; it was time for an altogether more strenuous and unforgiving style.

Just how powerful and reasonable their case was becomes clear if you compare a poem by, say, Swinburne—full of verbal color and rhythmic excitement, but very vague as to how the pieces fit together—with *The Waste Land*. It becomes even more powerful if you compare it with Eliot's notes to *The Waste Land*, which was where the real polemics were; they implied that the reader should have read books which had no obvious connection with poetry, should be able to work out the references, follow an argument, and so on. (My own belief is that if you read the poem itself, you got an utterly different impression: that of a precise, delicate, and not at all defended portrait of a man having a nervous breakdown; the notes were a way of confusing the issue.)

As it turned out, Eliot, Hulme, and the others were not wrong about classicism, they were simply optimistic. History was not on their side. Throughout this century the huge rational advances—in science, technology, social justice, the elimination of poverty, etc.—have been steadily balanced by crazed eruptions of irrationality and barbarism: world wars, genocide, endemic totalitarianism, symbolized most clearly and brutally by that peculiarly twentieth-century innovation, the death camp, where the technology was used to set up factories for the efficient mass production of corpses. In the fact of all that, it became increasingly difficult to believe in the supremacy of reason. Something more complex and less clear-cut seemed to be demanded.

A few years ago, in a book called *The Savage God,* I tried to suggest what that something might be. I called it Extremist art, by which I meant an art which goes out along that friable edge between the tolerable and the intolerable, yet does so with all the discipline and clarity and attention to detail Eliot implied when he talked of classicism. Where the Extremists—Lowell, Berryman, Plath, above all—part company with Eliot is in his doctrine of impersonality: "the continual extinction of personality," he called it. On the contrary, Extremist art uses inner strain and personal chaos deliberately, in order to set up a mirror to the chaos out there in the world. In other words, it is an existentialist art form, one in which the barriers between the artist's work and his life are forever shifting and crumbling.

By this I don't just mean that the art and the life illuminate each other, which is an idea at least as old as Samuel Johnson's *Lives of the Poets,* and too obvious to need arguing. For example, you can't properly understand the *Cantos* until you take into account how Pound dealt with his enormous energy and talent in his life. The force he dissipated in sheer literary busyness—founding magazines, laying down the law, pushing other writers' work—then later dissipated again in political and economic paranoia—ranting away in defense of fascism and Social Credit—is somehow reflected in what was to have been his great work. The dispersal and deliquescence of the later cantos is the aesthetic parallel of his own dottiness and fragmentation as a man. That idea is, as I say, self-evident.

What I mean is something more radical and confusing: the general belief—by the public as well as the artists—that the work and the life are not only inextricable but also virtually indistinguishable. Out of this a new and disturbing element has emerged during the last decade. I call it the myth of the artist and it is not, believe me, what I had in mind when I wrote *The Savage God*.

The myth is based, I think, on the terrible precedent set by Sylvia Plath and the tragic way in which her life and her art complete each other. In her collection of essays, *Seduction and Betrayal*, Elizabeth Hardwick has this to say: "She, the poet, is frighteningly there all the time. Orestes rages, but Aeschylus lives to be almost seventy. Sylvia Plath, however, is both heroine and author; when the curtain goes down, it is her own dead body there on the stage, sacrificed to her plot." Sylvia, of course, was by no means the first important artist to die dramatically by her own hand. Almost two hundred years before her, Chaterton committed suicide and became, as a result, a great Romantic symbol. But at least he didn't write about the act. Neither did Hemingway or Hart Crane or Randall Jarrell or even, in so many words, Virginia Woolf. To follow the logic of your art to its desolate end, as Sylvia did, and thereby turn yourself into the heroine of a myth you yourself have created was something unprecedented. It changed the nature of the game. Art, that most stringent and solitary of disciplines, suddenly came to resemble a high-risk activity, like hang-gliding.

If nothing else, it was one in the eye for the Freudian theory of art as compensation and self-therapy. Lawrence once wrote, "One sheds one's sicknesses in books—repeats and presents one's emotions to be master of them." I myself believe that this is the exact opposite of the truth: you don't shed your sicknesses, you dredge them up in writing and thereby make them readily available to you, so that you find yourself living them out. In other words, nature always imitates art, usually in a sloppy and exaggerated way.

John Berryman, for instance, began his great cycle of *The Dream Songs* as a kind of poetic daybook, recording his gripes, hangovers, alcoholic guilts, and very occasional highs. Then gradually he deepened it into an extended act of mourning for various friends tragically dead before their time. That, in turn, led back to what was, for him, the primal suicide: that of his

father, who shot himself when Berryman was twelve. And so
on, back and back, deeper and deeper, until in the end—
particularly in the beautiful series of Dream Songs entitled
"Opus Posthumous"—he seemed to be writing his own
epitaph, as if there were no one else he could trust with the job.
At which point, the way was clear to taking his own life. Which
he did. It seemed—perversity notwithstanding—the most logical means of completing his magnum opus.

That, anyway, is how the public seems to have read the
story of Berryman's desperate and messy last years. Portrait of
the artist painting himself into a corner. Portrait also of a
situation which has got out of hand, for it is based on a total
misunderstanding of the nature of art. It is utterly untrue to
believe that Extremist art, or any other art, has to be
vindicated or justified by an Extremist life, or that the artist's
experience on the outer edge of the intolerable is in any way a
substitute for creativity. In fact the opposite is true, as I have
written elsewhere again and again: in order to make art out of
deprivation and despair the artist needs proportionately rich
internal resources and proportionately strict control of his
medium. We have the collected works of Samuel Beckett to
prove the point. An artist is what he is not because he has lived
a more dramatic life than other people but because his *inner*
world is more substantial, variable, and self-renewing. I think
it was Camus who once remarked that Nietzsche proves that
you can live a life of wildest adventure without ever leaving
your desk. With all due deference to R. D. Laing, schizophrenia is not necessarily a state of grace and there is no shortcut to
creative ability, even through the psychiatric wards of the
most progressive mental hospitals.

But schizophrenia, alas, is a good deal more common than
creative ability, so it is not hard to understand why Laing's
theories should be so appealing. What is baffling is that real
poets should have gone along so readily with them. How else,
for instance, to explain the astonishing lack of professionalism
in Anne Sexton's books? Her trouble was not that she wrote
bad poems, as every poet does from time to time, but that,
instead of throwing them away, she printed them cheek by

jowl with her purest work. The reason was that the bad poems were bad in much the same way as the good were good: in their head-on intimacy and their persistence in exploring whatever was most painful to her. She was unable to resist the temptation to leave the effect to the material, as though whatever was sufficiently naked and overwhelming could not fail. As Randall Jarrell once wrote in an essay about unreviewable verse, "it is as if the writers had sent you their ripped-out arms and legs, with 'This is a poem' scrawled on them in lipstick." The truth is, great tragic poems are not necessarily inspired by great tragedies. On the contrary, they can be precipitated, like pearls, by the smallest irritants, provided the poet's secret, internal world is rich enough: Keats's "Ode to a Nightingale," for instance. By the same token, the more exposed and painful the theme, the more delicate and alert the artistic control needed to handle it. According to a psychoanalyst, Hannah Segal, there is one fundamental difference between the neurotic and the artist: the neurotic is at the mercy of his neurosis, whereas the artist, however neurotic he may be outside his work, has *in his capacity as an artist* a highly realistic understanding both of his inner world and of his relationship to the material of his art.

For example, Anne Sexton's good poems have an expressive tautness and inevitability in the rhythm which not only drives them forward but also keeps them whole. In her bad poems the need to express gives way to an altogether less trustworthy inspiration: the sheer pleasure of confessing in public, of letting it all hang out. Rhythmical control is replaced by a kind of hypnotic chanting. What begin as real poems often end in an operatic no man's land, the one between grand opera and soap opera, that shadow zone where it is hard to distinguish Giacomo Puccini from Al Pacino.

That in itself, you may say, is nothing very new. All sorts of talented writers have had their moments on the borderline of hysteria: Shelley, for instance, Lawrence, Dostoevski. To lose one's poise is an occupational hazard for the experimental artist, trying to make it new. The specifically modern ingredient Anne Sexton and lesser poets like her have added to the mixture is not that they occasionally lose control and thus become hysterical, but that they are hysterical *on purpose*.

This perhaps is the major danger of existential art. The theory can become a justification for letting go the art—by which I mean the solitary discipline and self-abnegation, the craftsman's patience and concentration in the face of his material. In the end, the poetry not only becomes indistinguishable from the psychopathology, it becomes secondary to it.

No doubt some of the blame lies with the media and their insatiable hunger for news. Art fashions may be news of a kind, but the scandalous lives of artists make much better news. "Real art," said Susan Sontag, "has the capacity to make us nervous." But real artists, God knows, do not. They tend to be battered, fallible, vain, boringly self-centered, and often seemingly stupid. So by concentrating on them and their unspeakable lives, you can sidestep the effects of their art. Nearly everyone, for example, knows about Sylvia Plath's broken marriage and despair and suicide. But I wonder how many of the thousands who fervently study the intensely autobiographical *The Bell Jar* have ever bothered with her sardonic, demanding, unforgiving, yet curiously detached poems?

Unfortunately, the artists themselves cooperate in this degradation. Writing is, after all, the most solitary of pursuits. It is easy, in your lighthouse keeper's isolation, to be taken in by your own propaganda and begin to believe the myth you yourself have created. Moreover, fame is addictive, particularly if you practice a nonpaying, minority art like poetry. Somebody—maybe Kenneth Patchen—once said, "The trouble with poetry is, there's no money in it." He meant, I assume, that the only rewards, apart from those of the art itself, are the most slippery ego gratifications: fame, if you can get it, and, if you can't, notoriety, malice, envy, backbiting and jostling for a place on the ladder. Whence the phenomenon of the stars of the poetry reading circuit, like Allen Ginsberg or the Liverpool poets, who, like American presidential candidates or the sacrificial kings in Fraser's *The Golden Bough*, offer their persons, their bodies, to the masses and simply use verse as an excuse for this strange, primitive, ritualistic exchange.

Ultimately, it is a form of sacrifice. The general public does not want poetry, but it does have a taste for licensed buffoons, scapegoats, and tragic heroes, or for a mixture of all three, such as Dylan Thomas. I wonder to what extent his so-called friends and admiring, ox-eyed public secretly envied him his genius and therefore encouraged him to drink himself to death in the name of good companionship and the romantic idea of what a bohemian poet's life should be like.

What, in all this, is the problem for the critic and the reader? In this age of public scandal and private psychoanalysis, the neoclassical solution convinces no one. Unless you approach literature simply as an excuse for an intellectual discipline like linguistics, it is impossible to brush the personal elements under the carpet and pretend they don't exist, as the New Critics did in the forties and fifties, or as Eliot (whose private life was for years unspeakable) wanted. They do exist, inescapably, and the artists seem determined that their audience should recognize this fact. Perhaps it is a way of insisting that what they are doing is deadly serious. Why else should they be willing to pay such a high personal price? So in the purest modern writing there is a curious two-way movement: the reader looks through the work to see the artist as he or she is, then out of it again to see just how perfect and detached and artistically self-contained the work is, how untroubled by the artist's nagging private disasters.

This is what happens in Sylvia Plath's late poetry or in the novels of Jean Rhys. Rhys's heroines move in an unremitting continuum of misery and drunkenness which, presented simply as such, would be not so much unbearable as merely boring. She redeems it with her elegantly casual, pared-down prose and her unwavering determination to fix the emotions in observed detail. By underpinning all that misery with the ordinary, indifferent business of living, she makes it, in the end, sharper and more painful. The detachment necessary to write as well as she does reflects back on the quality of the emotion portrayed.

Coleridge described this process eloquently in the *Biog-*

raphia Literaria: "himself meanwhile unparticipating in the passions, and actuated only by that pleasurable excitement, which had resulted from the energetic fervor of his own spirit in so vividly exhibiting what it had so accurately and profoundly contemplated." From this came what he called "the alienation, and, if I may hazard such an expression, the utter *aloofness* of the poet's own feelings, from those of which he is at once the painter and the analyst." Since Coleridge was writing about Shakespeare, the implication was that creative detachment of this order was the final criterion of great art.

It is not, alas, a criterion we seem to find particularly attractive at present. Even a poet as devoted, intellectually resolute, and lavishly gifted as John Berryman flinched away from it. He remarked, in a *Paris Review* interview: "the artist is extremely lucky who is presented with the worst possible ordeal which will not actually kill him. At that point, he's in business." This, I suggest, is the old Romantic Agony buttressed by peculiarly twentieth-century theories: a theory of existentialist aesthetics, a primitive psychoanalytic theory of the therapeutic relationship of art to life. If you think about this kind of statement, then remember how Berryman died, how Sylvia Plath died, how Anne Sexton died—all of them passionately believing that this was how the game was played—you have to conclude that no poetry, however fine, is worth that cost.

But there is another element involved, less tragic, less heroic: Berryman's remark, that is, was also influenced by his intense, competitive involvement with the media and with the idea of fame. He wrote an indifferent autobiographical novel about alcoholism called, ironically enough, *Recovery*. The hero is Alan Severance, M.D., Litt.D., a professor of immunology and molecular biology, who also teaches a humanities course on the side. Like Berryman, he is being dried out. Like Berryman too, he has been interviewed by *Time* and *Life* and can't get over it. He has this to say: "He had really thought, off and on for twenty years, that it was his duty to drink, namely, to sacrifice himself. He saw the products as worth it." I put it to you that the reverse may also be true:

given Berryman's belief in the connection between art and agony, given also the public's taste for bad behavior in its artists (which deflects it from the necessity of taking their work seriously), it may be that, for Berryman, the poetry was an excuse for his drinking.

At that point, art itself becomes a sideshow of no genuine intrinsic value. All that matters is the disturbance from which art might emerge, given the right talent and the right, disastrous circumstances. In other words, the contemporary artists whom the public finds most alluring are those who knowingly cooperate in their own destruction. Having created myths of themselves as a by-product of creating art, they finish by sacrificing themselves to those essentially trivial myths.

I may be wrong, I may be unduly pessimistic. But if I am right and that is, in fact, what is now beginning to happen, then, as they say in a ceremony rather different from the Hopwood lecture, God help the arts and all who sail in them.

1980

The American Writer:
The American Theater

Arthur Miller

It is quite beyond me to really do justice to this great occasion. The fiftieth anniversary of the Avery Hopwood awards deserves a thorough historical account of their impact on American literature. I do not mean a mere listing of the notable writers who were first recognized and encouraged by the awards, but perhaps, as important, the impact of the idea itself of a university that had the nerve not only to teach contemporary writing but, in effect, to act as its sponsor and to administer money prizes for student writing. I am not sure that this was a first, but I am certain that there could not have been many precedents fifty years ago. In fact, a look at the lives of some of our most distinguished writers who were born around the turn of the century and were of college age when universities were far more conventional in their attitudes toward the arts will show that a large number of them either never bothered to finish college or had no connection as writers with any such institution. The Hopwood awards, I believe, announced not merely annual winners but an attitude that has since spread through many other universities—that the writer can be just as valuable during his lifetime as he is afterward.

So rather than attempt some sort of historical appreciation, I think it wiser to stick to my own experience as a beginning writer, a more modest strategy, to be sure, but one that I hope will throw a more certain light on a far larger scene.

I believe I had two reasons for choosing Michigan, apart from its educational repute. The first was that they did not require mathematics. By the time I graduated from high school I was possibly the world's greatest expert on algebra;

having failed it twice, and only been passed a third time because they could not bear to look at me anymore, I came to a
certain intimacy with every problem in the textbook. All I
lacked was the remotest idea of how to solve them. The second
attraction was the astounding news of the Hopwood awards.
The idea of a university handing out cold cash to students was,
I confess, almost too glorious to contemplate. The money itself
was important of course—even on the lowest prize, $250, I
would later manage to live for a semester. And, of course, with
money so hard to come by in the Depression thirties, giving it
away for nothing more than words on a piece of paper had
miraculous overtones when I had been working in industry for
years for twelve and fifteen dollars a week. But the central
attraction was even more mysterious. The fact that money was
given out meant that the judges—unlike your mother or your
friends—could really tell good writing from bad. Thus, the
recognition of an award touched more than the pocket; it
might even point the future.

I am forced to wonder whether, if Avery Hopwood had
been a novelist and had neglected to give prizes for plays, I
would not have tried harder to become a novelist. For the
theater meant little to me when I began to write. I had seen
only a handful of plays and those had seemed so remote and
artificial that I could find no connection with myself at all in
them. It must be remembered that in the thirties there was
nothing that could be called an off-Broadway theater. It would
have been inconceivable to draw a separation between dramatic art and show business, which were treated as one and
the same. I had heard vaguely about a Provincetown Theatre,
an experimental place where Eugene O'Neill had started out,
but he, after all, had headed for Broadway as soon as producers would accept his plays. Later in the thirties there would be
two or three left-wing theater groups, most notably the Group
Theatre, but they, too, strove to succeed on Broadway even as
they pronounced anathema upon its commercial greed.

Whatever triggered my imagination toward the play form is
lost to me now, but it may well have been a production of an
early Odets play by the Group Theatre. Oddly enough, I can-

not recall which play; all I remember was seeing actors who for the first time in my experience were physically vivid, whose faces seemed to have commonplace outlines, palpable noses and eyes that moved, and hands with veins. The *moments*, so to speak, of the play seemed superheated, isolated one from the other so that they counted eloquently, while at the same time—and this was the weird paradox—everything flowed together. More than this, I found myself believing that offstage—and I had never set foot on a stage but could imagine what it must be like back there—offstage was not offstage at all but the city itself, the New York I knew. So that the play was not like a little isolated cell where things went on disconnected from the city around us, but was one cell among the myriad, part of the sound and the anxiety and the almost universal frustration of life at that time. Had I been capable, as I was not, of rationalizing the experience, I should have called it an experience of theater as life, as much a part of life as going into the subway or bringing home a bottle of milk or sitting in the back yard and wondering anxiously what was ever going to become of me after failing algebra three times.

It would be decades before I would see it all from the opposite side of the equation—life, that is, seen as theater. Politics as theater, love as theater, lecturing on Chaucer as theater, psychoanalysis as theater, the church as theater. But perhaps there won't be time to go into all that.

Anyway, having seen that acting was not, as it had seemed till then, the art of speaking with an English accent, and that a play had something to do with sweat and hunger, I was hooked. I am speaking personally, of course, but only to support my generalizations. For example, I am sure that had I come of age in any other time and had seen some other production of high excellence, I would also have been similarly inspired. But one can't really be sure. I can only be sure that it did happen then, and I know it was not only the acting or the crazy poetry of Odets's lines. It was also what he was saying and what this whole way of acting was saying. It is a convenience to call their message Marxist or revolutionary; but for me it was more like being provided with an emotion, an emotion appropriate to the frustrations of living in the early thirties, specifically, the verb, if you will, for protesting the cursed irrationality of our lives. For people were starving then in America, while food was being burned up on the farms for want of a price. Odets seemed to provide a license for outrage, which has to be the first step toward a moral view. To me, as to most of the critics and the media of the time, he was over-whelmingly the clarion playwright. It would be years until I discovered, quite by chance in a conversation with Harold Clurman, who had directed the Group, that Odets's plays themselves—I am not speaking of the royalties, but of his plays—never made any money. Nor, as a matter of fact, did most of O'Neill's, although his made more than Odets's. And I mention this crass subject for reasons that will be alarmingly clear in a moment, but one point needs making right now. The American theater at that time was not about O'Neill or Odets, quite obviously; it was about entertainment of a quite different kind, the kind that offers an escape from life rather than a confrontation with it. I would only add that this is what most theater in most places is about most of the time.

But when I set about writing a play for the first time, I shared a certain illusion of community, which, I think, is im-plicit in the act of writing for publication or production. I felt alone, of course, and I was scared of making myself ridiculous, and I felt light-years away from any suggestion of profes-sionalism, for I was painfully aware that I knew very little about plays and nothing at all about the theater. My only hope was that the other plays being written for the Hopwood con-test would be worse. This thought was the only one I had at the time that approached reason. The awards provided a world small enough to grapple with.

For the real world of theater was quite different than it is today. As I have suggested, it consisted of the commercial Broadway theater and, to all intents and purposes, that was it. How did one achieve the requisite professionalism? It was all a mystery too deep for me. I had by this time dipped into the contemporary Broadway plays, those that had been published, for very few were then, and found little I could relate myself to. For I did not understand about charm in those days. Unawares, I had come to connect plays and the theater with some sort of prophetic function. Again, I was not in the habit of rationalizing such things, but a playwright for me was a man with his own church. Not that it was a question of preaching but rather of being the vessel of a community's need to talk to itself and to the world. It was possibly my Jewish heritage that imposed such a burden, or, if you will, such a challenge. But O'Neill was not Jewish anymore than Ibsen was, or Chekhov, Strindberg, or the Greeks. (And, parenthetically, none of those writers could run very long on Broadway either, then or now.) How odd, then, to even imagine them as spokesmen, as prophets, for such they were to me then, and conventionally are still, even though we all know that the vast majority of plays are and always have been rearrangements of trivia.

It had not seemed to me to be too short a time—the five days of spring vacation—to write a three-act play. When it won a Hopwood award it was like an artillery shell fired right through the ranks of my opposing army—down went all my old algebra teachers, for one thing. Then, soon after, another award fell upon the same play, the Bureau of New Plays prize, administered by the Theatre Guild in New York. This was a nationwide contest for college students. Another winner was a Brooklyn student who is present today, Norman Rosten. Another was a fellow from St. Louis named Tennessee Williams.

The main thing about this prize was the money—$1,250. I had already earned more with my first play than I had in three years as a shipping clerk. Needless to say, the contrast was not lost to my mind. And if I seem to linger on the subject of money, it is, I assure you, at the center of the great tradition of playwriting. As George Bernard Shaw replied to a businessman who had asked to discuss art with him, "No, I am an artist, not a businessman; businessmen always want to talk about art, but artists only talk about money." But with all the luck I seem to have had with that first play, the idea of actually making a profession of the theater was still quite unreal.

One problem was that I had spilled out into that first play

everything I knew or could imagine about life. For I had hardly lived at all. I must invent something, I thought with sinking heart, and for this I supposed one had to have some kind of objectified technique. So, I promptly groped my way into Professor Kenneth T. Rowe's play-writing class. Such were the times—such was our theater, I should say—that one assumed to begin with that a certain technique could be learned that would more or less, if properly utilized, insure success. Again the Broadway theater loomed in the background, the only theater we had and that, indeed, rewarded certain formulas, as theater inevitably does at all times including the present. That formula had numerous variations, but if it had to have a name it might be the Theater of the Rational. A problem was put in act 1, complicated and brought to a crisis in act 2, and resolved or answered in act 3.

It is hard to define what I took from Professor Rowe's classes. Perhaps it was, above all, his enthusiasm for the catholicity of dramatic literature, the sheer variety of forms that time had developed. And, indeed, there was no single overriding style of writing in his class as there would be in the coming decades when fashion, for some reason, has so dominated and, I think, in many cases crushed invention. People then were writing Realism, Impressionism, Expressionism, poetic drama, verse drama, and Bronx comedies. It did not yet seem that there had to be obeisance to a prevailing mode. Perhaps fewer people were reading the arts section of the *New York Times* then.

I suppose it was somewhat like learning how to draw in order to go on to painting, liberated from the tyranny of line. In any event, I think I came to believe that if the dazzling glory of the masters was finally their poetry, the fundamental poem was the structure. The structure indeed, *was* the poem, the one element whose removal or disturbance collapsed the whole. One knew how Chekhov or Ibsen or Sophocles felt and *sounded*—now it was necessary to know how they were made. Paradoxically—or maybe it was quite logical—in less than ten years I would arrive on Broadway with a play, *The Man Who Had All the Luck*, that began with a problem and ended not with a solution, but at the door of the mystery of fate—why one person is chosen to win and another to lose, a question unanswerable whatever technique might be applied to it. I might add that the play lasted four nights. There was one encouraging review, but that from an alcoholic critic who was well on his way to the big bottle in the sky.

And speaking of the big bottle, it is time, I think, to talk about the critics. It is futile to criticize critics. It is quite enough to condemn them totally. Suffice it to say, I have never met a playwright who claimed he had learned anything from a review. Perhaps it can all be summed up in a story, which may just possibly be true, told me by the late Jed Harris who was the first director of *The Crucible* and in his best time, the twenties, one of the most creative men in the American theater. When he was directing *Our Town*, the most important critic, as always, was the man who happened to be on the *Times*, Brooks Atkinson, the very dean himself. Harris, concerned that Atkinson would not understand the play, which had certain innovations in staging, asked him to lunch, and there proposed to him that he begin a course of theater training by attending a few rehearsals. "I told him," said Harris, "that he really did not know very much about acting, directing, and scene design, and that I would be glad to teach him. He sat there very sweetly, listening to me and agreeing with me. But he didn't come to rehearsals because he felt it would be unethical and might tilt his opinion of the finished production."

Harris's point was one that everyone would have accepted in the decades before and after World War II—the New York reviewer was not necessarily a man who knew anything, he merely had to react with common sense in a manner representative of his readers. Thus, among the seven or eight main reviewers from the clutch of daily papers that still existed then, one found a remarkable number who arrived at the theater opening night on a tilting sidewalk. Others were unwashed refugees from the sports department, and one or two prided themselves on being professional humorists. The intellectual critics, exemplified perhaps by Joseph Wood Krutch, mattered very little to the box office, having disliked everything since the early Euripides. The reigning intellect of the Broadway scene was George Jean Nathan who, indeed, displayed occasional insights, but whose reviews, it seemed to me, most often consisted of lengthy lists of plays going back into antiquity of which the play at hand reminded him. To read American theater reviewing then and now is to be convinced that the reviewer owns a certain sacred space, which it is his moral duty to prevent the playwright from entering. It is quite as though the entire purpose of the whole theater enterprise, its very raison d'être, is to provide a subject for criticism. This might be acceptable if one could recall the name of a single critic who, for example, had wounded Chekhov, Ibsen, Strindberg, or O'Neill by dismissing their works out of hand.

I won a second Hopwood in my junior year, but I failed to win the big one as a senior. Nevertheless, it seemed possible to hope that I might become a professional playwright. The theater I was trying to enter seemed as always to be dominated by its critics, just as our immortal souls are dominated by our decaying flesh. But there was a certain illusion, shared, I think, by everyone involved, that I think helped to form a certain kind of play, and that kind, if I am not mistaken, was in the high tradition of the art. The illusion I speak of was that there was one single audience containing within itself in some mystical fashion the whole variety of America and Americans. The same audience that went to the Ziegfeld Follies one night might flock to O'Neill the next. And so it was not quite as odd as it might seem now that some of the reviewers would have been more at home at a ball game or a prize fight, for the same was true of much of the audience. In actual fact, of course, the audience may have been *emblematic* of American taste, but it was certainly not representative in the absence of blacks and workers in general. Still, there was a certain rough-and-ready air to its acceptance or rejection of a show.

The consequence to play writing, however, is what is important here. Facing such an audience, the playwright could not console himself with yearnings for another, more sensitive and cultivated audience. Balcony seats in the thirties cost fifty-five cents and in them, at least, if not in the orchestra, were the salt of the earth—the student and his teacher, the neighborhood intellectuals of modest means, the housewives and the more culturally hip of the working class. Downstairs in the orchestra were the business people and the professionals and, for certain shows, the usual sprinkling of café society. It may have been a better mix than we have today, but on the whole it never thought it owed anything to anyone, including even a minimal acquaintance with its own historical or literary culture. If a play had an idea, it had to be embodied in action; speeches had to be short, muscular, direct. If you had a message, said the prevailing wisdom, send it by Western Union, for it did not belong in a play. Plays were for fun, for obliterating your troubles, a chance to live other peoples' lives. It was a pragmatic, fundamentally uneducated audience, and if it simply turned its back on the poetic and the philosophical far more often than it should have, it could also make a quite proper demand upon a play; specifically, that its theme flow effortlessly from its action, and that meaning and viewpoint not be smeared all over it like mustard on a hotdog. It may be because of this kind of confrontation that I would find many years later a tendentiousness in so many absurdist plays that seemed to crudely slant life in favor of the meaningless conclusion, the hero slipping on a banana peel. It is a fact, nevertheless, that in the earlier time there was a dangerous intolerance of the ineffable unless even *it* were made active and packed with emotion, like *The Glass Menagerie*, for example. That play, I would remind you, was regarded as certain to fail on Broadway because it seemed so delicately inactive, so ineffable and talky, and when it did succeed, it proved yet again that this audience for prizefights and ball games could be stretched and lifted by poetry if it aimed for the heart rather than the education. In effect, then, the playwright was speaking to his country, and he had no other nor was it thought that he should have.

So, he was compelled to find language and theatricality broad enough in its humanity to hold such an audience. He could not rely for support on a clique pretuned to his cultural signals. Alienation in itself, in other words, had not yet become synonymous with style, let alone high art. And if it was mostly a theater of extroversion, its desire to make contact with the mass was not really different from that of the New and Old Testaments, the classical Greek theater, and the best of the Elizabethans. It was a brutal challenge and could be a brutal confrontation, even unfair; but to accept it was to know the difference between grace under pressure and grace before dinner.

Sometime in the mid-fifties the profound shift within the audience as well as in the organization of the Broadway theater changed all these elements forever. In a word, one became aware that the audience was losing even its former superficial unity; it had begun to atomize. In my case, it was at the opening night of *The Crucible* in 1952 that I realized I was no longer precisely among friends. I have written of this elsewhere at greater length; let it be enough to say now that I was obviously not to be a part of what was then extolled as The American Century, a dawning era when the United States was going to be the new imperium abroad while jumping with democratic prosperity at home. What it all looked like to me was fear and anxiety covered over with the same old self-infatuation that had always led us to our disasters.

I have always supposed, however, that it was *Waiting for Godot* that signaled this shift within the audience. Why precisely it should have occurred at that moment must be left to another time; it is sufficient to say now that the absurdities of life moved onto the stage as well as into the common wisdom of the time. But if the majority of the audience had no taste for shaggy dog stories and remained loyal to Broadway, most of the young left to support what now became known as the off-Broadway theater, a theater whose main stock in trade was the absurd. I cannot attempt a sociological explanation for that absurdist vogue, but I can say that until the mid-fifties it would have been impossible to have met an American who could believe that General Motors, Chrysler, and Ford would one day find themselves incapable of building an automobile competitive with, of all things the Japanese. It would have been equally hard to convince anyone that not only a president but his brother would be gunned down one after the other. The inconceivable, in short, had not yet become commonplace. And so, where before the structures of cause and effect, of fate and character-as-fate had supported the arch of dramatic structure, now it was the inconceivable itself that was raised up and given the kind of obeisance reserved for first principles. And in one sense, it was indeed a kind of naturalistic reportage of how the world was; for the concept of the absurd tended to legitimize the common conviction that absolutely nothing followed necessarily from anything else. One of the doubtful virtues of this philosophy was to liberate some of us from having to understand anything at all, and that included dramatic structure.

There were several reasons why I would find myself somewhat uneasy with this style. In principle, for one thing, it seemed odd that whether in Paris, London, Berlin, or New York, regardless of the great differences between these societies, precisely the same mode of feeling and writing should have spontaneously arisen. In short, it seemed too obviously a fashion rather than a truth that had taken hold of the western imagination. Secondly, our American despair is not quite the same as the European variety, for we have never ceased to hope, awkward as that may be to explain to strangers. So, it seemed somehow wrong that you should enter a theater and not be sure what country you were in. And, finally, so long as a writer writes, he hopes; this is what tragic writing assumes to begin with and black humor denies. I suppose what I am saying is that a work ought to acknowledge its premises.

With the atomization of the audience between avant-garde and rear guard, a new breed of critic came on the scene. He or she was far more literary than the roughnecks of the past, far better trained academically, making the new demand for a theater of ideas, and, in many instances, the more revolutionary the better. Some were brilliant stylists, others merely wished to be; the best that might be said of them is that their appearance was doubtless inevitable in the evolution of sophistication in American society, and the worst, that on the whole they seemed unwilling or incapable of admitting the contradictions of their own positions. Was it enough, for example, to abandon the majority audience in a democracy, or should play writing and theater in general persist in trying to find the key to that audience rather than to play reassuringly to enclaves of the washed, the already saved, and the elite?

Nor is it altogether wrong to note that some of these critics were not too revolutionary to resist the call to assume the role of critic for the better-paying magazines and even the *New York Times*. But perhaps their most harmful work was done upon the truth of history, for by the sixties they had all but persuaded their public that nothing in American theater was to be discussed in the same breath as the British, French, German—indeed nearly any other theater. Modernity was European; mere naive sentimentality belonged to us. This was more than misleading nonsense. In fact, it was almost diametrically the opposite of truth.

In the early winter of 1956 I happened to experience a moment of historical change that might throw some light on this question of the American contribution to international theater. I was in London at that time working with Peter Brook on his production of *A View From the Bridge*. At the same time my wife was starting a film, *The Prince and the Show Girl*, with Laurence Olivier. One evening soon after we arrived, he asked if there was anything in the London theater I wished to see. I glanced down the nearly full page of theater ads—there were many dozens of shows then—and was at a loss. Not only had I never heard of any of the titles, but they seemed to promise precisely the kind of precious, upper-middle-class nursery tales that had relevance, perhaps, to life among the fox hunters, but not very much else. My eye fell at last upon one title that I found intriguing—*Look Back In Anger*. It was not, of course, the looking back but the anger that seemed so un-British then. But Olivier dismissed it as an ugly travesty on English society. This made it even more interesting, and I persisted, and he finally agreed to get me a ticket. When I arrived at the Royal Court Theatre the follow-

ing evening, I found Olivier in the lobby awaiting me. He had
decided to see the play again.

To be brief about it, here was the first English play I had
any knowledge of that told me something about actually living
in England. And I had a strange déjà vu sensation when I
realized that it was doing for the English rather precisely what
Odets had done in the early thirties for New Yorkers—letting
loose a cleansing invective, an unbridled anguish and fury at
the hapless decrepitude of the social system, its injustices and
its frustrating stupidities.

Whether the author had ever read an Odets play was beside
the point; the quite similar style, a certain apt wedding of
lyricism and social outrage, had flashed out of the English sky
a quarter of a century after it had done the same thing in New
York, and doubtless for similar social reasons—namely, because a deadly formalized, polite and rather bloodless commercial play had dominated in both countries for several decades earlier. Incidentally, after his second viewing, Olivier
ended at the bar with the young Osborne who had written the
play, and while I talked with George Devine, the director of
the Royal Court Theatre, I overheard Olivier asking Osborne
whether he could write something for him. Which he
promptly did—*The Entertainer*.

I was invited to be one of the speakers at an informal rally a
few nights later in the Royal Court Theatre, where hundreds
of young actors and writers had jammed the place to discuss
the state of their theater. One of the recurrent questions directed to me was what they might do to begin creating plays
like the Americans, plays that seemed to them so vital, so alive
to current American life. There could simply be no mistaking
that for these young men and women it was the American play
and the American actor that had grasped the hour and the
style of contemporary existence. In a few short years, of
course, to listen to some of our own critics, it would be quite as
though the American play and the American playwright had
two left feet and could barely manage to read the hands of the
clock. Indeed, this self-rejection went to such an extreme that
nothing would do but an English critic had to be imported to

oversee the New York theater for the *New York Times*. Such is
the ineluctable power of fashion, I suppose. Indeed, the only
English-speaking place left where you could find any real critical understanding and enthusiasm for the American play, its
vigor and its poetry, was precisely in Britain, especially among
the British actors, authors, and directors.

I have talked far longer than I meant to, but before I finish I
must complete the winding of the noose from which American
theater currently hangs. I am speaking, of course, of the
Broadway theater, the so-called professional theater. If it was
once *the* theater in the sense that almost everything original
began on Broadway to be imitated by repertory and amateur
theaters, it is now quite the opposite. Nothing but musicals
now originates on Broadway; what serious work is shown, and
it is practically extinct, has been transferred from off-
Broadway or regional theaters across the country. Broadway is
hostile to serious work, that is no exaggeration, and so it
should be. Is it really too much to ask that people should
spend twenty-five to forty dollars a seat to watch painful scenes
and troubled characters? If it makes any sense at all, which I
doubt, it indeed is far more sensible for the entertainment-
seeker to spend that kind of money on song and dance shows,
and that is just what has happened. The great audiences,
which it used to be said great poets required, are no more.
The student, the teacher, the man of modest means, the working woman—these will hardly be found in a theater anymore,
not at such prices. But, as if this were not enough, we have the
monopoly of theatrical criticism exercised by the *New York
Times*.

Now the *Times* would doubtless deny this, pointing out
that its critic has sometimes praised a play that in short order
has closed anyhow. This is true but not particularly hearten-
ing. The far more decisive truth is that when the *Times* condemns a play it closes, and this regardless of how many other
papers may have praised it. In fact, in 1963, when the *Herald
Tribune*, the last of the *Times*'s competitors, shut down, the
editors of the *Times*, led by their chief, Clifton Daniel, were
sufficiently worried about the monopoly that had befallen

them to call a meeting of theater people, at which I was one of the panel of speakers, in order to gather suggestions as to how that monopoly could be mitigated. I suggested that they provide readers with a healthy variety of views, three, four or more critics to each show, but Mr. Daniel feared that nobody would know *who represented the opinion of the New York Times.* I thought this quite astonishing. It sounded suspiciously like an unacknowledged desire to wield the very power that they denied wishing to possess. But no matter—the absurdity remains, and given the massive domination of the *Times* over the theater, it is by no means an exaggeration to say that if every book published by a major American publisher—poetry, history, fiction, or whatever—were to be judged by a single individual and his word taken as to whether it ought to live or die, it would be an equivalent situation to the one obtaining on Broadway right now. Even in the Soviet Union plays can only be killed by a committee and not one man.

And on the outside chance that some of you may think me biased against the *Times,* let me say that in 1947 my first successful play, *All My Sons,* was recognized almost alone by Brooks Atkinson of the *Times,* his colleagues having been either indifferent or hostile to it. Having said that, I ought to add that the serenity of my confidence in critics is what it is because the same group of negative reviewers turned themselves around by the end of that season and voted *All My Sons* the best play of the year. Such is life among the playwrights.

It seems to me that after fifty years of Hopwood awards a cycle has been closed. I am sure that when Avery Hopwood conceived of financing prizes for young writers it was in some part an act of subversion against the commercial system of theater. I am also sure he wanted to encourage and support writers who would not only entertain but prophesy, and to give them a couple of years to strengthen themselves for a hard life. The Broadway theater today is, if anything, even more hostile to serious work than it was a half-century ago, but all is not by any means lost. Today, unlike in Hopwood's time, there is a truly decentralized system of theaters spread across this country. Much fine work is done in these theaters—indeed, much of their work is stolen by Broadway. If there is any note of lamentation in this speech it is not for a lost glory—there was never very much of that. But there was a level of professionalism in production, design, and performance that is not easy to find anymore. We have it still in the musical theater on Broadway, which is the best of its kind in the world. But the origination of serious theater is a thing of the past. Nor can one imagine how this will soon change; how forty-dollar seats will ever again come down in price, or how the monopoly of the *New York Times* will be broken, given the ingrained habits of theater-goers who follow the lead of that paper's tastes.

But maybe there is a disguised blessing in all this. A decentralized theater may turn out to be closer to the people than the New York–based one was, and perhaps this closeness will reflect itself in a more mature drama that reflects more of the balance of light and darkness in the country as a whole. I can see but one long-term danger, and it comes down to the problem of subservience. It is something that has cropped up frequently in the American theater since the early nineteenth century when Washington Irving complained that American authors and producers seemed to need the reassurance of foreign models for their works. Except in the musical, our most democratic form in the sense of its being adored and understood by the vast majority of the people, we seem uncertain about both the value of our own works as compared to foreign ones, and, more importantly, what the nature of serious theater really ought to be at this historical moment.

That last, of course, is a subject all by itself. Right now, one fundamental point might be made: what is evil in the United States and what is good, what is confused and what is clear, what is progressive and what is retrograde and reactionary, this whole crazy house—apart from this or that judgment upon it—is in the vanguard of history, and continues to create the century in ways that no other civilization can. Whether into the morass or onto the higher altitudes, we do break the ground. Our drama, therefore, has the right if not the obligation to see itself as a vanguard, as confronting human situations as though they had never existed before in quite the same fashion and bearing quite the same significance. I have traveled a great deal and in every kind of extant social system, and whatever may be the local opinion of us, it is from this land that they wait for news, for what's coming up, for word of our state of mind, our hopes, and our despair. Confronted by a professional theater that, between its greed and its irresponsibility, no longer has use for him, the American writer must now write for his own people, for the theaters he finds around him. There is no center anymore, and in this sense the writing of plays is no longer a profession but a calling to be practiced for the love of it or not at all.

I hope that what I have said has some truth in it. But since it is of the theater I have talked, and in a larger sense America herself, whatever is true now probably has been changing as we sit here. All I can hope for is that you will catch her on the wing, willing and ready to fly to wherever in her unpredictable wisdom she decides she wants to go.

1981

Biographical Notes

DONALD DAVIE (1922–), poet, critic, and teacher, was born in Barnsley, England, and educated at Cambridge University. He has published numerous volumes of verse and as a critic has explored poetic theory and technique in *Purity and Diction in English Verse* (1952) and in *Articulate Energy: An Inquiry into the Syntax of English Poetry* (1955). He has published critical studies of Sir Walter Scott, Thomas Hardy, and Ezra Pound, and is the recipient of a Guggenheim fellowship. He is a fellow of the American Academy of Arts and Sciences and an honorary fellow of St. Catherine's College, Cambridge. He currently teaches at Stanford University.

PETER TAYLOR (1917–), fiction writer and dramatist, was educated at Vanderbilt University, Southwestern College, and Kenyon College. He began writing and publishing short stories while an undergraduate and is the author of *A Long Fourth and Other Stories* (1948), *Happy Families are All Alike* (1959), a novel, plays, and other works. *The Collected Stories of Peter Taylor* appeared in 1969. Mr. Taylor has taught at Harvard, Oxford University, and the University of Virginia, and is the recipient of the National Academy award in fiction, a Fulbright award, a Guggenheim fellowship, and a Ford fellowship.

ROBERT BRUSTEIN (1927–), whose criticism of the drama has appeared in the *New Republic* and other magazines, was educated at Amherst, Yale, and Columbia. He has been a member of the faculties of Cornell, Vassar, and Columbia and was dean of the Yale School of Drama. His works include *The Theatre of Discontent: Studies in the Modern Drama* (1964), *Seasons of Discontent: Dramatic Opinions 1959–65* (1965), *Revolution as Theatre: Notes on the New Radical Style* (1971), and *Making Scenes*, 1980. Mr. Brustein is the recipient of the George Jean Nathan award for dramatic criticism and Guggenheim, Ford Foundation, and Fulbright fellowships. He has recently become artistic director of the American Repertory Theatre and director of the Loeb Drama Center at Harvard University.

DENISE LEVERTOV (1923–), poet and editor, was born in Ilford, England, and became a United States citizen in 1955. She was educated at home. Her books of poetry include *The Double Image* (1946), *Here and Now* (1957), *The Jacob's Ladder* (1961), and *The Freeing of the Dust* (1975). She has been a visiting lecturer at Vassar College, the University of Cincinnati, and Tufts University, an editor of the *Nation*, and has been honored by a grant of the National Institute of Arts and Letters, a Guggenheim fellowship, and by the degree of Doctor of Letters conferred on her by Colby College and by the University of Cincinnati.

PETER DE VRIES (1910–), novelist and editor, was educated at Calvin College. He has been coeditor of *Poetry* magazine and has served on the editorial staff of the *New Yorker*. His many novels include *The Tunnel of Love* (1954), *Mackerel Plaza* (1958), *The Vale of Laughter* (1967), and *The Glory of the Hummingbird* (1974). He is also the author of several books of short stories and a play. Mr. De Vries is a member of the National Institute of Arts and Sciences.

NADINE GORDIMER (1923–), South African novelist and short story writer, was educated in South Africa at the University of Witwatersr and Johannesburg. She has taught at many American universities including Harvard University, Princeton University, and the University of Michigan. Ms. Gordimer is the recipient of the Smith literary award, the Thomas Pringle award, the Black Memorial prize, and the Booker prize. Her works include *Face to Face* (1949), *A Guest of Honour* (1970), and, most recently, *July's People* (1981).

THEODORE SOLOTAROFF (1928–) has been an associate editor of *Commentary*, editor of *Bookweek* and of the *New American Review*, and is currently a senior editor at Harper and Row. He was educated at the University of Michigan where he won a Hopwood award in essay in 1952. His essays have appeared in *Esquire*, *Commentary*, *New York Times Book Review*, and other magazines, and a collection of his essays, *The Red Hot Vacuum*, was published in 1970. Volumes Mr. Solotaroff has edited include *Writers and Issues*, *An Age of Enormity*, and *Best American Short Stories* (1978).

CAROLINE GORDON (1895–), fiction writer and critic, was educated at Bethany College, West Virginia. She has served on the faculties of Columbia University, the University of Washington, and the University of California at Davis. Her novels include *Aleck Maury, Sportsman* (1934), *The Strange Children* (1951), and *The Glory of Hera* (1972). Along with several volumes of short stories, she is the author of *How to Read a Novel* (1957) and of a critical study of Ford Madox Ford. She is the recipient of a Guggenheim fellowship, an O. Henry award (1934), two National Endowment for the Arts grants, and the degree of Doctor of Letters conferred upon her by Bethany College and by St. Mary's College.

ROBERT W. CORRIGAN (1927–), critic and editor, was educated at Cornell University, Johns Hopkins, and the University of Minnesota. He has taught drama at Carleton College, Tulane University (where he was founder and editor of the *Tulane Drama Review*, now the *Drama Review*), the Carnegie Institute of Technology, and the University of Michigan. He has served as a dean at New York University and at the University of Wisconsin, Milwaukee. He has written and edited many studies of the drama including *Theatre in the Twentieth Century* (1963), *Masterpieces of the Modern Theatre* (1966), and *The Theatre in Search of a Fix* (1973). He is the translator of *Chekhov: Six Plays* (1962).

W. D. SNODGRASS (1926–), poet, was educated at Geneva College and the State University of Iowa. He has taught at Cornell University, Wayne State University, and Syracuse University. He is the recipient of numerous awards including the Poetry Society of America special citation (1960), the Pulitzer prize (1960), and the Miles award (1966). He is a member of the National Institute of Arts and Letters and a Fellow of the Academy of American Poets. Mr. Snodgrass's books of verse include *Heart's Needle* (1960) and *After Experience: Poems and Translations* (1968), and he is the author of *In Radical Pursuit: Critical Essays and Lectures* (1975).

JOHN SIMON (1925–), film and drama critic, was born in Subotica, Yugoslavia, and was educated at Harvard University. He has served on the faculties of the University of Washington, the Massachusetts Institute of Technology, and Bard College. Mr. Simon was the associate editor of the Mid-Century Book Society, the drama and film critic for the *New Leader*, the film critic for *Esquire*, the film and drama critic for *New York* magazine, and has been the drama critic for the *Hudson Review* since 1960. Mr. Simon's books include *Acid Test* (1963), *Private Screenings* (1967), and *Paradigms Lost* (1980). He is the recipient of the George Polk Memorial award in film criticism (1968), the George Jean Nathan award for dramatic criticism (1969–70), the literary award of the American Academy of Arts and Letters (1976), and has been a Fulbright fellow.

WALKER PERCY (1916–), novelist, was educated at the University of North Carolina, Chapel Hill and at Columbia University, where he earned an M.D. in 1941. His novels include *The Moviegoer* (1961), *The Last Gentleman* (1966), *The Second Coming* (1980), and he is the author of the nonfiction work *The Message in the Bottle* (1975). Mr. Percy is also the author of philosophical, critical, and medical essays which have appeared in various journals and magazines. He is the recipient of the National Book Award (1962), a National Institute of Arts and Letters grant, and is a fellow of the American Academy of Arts and Sciences.

TOM WOLFE (1931–), social critic and journalist, was educated at Washington and Lee University and Yale University. He worked as a reporter on the *Washington Post* and the *New York Herald Tribune* and became a contributing editor of *New York* magazine in 1968. He is a contributing artist of *Harper's* and his drawings have been exhibited in New York galleries. He is the author of *The Kandy-Kolored Tangerine-Flake Streamline Baby* (1965), *The Electric Kool-Aid Acid Test* (1968), *The New Journalism* (1973), and other works. Mr. Wolfe is the recipient of the Front Page awards for humor and foreign news reporting from the Washington Newspaper Guild (1961), an award of excellence from the Society of Magazine Writers (1970), and the Frank Luther Mott research award (1973).

JOAN DIDION (1934–), essay and fiction writer, was educated at the University of California, Berkeley. She was the associate feature editor of *Vogue* magazine, a columnist for the *Saturday Evening Post*, and a contributing editor of the *National Review*. Her novels include *Run River* (1963) and *Play It As It Lays* (1970), and her books of essays include *Slouching Towards Bethlehem* (1969) and *The White Album* (1979). She is the recipient of the *Vogue* Prix de Paris (1956) and a Breadloaf Writers' Conference fellowship.

AL ALVAREZ (1929–), poet, novelist, and critic, was born in London and educated at Corpus Christi College, Oxford. He has held various scholarships in England and America and has held several visiting professorships, including one at Princeton University. Mr. Alvarez has been a poetry editor and a regular contributor to the *Observer* since 1956 and was drama critic for the *New Statesman*. In 1961 he received the Vachel Lindsay prize for poetry from *Poetry* magazine. His books of verse include *Autumn to Autumn* and *Lost*, his novels include *Hers* and *Hunt*, and as literary critic and social commentator he has published *Beyond All This Fiddle*, *The Savage God*, and other works.

ARTHUR MILLER (1915–), playwright and essayist, was born in New York City and educated at the University of Michigan where he won two Hopwood awards. He is the author of *Death of a Salesman* (1949), *The Crucible* (1953), *A View from the Bridge* (1955), *After the Fall* (1964), and *The Price* (1968), among many other plays. He has received the Pulitzer prize, the Tony award, and a gold medal for drama from the National Institute of Arts and Letters. A past international president of P.E.N., he is also the author of a novel, a collection of essays, a collection of short stories, and three books of travel reportage written with his wife, the photographer, Inge Morath. He received an honorary degree, Doctor of Humane Letters (L.H.D.), from the University of Michigan in 1956.

The Hopwood Awards: A Brief History

The Hopwood Lectures, 1932–81

1932 Robert Morss Lovett. Literature and Animal Faith.
1933 Max Eastman. Literature in the Age of Science.
1934 Zona Gale. Writing as Design.
1935 Henry Hazlitt. Literature Versus Opinion.
1937 Christopher Morley. A Successor to Mark Twain.
1938 Walter Prichard Eaton. American Drama Versus Literature.
1939 Carl Van Doren. The First American Man of Letters.
1940 Henry Seidel Canby. The American Tradition in Contemporary Literature.
1941 Edward Weeks. On Counting Your Chickens Before They Hatch.
1942 John Crowe Ransom. The Primitive Language of Poetry.
1943 Mary Colum. Modern Mode in Literature.
1944 Louise Bogan. Popular and Unpopular Poetry.
1945 Struthers Burt. The Unreality of Realism.
1946 Harlan Hatcher. Towards American Cultural Maturity.
1947 Robert Penn Warren. The Themes of Robert Frost.
1948 J. Donald Adams. The Writer's Responsibility.
1949 F. O. Matthiessen. Responsibilities of the Critic.
1950 Norman Cousins. In Defense of a Writing Career.
1951 Mark Van Doren. The Possible Importance of Poetry.
1952 Horace Gregory. Dramatic Art in Poetry.
1953 Stephen Spender. The Young Writer, Present, Past, and Future.
1954 John Gassner. Modern Playwriting at the Crossroads.
1955 Archibald MacLeish. Why Can't They Say What They Mean?
1956 Philip Rahv. Literary Criticism and the Imagination of Alternatives.
1957 Malcolm Cowley. The Beginning Writer in the University.
1958 John Ciardi. The Silences of the Poem.
1959 Howard Nemerov. The Swaying Form: A Problem in Poetry.
1960 Theodore Roethke. The Poetry of Louise Bogan.
1961 Saul Bellow. Where Do We Go From Here? The Future of Fiction.

1962 Mark Schorer. The Burdens of Biography.
1963 Arthur Miller. On Recognition.
1964 Alfred Kazin. Autobiography as Narrative.
1965 Donald Davie. Sincerity and Poetry.
1966 Peter Taylor. That Cloistered Jazz.
1967 Robert Brustein. No More Masterpieces.
1968 Denise Levertov. Origins of a Poem.
1969 Peter De Vries. Exploring Inner Space.
1970 Nadine Gordimer. Modern African Writing.
1971 Theodore Solotaroff. The Practical Critic: A Personal View.
1972 Caroline Gordon. The Shape of the River.
1973 Robert W. Corrigan. The Transformation of the Avant-Garde.
1974 W. D. Snodgrass. Moonshine and Sunny Beams: Ruminations on *A Midsummer Night's Dream.*
1975 Pauline Kael. On Movies.
1976 John Simon. The Word on Film.
1977 Walker Percy. The State of the Novel: Dying Art or New Science?
1978 Tom Wolfe. Literary Technique in the Last Quarter of the Twentieth Century.
1979 Joan Didion. Making Up Stories.
1980 Al Alvarez. The Myth of the Artist.
1981 Arthur Miller. The American Writer: The American Theater.

Publications

The following prize-winning Hopwood manuscripts have been published:

Whatever You Reap, by Annemarie Persov, Schuman, 1933.

Fireweed, a novel, by Mildred Walker, Harcourt, Brace, and Co., 1934.

Books for the Dead, a play, by Hobert Skidmore, in *The One-Act Theater*, Vol. II, Samuel French, 1936.

Swamp Mud, a play, by Harold Courlander, published by Maurice Kaplan, 1936.

I Will Lift Up Mine Eyes, a novel, by Hubert Skidmore, Doubleday, Doran, and Co., 1936.

Straw in the Wind, a novel, by Ruth Lininger Dobson, Dodd, Mead, and Co., 1937.

The Stubborn Way, a novel, by Baxter Hathaway, Macmillan Co., 1937.

The Well of Ararat, a novel, by Emmanuel P. Varandyan, Doubleday, Doran, and Co., 1938.

The King Pin, a novel, by Helen Finnegan Wilson, Macmillan Co.,
1939.

Lucien, a novel, by Vivian La Jeunesse Parsons, Dodd, Mead, and
Co., 1939.

The Loon Feather, a novel, by Iola Fuller, Harcourt, Brace, and Co.,
1940.

Return Again, Traveler, poems, by Norman Rosten, Yale Series of
Younger Poets, Yale University Press, 1940.

Heart-Shape in the Dust, a volume of verse, by Robert E. Hayden,
Falcon Press, 1940.

Homeward to America, a volume of poems by John Ciardi, Henry
Holt and Co., 1940.

Whistle Stop, a novel, by Maritta M. Wolff, Random House, 1941.

American in Search of a Way, selections from journals, by Walter
Morris, Macmillan Co., 1942.

The Garden Is Political, a volume of verse, by John Malcolm Brinnin,
Macmillan Co., 1942. Many of the poems in this book were in
volumes with which Mr. Brinnin won Hopwood prizes in 1938,
1939, and 1940.

Lincoln Lyrics, a volume of verse, by John Malcolm Brinnin, New
Directions, Poet of the Month series, 1942.

Nearer the Earth, a novel, by Beatrice Borst, Random House, 1942.

Rising Wind, a volume of verse, by Sister Mary Edwardine, Bruce
Humphries, 1942.

November Storm, a novel, by Jay McCormick, Doubleday, Doran,
and Co., 1943.

Dancing Saints, a novel, by Leslie G. Cameron, Doubleday, Doran,
and Co., 1943. The writer published under the name of Ann
George Leslie.

Golden Apples of the Sun, a novel, by Rosemary Obermeyer, E. P.
Dutton and Co., 1944.

Delay Is the Song, a volume of verse, by Rosamond Haas, E. P.
Dutton and Co., 1944.

The Chapin Sisters, a novel, by Fynette Rowe, Current Books, 1945.

The Task, a volume of verse, by Robert Bhain Campbell, Farrar and
Rinehart, 1945.

The Broken Pitcher, a novel, by Naomi Gilpatrick, Dial Press, 1945.

Years Before the Flood, a novel, by Marianne Finton Meisel, Charles
Scribner's Sons, 1945. The writer published under the name of
Marianne Roane.

34 Charlton Street, a novel, by Rene Kuhn, D. Appleton-Century
Co., 1945.

Family Tree, a novel, by Florence Maple, Alfred A. Knopf, 1945.

A Sweep of Dusk, a novel, by William Kehoe, E. P. Dutton and Co.,
1945.

The Gifts of Love, a novel, by Andrina Iverson, Farrar and Strauss,
1946.

Clementine, a novel, by Peggy Goodin, E. P. Dutton and Co., 1946.

Rip Van Winkle's Dream, a poem, by Jennette Haien, Doubleday and
Co., 1947.

April Trees, a volume of verse, by Beth Merizon, privately printed,
1947.

By Their Fruits, a nonfiction book, by Julia Neal, University of North
Carolina Press, 1947.

No More with Me, a novel, by Russell La Due, Doubleday and Co.,
1947.

The Practicing of Christopher, a novel, by Josephine Eckert, Dial
Press, 1947.

Not Quite a Dream, a novel, by Kathleen Hughes, Doubleday and
Co., 1948.

I, A Stranger, a play, by Grace E. Potter, Baker's Plays, 1949.

The Bending Cross, a biography of Eugene Victor Debs, by Ray
Ginger, Rutgers University Press, 1949.

Bent Blue, poems, by Charles Madden, Decker Press, 1950.

A Man from South Dakota, an autobiography, by George Reeves,
E. P. Dutton and Co., 1950.

The Toy Soldier, a volume of poetry, by Donald C. Reaser, Exposition Press, 1951.

The Dark and the Damp, an autobiography, by Jock Wilson, E. P.
Dutton and Co., 1951.

Autographed Copy, poems, by Constance Rinehart, Dierkes Press,
1951.

Little Benders, a collection of stories, by Joe Knox, J. B. Lippincott
Co., 1952.

Ketti Shalom, a novel, by James Murdock, Random House, 1953.

The Far Command, a novel, by Elinor Chamberlain, Ballantine
Books, 1953.

Now and at the Hour, a volume of short stories, by Aida I. Rivera,
Benipayo Press, Manila, P. I., 1957.

Somewhere There's Music, a novel, by George Lea, J. B. Lippincott
Co., 1958.

A Dream of Falling, a novel, by Mary O. Rank. Houghton Mifflin Co., 1959.

Nude Descending a Staircase, a volume of poems, by X. J. Kennedy, Doubleday and Co., 1961.

The Praying Mantis, a novel, by H. Gordon Green, Brunswick Press, 1963.

Plans for an Orderly Apocalypse, poems, by Harvey Gross, University of Michigan Press, 1968.

The Right Trumpet, a novel, by John Roberts, McGraw-Hill Book Co., 1968.

Summer's Lie, a novel, by Alan Boatman, Harper and Row, 1970.

Hurt, Baby, Hurt, an autobiographical essay, by William Walter Scott, III, New Ghetto Press, 1970.

The Collected Poems of Frank O'Hara, edited by Donald Allen, Alfred A. Knopf, 1971. This volume includes O'Hara's Hopwood manuscript of 1951, *A Byzantine Place*.

Someone to Hold Onto at the Bottom of the Stairs, a volume of verse, by John Allen, privately printed, 1972.

Coigns of Vantage, a collection of stories by Padma Hejmadi, Writers Workshop, Calcutta, India, 1973.

Winter in the Rex, poems, by William D. Elliott, privately printed, 1973.

See the Lighthouse Burning, poems, by James B. Allen, Peter Quince, 1976.

Willo, a novel, by Karen Snow, Street Fiction Press, 1976.

Pardon Me, Your Honor, poems, by Robert E. Clifford, Crowfoot Press, 1979.

Hawk of May, a novel, by Gillian Bradshaw, Simon and Schuster, 1980.

Forget Harry, a novel, by Carrie Smith, Simon and Schuster, 1981.

Judges in the Major and Minor Hopwood Contests, 1931–81

DRAMA

John Anderson	Charles S. Brooks
Brooks Atkinson	John Mason Brown
Marston Balch	Kenneth M. Cameron
Mark Barron	F. Curtis Canfield
Eric Bentley	John Chapman
Herschel L. Bricker	Robert H. Chapman

Harold Clurman
Robert W. Corrigan
Alexander Dean
Thomas Dickinson
Alan Downer
Martin Duberman
Walter P. Eaton
Sawyer Falk
Lewis Funke
Robert E. Gard
John Gassner
Jack Gaver
Will Geer
Wolcott Gibbs
Rosamond Gilder
Richard Gilman
Susan Glaspell
Melvin Gordon
Kenneth L. Graham
Paul Green
John Guare
Walter Hadler
T. Edward Hambleton
Hubert C. Heffner
Teresa Helburn
Lillian Hellman
Henry Hewes
Norris Houghton
John K. Hutchens
Edith Isaacs
Margo Jones
Frederick Koch
Fred Koch, Jr.
Jan Kott
Alfred Kreymborg
Joseph Wood Krutch
John Lardner
Jerome Lawrence
Barclay Leathem
Robert Littell
Richard Lockridge

Charles MacArthur
Burns Mantle
Margaret Mayorga
Frederic McConnell
Arthur Miller
Ward Morehouse
Mary Morris
Lewis Nichols
Allardyce Nicoll
Clifford Odets
Edith Oliver
Paul Osborn
Brock Pemberton
Thomas E. Porter
Daniel L. Quirk
Norman Rosten
Kenneth T. Rowe
Arthur Ruhl
Samuel Selden
Robert G. Shedd
Betty Smith
Robert L. Snook
Thomas W. Stevens
Milan Stitt
F. Cowles Strickland
Dan Sullivan
Peter Taylor
Howard Taubman
Carl Van Vechten
Theodore Viehman
Walter H. Walters
Gerald Weales
Geroge E. Wellwarth
Percival Wilde
Kirk Willis
Stark Young

ESSAY

Louis Adamic
Franklin P. Adams
J. Donald Adams

James Truslow Adams
Phoebe Adams
Nona Balakian
Jacques Barzun
Joseph W. Beach
May L. Becker
R. P. Blackmur
Bruce Bliven
Catherine D. Bowen
Mary C. Bromage
Van Wyck Brooks
Henry S. Canby
Robert Coles
Mary Colum
Norman Cousins
Malcolm Cowley
Frederick Crews
Alan Devoe
John Erskine
John Fischer
Esther Forbes
Katherine F. Gerould
Harry Hansen
Elizabeth Hardwick
Harlan Hatcher
Baxter Hathaway
Hiram Haydn
Harold Hayes
Henry Hazlitt
Robert Hodesh
Irving Howe
Katherine G. Jackson
Randall Jarrell
Burgess Johnson
Alfred Kazin
Hugh Kenner
John Kieran
Freda Kirchwey
Joseph Wood Krutch
Lewis Lapham
Amy Loveman

Robert M. Lovett
Robert Lucid
Dwight Macdonald
Dumas Malone
Steven Marcus
Margaret Marshall
Dorothy McGuigan
Francis Meehan
H. L. Mencken
Michael Millgate
Arthur Mizener
Christopher Morley
Charles Morton
Marjorie Nicolson
Sterling North
John H. O'Brien
William Van O'Connor
Donald C. Peattie
Howard Peckham
George Perkins
William Phillips
Norman Podhoretz
Philip Rahv
John Crowe Ransom
Louis D. Rubin, Jr.
Tony Schwartz
Odell Shepard
Robert B. Silvers
Bernice Slote
Harrison Smith
Theodore Solotaroff
Monroe K. Spears
Donald E. Stanford
George Stevens
Martha Bennett Stiles
Dorothy Thompson
Willard Thorp
Carl Van Doren
Peter Viereck
Charles C. Walcutt
Chad Walsh

Austin Warren
George F. Whicher
Helen C. White
Edmund Wilson
John T. Winterich

FICTION
Alice Adams
Renata Adler
Max Apple
Harriette Simpson Arnow
Don Barthelme
Alice Bensen
James Boyd
Herschel Brickell
Paul Brodeur
Louis Bromfield
Roger Burlingame
Hallie Burnett
Whit Burnett
Struthers Burt
Taylor Caldwell
Carl Carmer
R. V. Cassill
John Chamberlain
Mary E. Chase
Walter Van Tilburg Clark
Robert P. T. Coffin
Malcolm Cowley
A. J. Cronin
Wilbur L. Cross
David Daiches
Marcia Davenport
Bernard DeVoto
E. L. Doctorow
Walter D. Edmonds
George P. Elliott
Seymour Epstein
Clifton Fadiman
Dorothy C. Fisher
Martin Flavin

Martha Foley
John T. Frederick
Anne Fremantle
Lewis Gannett
George Garrett
Brendan Gill
Ellen Glasgow
Albert J. Guerard, Jr.
Mark Harris
Ihab Hassan
Harlan Hatcher
Granville Hicks
James Hilton
Helen Hull
Katherine G. Jackson
Elizabeth Janeway
Alfred Kazin
Oliver LaFarge
Sinclair Lewis
Edmund Love
Robert F. Lucid
Andrew Lytle
Robie Macauley
John P. Marquand
Jack Matthews
Jay McCormick
Arthur Meeker
Nolan Miller
Joyce Carol Oates
Tillie Olsen
Martha Ostenso
Walker Percy
Padma Perera
Victor Perera
Katherine A. Porter
J. F. Powers
Kerker Quinn
Marjorie K. Rawlings
Ishmael Reed
Conrad Richter
Elizabeth M. Roberts

Kenneth Roberts
Roger Rosenblatt
Arthur Schlesinger, Jr.
Robert Scholes
Harvey Shapiro
Alfred Slote
Harrison Smith
Jean Stafford
Wallace Stegner
Phil Stong
T. S. Stribling
Ruth Suckow
Ronald Sukenick
Harvey Swados
Caroline Gordon Tate
Peter Taylor
Lionel Trilling
Agnes S. Turnbull
Henry Van Dyke
Webb Waldron
Mildred Walker
Edward Weeks
Eudora Welty
Anthony West
Ray B. West
Thornton Wilder
John Williams
Thomas Williams
L. Woiwode

POETRY
Leonie Adams
Conrad Aiken
A. R. Ammons
John Ashbery
W. H. Auden
Joseph Auslander
Gerald Barrax
May L. Becker
Marvin Bell
Stephen Benet

Robert Bly
Louise Bogan
John M. Brinnin
Witter Bynner
Oscar J. Campbell
Hayden Carruth
John Ciardi
Mary Colum
Padraic Colum
James V. Cunningham
Donald Davie
Babette Deutsch
James Dickey
George Dillon
Max Eastman
Richard Eberhart
John G. Fletcher
Frances Frost
Horace Gregory
Arthur Guitermann
Thom Gunn
Donald Hall
Michael Harper
Robert Hillyer
John Hollander
Edwin Honig
Robert Huff
Randall Jarrell
Donald Justice
X. J. Kennedy
Jascha Kessler
Galway Kinnell
Maxine Kumin
Laurence Lieberman
Archibald MacLeish
Edgar Lee Masters
David McCord
W. S. Merwin
Josephine Miles
Harriet Monroe
Marianne Moore

Frederick Morgan
Howard Moss
Robert Nathan
John G. Neihardt
John Frederick Nims
Robert Pack
Ron Padgett
Dorothy Parker
Frederick Pottle
Ezra Pound
Henry Rago
John Crowe Ransom
Jessie Rittenhouse
Theodore Roethke
M. L. Rosenthal
Muriel Rukeyser
Delmore Schwartz
Karl Shapiro
Louis Simpson
William Jay Smith
Gary Snyder

Ann Stanford
Wallace Stevens
Marion Strobel
Dabney Stuart
May Swenson
Allen Tate
Charles Tomlinson
Louis Untermeyer
Mark Van Doren
Peter Viereck
Anne Waldman
Edward Weeks
Theodore Weiss
John Hall Wheelock
Reed Whittemore
Margaret Widdemer
Miller Williams
John Woods
Ann Winslow
James Wright